Childhood Experiences
of Domestic Violence

of related interest

Making an Impact
Children and Domestic Violence
A Reader
Marianne Hester, Chris Pearson and Nicola Harwin
ISBN 1 85302 844 4 pb

State Child Care
Looking After Children?
Carol Hayden, Jim Goddard, Sarah Gorin and Niki Van Der Spek
ISBN 1 85302 670 0 pb

Effective Ways of Working with Children and their Families
Edited by Malcolm Hill
ISBN 1 85302 619 0 pb
Research Highlights in Social Work 35

Social Work with Children and Families
Getting into Practice
Ian Butler and Gwenda Roberts
ISBN 1 85302 365 5 pb

Child Development for Child Care and Protection Workers
Brigid Daniel, Sally Wassel and Robbie Gilligan
ISBN 1 85302 633 6 pb

Troubles of Children and Adolescents
Edited by Ved Varma
ISBN 1 85302 323 X pb

Domestic Violence
Guidelines for Research-Informed Practice
Edited by John P. Vincent and Ernest N. Jouriles
ISBN 1 85302 854 1 pb

Homeless Children
Problems and Needs
Edited by Panos Vostanis and Stuart Cumella
ISBN 1 85302 595 X pb

Childhood Experiences of Domestic Violence

Caroline McGee

Foreword by Hilary Saunders

Jessica Kingsley Publishers
London and Philadelphia

First published in the United Kingdom in 2000 by
Jessica Kingsley Publishers
116 Pentonville Road
London N1 9JB, UK
and
400 Market Street, Suite 400
Philadelphia, PA 19106, USA

www.jkp.com

Copyright © Caroline McGee 2000
Second impression 2001
Third impression 2003
Fourth impression 2004
Printed digitally since 2005

Library of Congress Cataloging in Publication Data
McGee, Caroline, 1965–
        Childhood experiences of domestic violence
        Caroline McGee.
             p.   cm.
        Includes bibliographical references and index.
        ISBN 1 85302 827 4 (alk. paper)
        1. Child abuse--Great Britain--Prevention. 2. Family violence-
-Great Britain--Prevention. 3. Abused children--Services for--Great Britain.
4. Victims of family violence--Services for--Great Britain. I. Title.
HV6626.54.G7M34   1999
362.76'7'0941--dc21   00-027363

British Library Cataloguing in Publication Data
McGee, Caroline
        Childhood experiences of domestic violence
        1. Child abuse 2. Wife abuse
        I. Title
        362.7'6

ISBN-13: 978 1 85302 827 4
ISBN-10: 1 85302 827 4

Contents

Part V Overcoming the obstacles

Foreword

This book is essential reading for anyone who needs to understand the effects of domestic violence on children – particularly those who are responsible for providing or funding services for children who have experienced domestic violence.

Instead of focusing on incidents of physical abuse (the standard approach taken by many professionals), this research looks at domestic violence in the context of everyday living. What emerges is a picture of abusive men seeking to control every aspect of the lives of women and children by using not only physical or sexual violence but also constant intimidation, humiliation and other forms of emotional or psychological abuse.

It would be comforting to think that many children are not affected by domestic violence because they are too young to notice or understand what is happening. However, the statements by children involved in this research show that they are very aware of the violence and not fooled by their mothers' attempts to conceal this. One child remembers seeing Daddy hurting Mummy, even though her parents separated when she was aged 1.

The children also make it clear that they feel very strongly about the violence that they have heard, witnessed or experienced personally. They struggle to express intense feelings of fear, sadness, anger, shame, guilt, confusion and despair – feelings which inevitably affect their self-esteem, their behaviour, their education, their health, their ability to make friends and their relationship with their mother.

Recognising their own powerlessness to deal with domestic violence, children look to adults to 'sort it out'. How we respond sends a clear message about our society's determination or inability to tackle this issue. If helping agencies provide emotional support and practical help, they are 'brilliant'. Conversely, if the abuser manages to escape prosecution, children cannot understand how he 'got away with it' and this reinforces their belief that 'he's invincible' and 'nobody can do anything about him'.

However, the major question posed by this research – and it is an important one – is how we as a society can help children to deal with the huge emotional burden inflicted by their experiences of domestic violence. These children want to talk!

This is not as straightforward as it might seem. It is not easy to communicate openly about domestic violence, when it is still regarded as shameful and when it could erupt at any moment. This research shows that children and their mothers frequently try to protect each other by *not* discussing what they have suffered, and often it is only after leaving the family home that they can begin to talk freely about the violence.

Unfortunately for many abused women and children the danger continues after separation, because abusive fathers can use the family courts to track them down and contact orders are almost always granted. In these circumstances the children's worries about saying anything that might 'get back' to the abuser are absolutely critical, and clearly they need to know that they will be protected if they disclose abuse. These issues need to be addressed to enable the courts to take account of children's wishes and feelings and make decisions that are in their best interest.

The mothers involved in this study say that they want their children to have counselling, while the children themselves say they want to talk to other children who have had similar experiences. The children also stress the need to make services accessible, child-centred and child-friendly.

This is a good time for these needs to be identified. The government is committed to tackling domestic violence and its national strategy must surely include measures to help children recover from the trauma of domestic violence. Such a development would highlight the child protection implications of domestic violence, while also reflecting the new emphasis on intervening early to provide support services for 'children in need'.

Local authorities need to be involved to ensure that appropriate services are made available in every area, but it is important that statutory agencies are not the main providers of these services. This research confirms a previous finding (Abrahams, 1994) that abused women are reluctant to seek help from statutory agencies for fear that social services will remove their children. Two mothers also reveal that their children have refused counselling provided within the psychiatric service, as they did not want to be 'labelled'.

A range of essential services are already being provided within the voluntary sector for women and children survivors of domestic violence. These services have been developed mainly by Women's Aid since the mid-1970s and in recent years the children's charities and other voluntary groups have also set up support services. More than 85 per cent of refuges now offer children's services, which are much appreciated but chronically under-resourced. This is the ideal location in which to work with children and their mothers, but these services need adequate funding. They also need to be extended in partnership with other local projects to include outreach, aftercare, specialist counselling for children and services which meet the particular needs of abused women and children from different cultures.

I would like to thank Caroline McGee for writing an excellent report which provides a clear signpost for the development of services to meet the needs of children who have lived with domestic violence. These children deserve a better future. Let us make this possible.

Hilary Saunders
National Children's Officer
Women's Aid Federation of England

Acknowledgements

This book is a testament to the courage of the children and women who took part. They unselfishly retold their painful stories in the hope that things could be improved for others living through the horror of domestic violence. It seems trite to acknowledge that without them this book would not exist. Heartfelt thanks go out to these children and women, not only for describing their experiences but also for trusting us with their stories and inviting us into their homes as guests.

A big thank you also goes to Catherine Crabtree, co-researcher, who shared not only the workload but also the outrage and sadness. I would also like to thank Caroline Boyle for her excellent administration and organisational skills and who many, many times calmly converted chaos into order.

I would like to acknowledge the financial support of the BBC Children in Need Appeal and also Dr Pat Cawson of the National Society for the Prevention of Cruelty to Children (NSPCC) for her commitment to embarking on this project.

Thanks are due to all those individuals and agencies who introduced us to the children and women who took part. I would like to acknowledge the advice of those who commented on an earlier draft of this book, particularly Marianne Hester (University of Sunderland) and Audrey Mullender (University of Warwick), also Catherine Crabtree (Westminster Women's Aid), Pat Cawson (NSPCC), Una Fisher (NSPCC), Gill Hague (University of Bristol) and Hilary Saunders (Women's Aid Federation of England).

Caroline McGee

Research for the book was carried out by Caroline McGee and Catherine Crabtree

Disclaimer

The views expressed here are those of the author and do not necessarily represent those of the NSPCC.

PART ONE

Literature Review and Method

CHAPTER ONE

Introduction and Overview of Literature

Introduction

This book reports on a research project that was undertaken in order to elicit the views of children and young people about their experiences of domestic violence and support services. Although research is frequently carried out *on* children and young people, they are not so commonly directly involved and asked for their own views of their experiences. Instead researchers approach professionals or carers to describe their perceptions of children's experiences. These significant adults may be asked to rate children's behaviour on a number of scales so that inferences can be drawn regarding the impact on children of adverse experiences such as domestic violence. The discrepancies that may exist between the carer's and child's perspective are highlighted by Jaffe, Wolfe and Wilson's (1990) observation that interviews with children demonstrated that they could reveal detailed accounts of violent behaviour that their parents were unaware they had witnessed. In order to support most effectively children who have experienced domestic violence, it is crucial that we listen to what children themselves have to say, both about their experiences and the types of intervention they believe would be most useful. This book draws on the interviews with children and their mothers to illustrate children's perceptions of their experiences. **All names have been changed.**

There are a number of themes underlying the rationale of the present research:

1. A growing body of literature indicating that domestic violence was overlooked as a risk factor in child protection work.

2. Practice experience with women and children escaping domestic violence.

3. Recognition that difficulties exist in accessing support services for women and children experiencing domestic violence.

4. A lack of attention to seeking out the views of children and young people themselves.

Aims

The aim of this research is to explore issues around the protection of children who experience domestic violence and to establish the best way of meeting that need. The focus of the project is specifically on giving children and young people a voice. As more attention is being focused on listening to the experiences of children and young people who have been involved in the child protection system (McGee and Westcott 1996) it is crucial to listen to the views of children who have experienced domestic violence.

The study aimed to explore:

1. How can we best support children when there is domestic violence?

2. What do children and mothers themselves have to say about support services they have wanted or received?

3. Whom do children and mothers most often approach for help?

Research methodology

The research used a qualitative approach to obtain information from women and children who had experienced domestic violence. Due to the highly sensitive nature of the research, which would include questions on both domestic violence and possible involvement in investigations into alleged child abuse or neglect, it was felt that it was most appropriate to use qualitative interviews rather than quantitative methods such as surveys. Domestic violence is a very complex issue, as is the whole area of child protection. Qualitative methods allow for more exploration of issues so that a fuller picture can be obtained in a contextual way. In addition, the age range of children involved in the study meant that methods such as questionnaires, which require respondents to be able to read and write, would be unsuitable.

The study used an 'opt-in' procedure for recruiting mothers and children to take part in the research. This means that participants have to make an active decision to become involved in the research and contact the researchers themselves. This method is in contrast to the 'opt-out' procedure where researchers will contact those they wish to interview (usually first obtaining names and addresses through an agency providing a service to the people contacted). It is then up to the person contacted to make an active refusal to be involved in the research. Many researchers feel that an opt-out procedure raises ethical questions and certainly in the current study it would have been an extremely inappropriate method to use, not least because of the risk of further violence to women and children caused by the violent partner intercepting the contact by the researcher. Using an opt-in procedure meant that women and children were free to decide whether or not to take part in the research once they had seen publicity or received information about it. In addition this approach did not violate the confidentiality of agency records by researchers having access to these records. As will be explored later, women and children who have experienced domestic violence face many obstacles in seeking help. A research project which used agency records to make contact with women and children who have experienced domestic violence would very likely generate mistrust of not just the research project but also the agency that supplied the information. This could lead to women and children feeling that they had to cut off contact with this agency in order to protect themselves. It could also inhibit them from seeking support from other agencies, fearing that their confidentiality and ultimately their safety would not be respected. Details of the interview procedure can be found in the appendix.

Description of the sample

Fifty-four children and forty-eight mothers took part in the research. Mothers and children were contacted in a variety of ways using publicity mail-outs to relevant organisations, direct media publicity, and approaches from workers in statutory (social services) and voluntary (refuges, social care and counselling agencies) groups. Interviews were carried out throughout England and Wales. Just over half of the mothers and children were living in towns at the time of the interview (53%) with 27 per cent living in cities and 20 per cent in rural areas; 13 per cent of the sample described themselves as black and a further 13 per cent had a disability. It was originally planned to incorporate interviews with Asian women in Asian languages. Unfortunately the interviewers who were to carry out this piece of the research were unable to do it and there was not time to recruit others to continue the work. Similarly, an interviewer was recruited to carry out interviews with children using assisted communication methods. Again the interviewer was not in the end able to take part in the research. These areas remain in need of research attention, particularly from the perspective of the children.

During the period in which they were experiencing the domestic violence, in 60 per cent of the families the mother was married to the violent man and in 40 per cent they lived together. In two-thirds of cases the man was the children's father and in the other families he was a father figure.

The age of children interviewed ranged from 5 to 17 years with a woman of 19 and one of 24 also taking part to discuss their experiences of growing up with domestic violence; 55 per cent of children were born into a family where the man was already violent and 72 per cent of children were exposed to between one and six years of violence. The average length of time children were exposed to domestic violence was six years.

Terminology

For the purposes of the research, domestic violence is defined as the emotional, psychological, physical and sexual abuse of a woman and possibly her children by a man in a present or previous close relationship with the woman. The term 'domestic violence' is chosen because it has become easily identified shorthand for a range of gendered abusive behaviours. The term is used, however, with recognition of the many shortfalls that have been identified. This is particularly the case in terms of minimising and obscuring the gendered nature of the crime (Dobash and Dobash 1980; Hague and Malos 1998; Hester and Radford 1996; McGee 1997).

The term 'black' is used throughout this book to denote those of African, Caribbean and Asian origin. 'Survivor' is used in preference to 'victim', as it is generally perceived to be a much more positive and accurate description of women's and children's status. The term 'children' is used frequently as shorthand to refer to both children and young people and the term 'father' is similarly used to refer to both birth fathers and non-related father figures.

Violence towards men

Domestic violence towards men from women can and does occur, as does violence in gay and lesbian relationships. However, the vast majority of studies on domestic violence have focused on heterosexual relationships and illustrate that by far the most common form of this violence is from men to women. While women may be violent to male partners it is often in self-defence as a response to long-term abuse from those male partners

(Dobash and Dobash 1992; Hague and Malos 1998). Nazroo (1995) reports on an innovative study exploring domestic violence by interviewing both partners. He highlights the importance of utilising a methodology that addresses the context and meaning of the violence:

> Gender-neutral approaches, which claim women are as violent as men in marriage, are misled by their use of a structured questionnaire methodology which simply focuses on acts of physical aggression. This obscures the meaning of such acts, which leads to an inability to demonstrate crucial differences between male and female violence in marriage (Nazroo 1995, p.475).

His study concluded that male violence is considerably more likely than female violence to be dangerous and threatening and also more likely to lead to serious injury and increased anxiety for women whereas female-perpetrated domestic violence has none of these outcomes.

Prevalence

There are no national statistics maintained in the UK regarding either the incidence or prevalence of domestic violence. Incidence refers to the number of incidents of domestic violence whereas prevalence refers to the number of people experiencing domestic violence. Thus different aspects are measured as one person may experience a number of incidents of violence. However, available studies highlight how common domestic violence actually is (see also Hester, Pearson and Harwin 1999).

- Dobash and Dobash (1980) reported that domestic violence forms the second most common type of violent crime reported to the police in Britain. Specifically these researchers found that it comprises more than 25 per cent of all reported violent crime.

- Mooney (1994) found a prevalence rate for women of 30 per cent using a definition which excluded 'mental cruelty, rape, threats of violence, and the "less severe" forms of actual violence; grabbed, pushed or shaken' (p.28).

- Stanko et al. (1998) estimated that one in nine women and over 5000 children a year experience domestic violence.

- Women's Aid Federation of England (WAFE 1997) reported that approximately 32,017 children were accommodated in Women's Aid refuges during the year 1996–97.

- In an international context, studies that focused only on physical abuse yielded a prevalence rate of between 25 per cent and 60 per cent (McGee 1997).

Thus, although it is difficult to measure the prevalence and incidence of domestic violence, the available evidence points to a widespread phenomenon of abuse within the home. Some of the factors that have been reported as contributing to this underestimation include:

- the use of 'forgetting' as a coping strategy by women (Kelly 1988)
- fear of losing their children (Kelly 1994)
- fear of the violent man, or women learning to define their experiences as unimportant (Kelly and Radford 1991)
- fear of not being believed, shame, pride, self-blame and lack of self-confidence (McWilliams and McKiernan 1993).

Prevalence and incidence statistics should be interpreted with these factors in mind.

Domestic violence is experienced by women and children of all social classes, ethnicities and abilities. However, women's and children's experiences of domestic violence, and particularly of help-seeking, may vary across different groups (Hester and Radford 1996; Imam 1994; Mama 1996).

There are a number of ways in which children might witness the abuse of their mother. McGee (1997) and Silvern and Kaersvang (1989) conclude that witnessing the violence to their mother is sufficient to cause children to be traumatised. For an overview of the current knowledge of the impact of domestic violence on children see Hester *et al.* (1999, ch. 3). Witnessing the physical or sexual abuse of their mother is undoubtedly distressing for children but it is important that the impact of other forms of domestic violence such as psychological or emotional abuse are not overlooked or minimised. Experiencing domestic violence means that children are exposed to and affected by a range of abusive behaviours and it is important to acknowledge that it is not only the extreme forms of physical violence which may lead to adverse outcomes for children. In addition to witnessing the abuse of their mother, children may be directly abused themselves. Table 1.1 summarises some of the main studies demonstrating the links between domestic violence and child abuse.

Table 1.1 Links Between Domestic Violence And Child Abuse

Study	Where	Sample	Main findings
Bowker, Arbitell and McFerron (1988)	US	1000 'battered' women, 775 with children	70% of male partners also physically abused the children: 'the severity of the wife beating is predictive of the severity of the child abuse' (p.165).
Stark and Flitcraft (1988)	US	116 abused/ neglected children	45% of the children had mothers who were subject to physical violence: 'the battering male is the typical child abuser' (p.97).
Hiller and Goddard (1990)	Australia	Survey of 206 cases of child abuse	Domestic violence was present in 40% of child sexual abuse cases and in 55% of physical abuse cases.
London Borough of Hackney (1993)	UK	Children on the child protection register	At least one-third of registered children had mothers who were subject to violence themselves.
Cleaver and Freeman (1995)	UK	30 families with 61 children involved in an alleged child abuse investigation	In 12 out of the 30 families (40%) there was domestic violence.
Farmer and Owen (1995)	UK	44 children whose names had been placed on the child protection register	Where there was physical abuse, neglect or emotional abuse of the children, in 59% of cases there was domestic violence, usually from the father figure to the mother: 'Domestic violence was a feature of most of the cases with the worst outcomes.' (p.63)
Gibbons, Conroy and Bell (1995)	UK	1888 child protection referrals	Domestic violence was recorded in 27% (taken from records, not in response to specific questions regarding domestic violence).
Brandon and Lewis (1996)	UK	105 maltreated or neglected children	46% were also witnessing domestic violence (interviews carried out to ascertain the presence of domestic violence).
Ross (1996)	US	A representative sample of 3363 parents.	The authors concluded that 'there is a statistically significant relationship between marital violence and child abuse within a community sample' (p.596).

In a review of studies, Hughes (1992) found correlations of 40–60 per cent between child abuse and domestic violence. In a later review, Edleson (1995) reported that in 32 per cent to 53 per cent of all families where the men are physically abusive to their female partners, the men were also abusing the children. As Morley and Mullender (1994, pp.29–32) point out, studies aiming to examine the links between domestic violence and child abuse may be limited by such methodological shortcomings as how domestic violence is defined or how the presence of violence is identified. Despite these limitations there is enough evidence to be concerned about the co-occurrence of child abuse and domestic violence.

Responses to domestic violence

There are a number of agencies who have contact with women and children experiencing domestic violence. However, there has been a tendency for domestic violence to be considered as a problem to be addressed only within the remits of the police, social services, housing and refuges (McGee 2000). This section will consider the available research examining agency responses to domestic violence.

Social services

A number of studies have highlighted that women believe that if they tell social services about the domestic violence they are experiencing, their children will be removed (Abrahams 1994; Clifton, Jacobs and Tulloch 1996; Dominy and Radford 1996; McWilliams and McKiernan 1993; Mooney 1994). In the study carried out by Abrahams (1994) young people also reported fears that social workers would remove them if they told anybody about the domestic violence. This fear may be particularly pronounced for those from ethnic minorities (Clark 1994). Bernard (1997) suggested that black mothers' fears of having their children removed may not be groundless as black, particularly African-Caribbean, children are over-represented in the public care system. A study carried out in Coventry (Humphreys 2000), found that two-thirds of the women in the study were either threatened with the removal of their children or did in fact have their child accommodated.

Concerns have been identified with regard to training on domestic violence in social work courses (Jones 1989; Mullender 1996) and this is especially the case with a family therapy focus, which may overlook or minimise domestic violence. O'Hara (1994) has identified the following four key areas in the development of effective professional practice in child protection work:

- supporting the mother
- consulting the child
- confronting the violent man
- developing strategies to protect workers as well as children and women from violence.

In addition Lloyd (1995) emphasised the importance of individual workers' attitudes and value systems and the central role of initial and ongoing training programmes in raising awareness about domestic violence issues.

Housing

Access to good-quality, safe temporary and permanent housing is a crucial resource for women and children attempting to escape domestic violence. Having to flee their home, often without many of their possessions, is undoubtedly a big upheaval and Hague and Malos (1994) have highlighted the impact on women and children of being made homeless because of domestic violence. Black women and children may face further complications in their bid to be rehoused following domestic violence in that they may have a limited choice of areas where they can be safe not only from the violent man but also from racism (Imam 1994). In a study carried out in Surrey, Dominy and Radford (1996) raised concerns about the poor provision for housing applicants needing translation services, particularly Asian women. Overall Dominy and Radford's (1996) study uncovered high levels of dissatisfaction (53%) with housing departments due in part to insensitive questioning by housing officers in relation to the domestic violence but also because the lack of housing resources meant that women and children had to wait a long time for permanent housing. In a Sussex study, Clifton, Jacobs and Tulloch (1996) found that women escaping domestic violence had 'widely varying experiences of applying for housing' (p.200). Since these studies the Housing Act 1996 has been implemented. This Act incorporates two major changes to the previous legislation with regard to domestic violence. Local authorities now have a temporary but renewable two-year duty to house certain applicants including women and children escaping domestic violence whereas previously an application could be made for permanent housing. The second major change of the Act is to introduce the concept of associated persons such that whereas the previous legislation recognised violence or the threat of violence only from people living in the home, the new Act defines domestic violence as violence or threats of violence from a person who is associated with the person under threat.

Health

Health professionals are more likely to have contact with women and children experiencing domestic violence than any other professional group (Casey 1987; Pahl 1995). Indeed women frequently approach their general practitioner (GP) first for help (Dominy and Radford 1996). However, the evidence suggests that women do not get the help they need from health service professionals (Pahl 1995). For example, McWilliams and McKiernan (1993) reported that of the women in their study who told their GP about the domestic violence, only one-third found the GP's response to be helpful. In Clifton et al.'s (1996) study, although women who had approached their GPs for help did not feel dismissed by them, the authors conclude, '[GPs] are poorly informed about the causes of domestic violence and what can be done to help women' (p.190). Related to this finding Hague, Malos and Dear (1996) observed that health service providers and practitioners tend to be under-represented on domestic violence forums and inter-agency initiatives. Confidentiality appears to be an important issue in relation to women talking to their GPs about domestic violence. Both Dominy and Radford (1996) and McWilliams and McKiernan (1993) found that women were inhibited from telling their GP about the domestic violence because of their fears that the GP would tell their partners what they had disclosed (particularly if their partner was also a patient of the GP). In addition, particularly in relation to health visitors, women have been found to fear that telling them about the domestic violence could mean that their children are removed (Clifton et al. 1996; Dominy and Radford 1996). Frost (1997) found that a lack of initial and subsequent training for health visitors concerning domestic violence increased the vulnerability of health visitors and clients. Pahl (1995) suggested that health professionals can best help women experiencing domestic violence by

- respecting the woman's account
- knowing the relevant information (particularly with regard to local agency provision)
- keeping careful records
- giving women enough time to make their own decisions.

Police

A common perception of police responses to domestic violence is that they will not take it seriously although actual police responses showed evidence of positive change during the 1990s. This is particularly so in relation to the establishment of domestic violence units. One of the issues identified by research is women's reluctance to involve the police in domestic violence. Dominy and Radford (1996) found that only 23 per cent of women in their study who had sought formal help had approached the police. Mama (1996) reported that 53 per cent of the women in her study had contact with the police; however, a 'significant proportion' of these women did so only because neighbours or friends had called them. Mama (1996) stressed that despite the extreme violence women were suffering,

> many black women will be severely injured, and face the other dire consequences of violence rather than involving the police or making use of the law. Quite apart from the poor opinion that women, and particularly black women, have of the police there is also some evidence to suggest that fear of reprisals combines with a sense of loyalty to deter black women further. (Mama 1996, p.173)

McWilliams and McKiernan (1993) reported that only 26 per cent of women who had contact with the police found them to be helpful, usually because they removed the abuser. Nearly half (48%) of women who contacted the police in Dominy and Radford's (1996) study were dissatisfied with the response they had received leading the authors to conclude: 'Levels of dissatisfaction declined since the setting up of DVUs [domestic violence units] but nonetheless remains unacceptably high' (p.75). Kelly (1999) found that most women in her study reported that they perceived the police response as sympathetic and supportive. However, in only 28 per cent of cases did the police give women information about refuges and in 14 per cent information was given about other agencies. It is also noteworthy that the police checked whether children were present in only 33 per cent of cases. Kelly (1999) concluded:

> Police officers currently do not agree as to what counts as domestic violence, or what their role in response to it should be. This creates a lottery for victims, in which one officer will define her experience as violence, and respond to it as a crime, whilst another will not. (Kelly 1999, p.115)

PART TWO

What Does it Mean to Experience Domestic Violence?

CHAPTER TWO

Forms Of Domestic Violence and Child Abuse

Domestic violence incorporates a range of controlling and abusive behaviours. This chapter explores the context of this violent behaviour for both mothers and children. The chapter begins by examining the man's violence to his partner before going on to detail the specific forms of abuse experienced by children living with domestic violence.

Triggers

Women were asked if they could identify any particular things that would trigger their ex-partner's violence. The majority said that it was either random, anything could trigger it, 'life's experiences, everyday things, normal things' (seventeen women), or connected to accusations of infidelity (seventeen women). Women frequently said that initially they tried to make excuses for their partners' violence but then realised that it could not be blamed on external factors.

> If something wasn't as clean as it should have been or the meal wasn't cooked quite right – he started to drink, but not until we had been married about five years so I can't put it down to drink. I think it was just male dominance over women. (Camilla)

A number of young people discussed at length how they had tried in vain to find reasons for their fathers' violence. They described how they came to see that there were no reasons as such, that the behaviour was concerned with control.

> If my mum had left the door open, [he'd say] 'Close the door, close the door' and then if she closes the door, [he'd say] 'Why are you closing the door? What are you doing out there? Who are you going to see?' (Mona, aged 17)

Accusing women of infidelity

Seventeen women volunteered that a theme underlying all forms of violence they suffered was their partner accusing them of having affairs. In all cases there was no justification for the claim and in some cases the accusation appears to be the man's projection of his own behaviour, as Denise explained:

> Then he started going with other women, he used to lock me in the house, the postman once knocked and I had to sign for this recorded delivery thing and he actually beat me and accused me of having an affair with the postman. (Denise)

Others could see that as the intensity of the violence increased, so did the claims that the woman was unfaithful. Marianne described how the accusations of infidelity were used both to control her movements rigidly and to humiliate her, to the extent of having an impact on her health.

> I wasn't allowed to go to the doctors, I wasn't allowed. I had a dentist and if I was too long in the dentist, he'd knock the fillings back out and say that I was having an affair with the dentist. [According to him] I was having an affair with everybody, even my own father and my own son I was having an affair with, if I was too long in a room with him. He was crude. And he didn't say it quietly either. (Marianne)

Another woman interviewed recounted how her ex-partner would quiz her child about her seeing other men. When the child would reply that she was not seeing anyone, he would be called a liar.

This belief of the woman's infidelity on the part of the violent man and subsequent violence appeared to represent not so much a jealous rage as another aspect of the need to control and totally dominate the woman. There was nothing in the woman's behaviour to suggest that she was seeing someone else and the accusation seemed to be used primarily to control the woman's movements on a day-to-day basis or as a precursor to a specific violent attack. For example one woman woke up in the middle of the night to find her partner's hands round her throat. He was accusing her of just having slept with someone else. (She had been sleeping beside her partner all night.) He then raped her.

Alcohol

Eleven of the women said that their partners used alcohol in connection with their violence:

> sometimes it was drink, sometimes it wasn't drink, the emotional abuse was worse and then if that got really bad, there'd be a belting, a push down the stairs. (Bea)

A small group of these violent men were alcoholics, and, as one woman pointed out, although her ex-partner was drinking constantly, he would not actually get drunk. He drank until he passed out at night. This woman did not feel that his violence could be attributed solely to his drinking, as he had been violent before he started abusing alcohol.

Most of the women in the group felt that alcohol could make their partner's violence worse but they were frequently violent when not drinking also. There was nothing to indicate that these men were violent to others when they were drunk, only to their partners. Some women felt that their ex-partners had used alcohol as an excuse for their violence. Only two women felt that their ex-partners' violence was more or less completely associated with their alcohol use and only two with their drug use.

Six women specifically referred to the fact that their ex-partners' violence was not connected to their use of alcohol. Women were not asked about the connection between their ex-partner's violence and alcohol use. However, as one of the myths around domestic violence is that it is caused by alcohol use, women had considered the connection in order to make sense of what was happening for themselves. In the interview situation women referred to their ex-partners' alcohol abuse in order to explain the context of the violence they had experienced.

> No, I actually stupidly said that to him one night [that he was only violent when drunk]. So he woke up the next morning and started again. (Cheryl)

> I used to think, well, at least if he was drunk, you know, he'd have a reason, but he didn't drink, I just couldn't understand it at all. (Denise)

Other triggers for their ex-partners' violence identified by women included:

- money
- disagreeing with him

- if the children cried
- when the man was having affairs
- the man's religious faith
- when the woman would try to leave the relationship
- when anything would go wrong in the man's life.

Onset of the violence

Only three of the women said that the abuse started with overt physical violence then was followed by emotional and psychological abuse. Ten women reported that the violence started within the first few months of the relationship beginning. A further ten women found that their partners became violent to them when they made some form of commitment to the relationship, either living together or getting married.

And the day after we got married was the first time he hit me. (Margo)

First of all it was just mentally, started actually the day after I had married him. Up to us getting married, I lived with him and he was fine. (Denise)

Six women said that their partners became violent seemingly out of the blue after at least one year, but more commonly, several years into the relationship.

The onset and form of violence during pregnancy will be dealt with in a separate section. In addition to the onset of violence during pregnancy, ten women said that their partners first became violent or the violence significantly worsened after the birth of their child. Women often said that they felt that their partners were jealous of the attention the women gave to the children. Women also felt that the men could not cope with the responsibilities of fatherhood and so became violent.

No everything was very ideal to begin with, until the kids come along. Until I had my eldest son, and that's when he changed. (Dawn)

The largest single group of women were those who said that there had been a gradual onset of their partners' violence. Usually this gradual process started with verbal abuse, progressed to pushing and then developed into slapping, punching, kicking and other forms of brutality.

But I think it probably starts with the pushing, you know, pushing you back into a chair and you don't think anything of it, initially you know it's just a push, you know. And then before you know it you're getting the fists and kicked and spat at and sworn at. (Zoe)

Women described how this build-up to the physical violence often made it difficult for them to name what was happening to them as domestic violence.

There would be, there would be things that I didn't recognise as abuse like pushes and shoves and threats, that I never really thought were but ... and the way he spoke to me. And even when he'd actually hit me a few times I always felt that it was my fault. (Danielle)

For many women the verbal abuse they had been subjected to before the physical violence meant that their self-esteem had already been worn down. Consequently, some believed the messages that their partners were consistently giving them, that they were worthless. As a result they frequently blamed themselves for the physical violence.

It makes you feel, how can I say it, that you're worthless, because that's all, because he said to me a lot of the times, 'You provoke me', or, 'You deserve it', and in the end you think maybe you have done it and in the end you think, 'Well what did I say to make him do that?' (Vivien)

Control

The most central aspect to domestic violence is the violent man's need to control totally every aspect of the woman's (and sometimes the children's) life. Other forms of violence such as physical violence may be completely gratuitous but usually fulfil the function of enforcing the man's power and control over the woman and her children. A failure to recognise the extreme nature of this controlling behaviour or not putting isolated incidents in the context of control exerted by the man means that the perception of the violence will be minimised. Women in the study described how every aspect of their lives was controlled by their violent partners:

He'd do things like take the car keys away, couldn't have any money for shopping, had to have receipts, you couldn't watch what you wanted on telly, had to go to bed when you were told, you couldn't do this, you weren't allowed to use the telephone. (Kim)

The effect of this controlling behaviour was to make women totally objectified:

He wants to own you, you are a possession. You belong to him. (Kim)

The most common form of controlling behaviour that women reported being subjected to was isolating them and their children from family and friends. This ranged from making people feel so uncomfortable that they stopped coming to the house, to being violent to the woman's friends and family also. Threats to family and friends served the dual purpose of · isolating the woman from any support networks and ensuring that she stayed in the relationship in order to protect the threatened friends or family members.

Another form of control that women talked about in interviews was restricting their movements so that they were kept in the house. Some women reported being timed when they went out, especially to pick the children up from school. If they did not return within the allotted time they would be physically assaulted. Other women were allowed out on their own only once a week to do the shopping and pay the bills. If anything was forgotten it would have to wait until the next week. Some women were locked in and denied access to medical care, particularly for injuries inflicted by their violent partner. In this way, not only were others unaware of the extent of the violence but also there were no medical records of the numerous injuries sustained by the women. These medical records could have been used to bring a conviction against the violent man or could have been considered in any legal decisions concerning the children. June described how she was not only locked in but also tied up to prevent her escaping.

> Like he locked me in the house and I climbed out the window and down the drainpipe. Don't ask me how! I mean he'd tie me up before he would go out or even get a friend to stand and make sure that I can't go out the door. (June)

Violent men frequently tried to stop their partner talking to anyone else, especially other men. Some of the examples that women gave of the extremes their partners went to in order to control their communication with others were: searching her handbag for phone numbers; always dialling 1471 after incoming calls in order to get the number of the person she had just been talking to; and surreptitiously tape-recording the woman and children's phone calls.

As has been pointed out by Hester *et al.* (1994), Hester and Radford (1996) and Kelly (1988), this control of the woman and children does not automatically stop with the end of the relationship. It is certainly not unusual for violent men to stalk their ex-partners. Interestingly, in this study one man, who had been stalking his ex-partner and children for some time, actually stopped when the new stalking legislation (Protection from Harassment Act 1997) was implemented. A very important aspect of stalking described by women interviewed was how friends and family of the violent man assisted him in tracking down and following the woman and children once they had left him. In this way, as was the situation with one woman and her daughter in this study, the violent man has been able to continue controlling and harassing the woman from prison by having her stalked by his friends. Deirdre explained how she had escaped and gone to a refuge with her children but was tracked down by her ex-partner when one of his family found her file in the housing office and gave him the address of the refuge:

> and he said, 'Don't think you can ever run away from me, because I know your every move, if you sign on at a different social office, I've got people who work for the social, I can find out where you are'. He said, ' ... I can find you wherever you are'. (Deirdre)

Seven women said that when they separated from their ex-partners they had been subjected to stalking and further harassment. Margo recounted how her ex-partner used to leave dozens of messages on her answerphone every day, starting with saying he loved her and wanted her back and finishing with threats against her and her family. Another woman was threatened with having her home set on fire while her children were inside.

Other forms of controlling behaviour women experienced were:

- threatening to injure or kill
- controlling the finances and not giving her any money
- controlling what she could wear, perhaps even buying her clothes
- attempting suicide (sometimes in front of the woman and the children) so that she would not leave
- threatening to take the children if she left
- making sure she could not tell professionals about the violence by staying with her or within earshot when she was talking to them
- claiming she has mental health problems
- stopping her contact with the children when they lived with him
- not allowing her to go to bed until he said she could
- making all the decisions in the house

- not letting the woman get employment outside the home
- not allowing her to attend to the needs of the children.

Another form of control and intimidation used by the violent partner was to smash the woman's possessions or damage the house, for example, ripping up her clothes so that she could not go out. Others felt that it was used more as revenge after they had left. The man would find out where she lived, break in and wreck her new home.

Women were affected by this damage to their property in several ways. First, to watch the level of violence used was very intimidating for both the women and the children; there was always the threat that the violence could be turned on them. Second, women found it very hard financially to try to create a nice home when things were being constantly destroyed. Third, women were very hurt by what they felt these acts of destruction meant, particularly when items of particular sentimental value were destroyed. Some women were saddened that they had no photographs of their children when they were small because their ex-partner had destroyed them.

> It's a regular thing you know to tear up my photos so that I've got no photos, things like that that really hurt. I mean it doesn't sound like it's a lot but you know it's really hurtful to think you had something and it's just been destroyed, just gone just like that. (June)

Children too can be directly affected by having their toys broken or, in some instances, sold. A young person explained:

> He'd tip up everything in my room like, knock everything down and perfume would get smashed and all the curtains would be ripped, throw things on my wall. My mum used to paint my bedroom. I always wanted my bedroom peach, and Mum just painted it peach and I don't know what he threw on it, but he threw something on it and all down the walls. (Mona, aged 17)

In addition to the control that violent men exerted over their partners, women were subjected to specific emotional and psychological abuse, physical and sexual violence, as will be described in the next sections.

Emotional and psychological abuse

> He seemed to shift after Ralph was born, the physical abuse wasn't there but the threat of it, the emotional abuse and the threat of it was always there. So to me it didn't feel any better. (Cheryl)

The majority of women reported that they suffered different forms of abuse concurrently, while others found that their ex-partner used different forms of abuse at different times. Some men stopped using physical violence but continued to use psychological or emotional abuse, and women made the point that this was equally, if not more, intimidating than physical violence was:

> the physical stuff really deteriorated because I think he discovered that it was much more effective to manipulate me and manage and control me if I felt really bad about myself. So it was mostly insults and abuse. (Sheila)

Women described their experiences using words like cruelty and torture and emphasised how the emotional and psychological abuse was a systematic way of wearing down their self-confidence and self-esteem.

> I think in my experience that's how they work, they grind you down mentally, they make you feel totally useless and inept and unable and incapable, and then it's easy for them to just intimidate you without ... just the threat of physical violence is enough, you know, without the actual going through with it. (Lucy)

The most frequently reported form of emotional abuse was constantly belittling the woman, usually by name-calling and criticising everything that she did. Women spoke of not being able to do anything right in their partners' eyes, and they would then be beaten or humiliated.

Using the children against their mother was the next most frequent method of emotional abuse used. This usually involved constantly telling the woman (and sometimes others) that she was not fit to look after the children, that she was a dreadful mother. Other methods used were stopping the woman's contact with her children, sending abusive messages back to the woman through her children, trying to turn the children against their mother and threatened or actual abduction of the children.

Another tactic used against women was sleep deprivation. One woman described the impact on her son:

You know, at one stage I had to go to school and explain to them why he was so tired, because his father woke us up every single, solitary night in the middle of the night, shouting, screaming and swearing. (Kim)

Accusing the women of mental health problems or alcohol abuse was also used, and Danielle described how her partner used this to stop her seeking help:

When I'd had the police here, he said after the policeman had gone, the police actually went out to talk to him and he'd said that the police had said to him, 'God mate what's she on, there's something wrong with her.' You know, and he'd always prey on my mind thinking that there's something wrong with me mentally, that I was unstable. (Danielle)

Other women were subjected to death threats:

And the times he'd told them [the children] things like 'I'm going to strangle your mum, I'll go to Broadmoor and I'll still see my children'. I think he knew what the fashion was in the family court, it doesn't matter what a father does, the attitude is that the mother is causing this. (Marcia)

On the other hand three men injured themselves or threatened to commit suicide in front of the women and their children:

one of the threats he'd made was to kill the two children, him and the children in the car. (Danielle)

Other forms of emotional and psychological abuse women reported were:

- not allowing the woman to have a light on while bathing and telling the woman that men had been spying on her getting dressed in her home

- when angry, sitting in the car blowing the horn continuously

- leaving lists of things for the woman to do while he was at work; if she did not or could not do them (for example, fix the car) she was beaten up

- making women do their hair and make-up a certain way

- mocking the woman's grief at her father's death

- forcing the woman to have an abortion, then shouting round the neighbourhood that she was a 'baby killer'

- blaming the woman because her uncle sexually abused her daughter

- having affairs and taking girlfriends on holiday while the woman and children never had a holiday

- trying to match the woman up with his friend so he could see someone else

- blaming the woman for everything that went wrong in his life

- making the woman sleep on the floor.

The following quotes illustrate the irrationality of the man's behaviour and how difficult it is for the woman to find ways of coping. It is worth noting that none of the men in the following examples had any mental health problems.

Margo had a benign breast lump; her ex-partner told everyone she was dying of cancer and had only six months to live.

> I had developed a lump, but I'd had the biopsy done and had the all clear but he was telling everyone. I had six months. No until 18, he tells people that I'm in a hospice now with a few weeks to go. And he's actually got a few people take him around money to buy flowers for me. He's actually got people who still think that I'm there. (Margo)

Judith described her experiences:

> He would lash out, he'd throw things, not always at me, the big thing was throwing himself on the floor and pretending to like knock himself out and he would just lay down on the floor for about ten minutes. And then he would get up, pretend he didn't know where he was. But if anybody came knocking on the door he would get up and sort of disappear for a bit, so I knew he was just pretending. I soon learned very, very quickly that that was just pretending. I just left him to it and would walk away from him. (Judith)

Camilla's ex-partner broke into her new home, stole her underwear and set her bed on fire.

> He even broke in and set light to my bed which was quite frightening the way he did it, he done it all with the bible and just laid it under the bed and set light to it. We had the police involved and everything again and to me that was really freaky, that was more psychological abuse than physical ... And the bible was laid under the bed, there was this little pot of water

which was I presume must have been blessed water or whatever he thought it was, and there was a big ritual in my bedroom, and it really did freak me out. (Camilla)

The effect of such behaviour was that the women and children lived in constant anticipation of an abusive incident, trying to second-guess what mood the man would be in.

But it's more like the mental cruelty, the mental things that drive you mad, it's like not knowing when he comes in, is he gonna start? Loads of things, it's the thought of him starting that is more frightening than the hitting. (Vivien)

A number of women made the point that it was much harder to 'get over' the emotional and psychological abuse than the physical violence. As Bernice explains, perhaps the reason or one of the reasons for this is that things constantly trigger the feelings associated with the emotional and psychological abuse.

I could handle the mind games but that leaves you ... actually damaged for a lot longer, because I still hear something or see something that sets this fear off. I don't like people knowing me thoughts too much or trying to get into me head so that leaves you a lot more emotionally scarred than anything that they can do. I mean he could have broke me leg in fifty places and I could walk with a limp for the rest of me life but it would heal but it's taken a long time to get me head together, and for Kara [my daughter] to get it together as well really. (Bernice)

Physical violence

Forty women (83%) said that they had experienced physical violence. Thirty-one of these described being hit or punched, and seven reported that the violence was specifically aimed at their heads. June suffered a brain haemorrhage and thereafter her partner always targeted her head. Six women had been knocked unconscious. Cheryl had been nearly killed when she had been punched, knocked down the stairs and hit her head on a concrete post. Marina talked about how her partner had walked out after hitting her, leaving her two small babies alone with their unconscious mother.

A small number of women were hit where the bruising would not show; one abusive man told the woman that he would never hit her on her face because then people would know what was happening. Women who do not have obvious physical marks of the violence can find it difficult to make others believe them when they need help.

Five women talked about their partner being violent when they had been holding a child, and how frightening that had been for the woman and child:

> he came at me with a broken bottle and I was holding one of the twins then and he came at me. I mean the children weren't actually harmed but it is a possibility. (Marina)

Contrary to the popular notion that mothers fail to protect their children from the violence, as the following quote illustrates, protecting the children was uppermost in the women's minds, even when they were being brutally attacked themselves.

> And he picked up a wooden coat hanger and started hitting me with it and I had Francis in my arms so I'm using my body to shield Francis to make sure that he couldn't hit Francis. (Judith)

These were not situations of children being caught in the crossfire. There was no crossfire: it was unidirectional. Women were attending to the children's needs and were attacked. These men chose to be violent to the women irrespective of the children's safety. The mothers' fears for their children's safety may give an added dimension to the abusive men's feelings of power. Jasmine was very clear that her partner was totally in control and 'knew exactly what he was doing'. She was holding her newborn baby at the time of the attack.

> I mean after Fred was born, and then he was only 3 days old, and he got this knife and he run it down my neck, he only caught my neck, I mean he was going to kill me, I know he was, oh it was terrible. (Jasmine)

Women most commonly were attacked by men using their fists and/or feet. Occasionally men would use objects or weapons, including threats to shoot. Other everyday objects which were used by the violent men as weapons were a broken bottle, a spirit level, a baseball bat and a wooden coat hanger. In addition one woman was strangled with a cord and women reported that men threw glasses or knives.

Women were subjected to severe violence leaving them with both short- and long-term injuries. In this study abusive men were responsible for women having bruised eyes, broken bones (jaw, noses and fingers), burst lip, a burst ear-drum, hair ripped out and miscarriages; one woman had a cigarette extinguished on her foot, and another suffered a brain haemorrhage. Margo was diagnosed as having multiple sclerosis shortly after being interviewed for the study. She felt that it might be attributable (at least in part) to all the head injuries she received at the hands of her husband.

A number of women reported that their partners threw things at them, including glasses, keys, knives, ashtrays or bowls. Kim explained how the physical violence started with her partner throwing things:

> he threw that brass ashtray at me. I had seven stitches in my head – that was the start of it, and once they've done it once it just goes on and on and on, you know. (Kim)

Sexual violence

Fifteen women (31%) reported that they had experienced sexual violence from their ex-partners. Women were not asked specifically about sexual violence, so the responses were dependent on how women defined forced sex, how comfortable they were in talking to the interviewer about it and how relevant they saw it to the study. The latter point is particularly important as the question on violence or abuse experienced was couched in terms of how much the children were aware of the violence or how it impacted on the children. In fact a number of the women referred to their difficulty in naming their experiences as rape because they were married to or living with the offender. Rape is generally viewed as something committed by strangers. Some women said that the sexual violence was temporally linked to other forms of abuse they experienced; usually after an incident of physical or psychological abuse they would then be raped.

Three of the women interviewed specifically referred to the children witnessing the rapes. Margo said:

> He just didn't care, he knew that they were there, I mean Sabrina would be trying to pull him off of me. And he didn't give a damn, he just didn't care. (Margo)

Camilla spoke of her fears that he would rape her daughter.

> He raped me once, and it frightened me that he would actually do it to Marilyn. And I think he must have known what was frightening me because he said, 'When you've outgrown your usefulness there's another female in the house', and that is what frightened me. (Camilla)

Marianne was raped by her ex-partner and when she managed to leave was forced to return to the relationship when he threatened to have her eldest daughter raped. Two women were raped by their partners during pregnancy and a further two women became pregnant as a result of their partners raping them.

Economic abuse

> As long as he's got the money you know, he's got the power, he's got a hold over you. (Kim)

Seven women (15%) mentioned specifically that they had been controlled by being deprived of money. Five of these women reported that their ex-partner would not give them money towards food or clothes for the children or that he would take money off them that they needed for the children. As Margo pointed out, not having any money hinders women getting help.

> Because my problem was I had to go to a solicitor's in one place, the housing office somewhere else, the benefits office somewhere else. You've got no money so you're walking everywhere. (Margo)

Another woman had her clothes ripped up and as her money was taken from her every week by her ex-partner, she had to stay in the house as she had no clothes in which to go out. Finally, Lana was left with a lot of debt as her ex partner would order from catalogues in her name and then not pay the bills.

Violence to others

Nine women and their children talked about the man being abusive or violent to others outside the immediate family. In these situations, the violent man would harass the woman's family or friends in an attempt to find her and the children.

> And now even when we're not there, he keeps on phoning up my grandma and my auntie because he can't get through to us. (Regina, aged 9)

The result of the threat of or actual violence to those close to the women meant that they felt responsible for the safety of family and friends. Therefore women tried to protect others by not telling them about the violence. As well as increasing the isolation of women while in the relationships, it meant that they felt trapped, unable to find a way out of the relationship without putting others at risk:

> because I knew the hassle he was gonna give to other people as well, and that's another thing, that's why a lot of women even in here [the refuge] say why they have never done it earlier is because of the hassle the partners are going to give everybody else. (Dawn)

Violence during pregnancy

Previous studies have drawn attention to the particular issue of domestic violence during pregnancy. Andrews and Brown (1988) reported that women who were experiencing violence reported more severe violence when pregnant than at other times and because of the violence women were twice as likely to suffer miscarriages. Mezey and Bewley (1997) further found that the risk of moderate to severe violence to the woman appears to be greatest in the period after the baby is born.

The present study found that violence during pregnancy was a theme that arose again and again in the interviews with mothers. Some women found that the violence first started when they were pregnant, others said that the violence continued despite the pregnancy. Generally being pregnant may serve to increase women's vulnerability rather than affording any protection from the violence.

Eight women said that their partners' violence first started when the woman was pregnant. Women themselves suggested that the reason for the violence was that their partners were jealous: they felt excluded by the fact of the woman's pregnancy. Kim found that the violence started when her pregnancy began to show.

> It was great before Seamus was born, we did everything together. We partied together, we did everything, we shared our own friends, we went out to parties, we had great times, we shared everything. From problems to good times, we shared everything, it was a really solid, well, what I considered a solid relationship. As Seamus arrived, when I fell pregnant with Seamus it almost immediately, it changed as when I started showing. That's when his attitude towards me changed, he seen my role to have changed. (Kim)

A number of women said that once they told their partners that they were pregnant, the men accused them of being unfaithful and insisted that the baby was someone else's. Pregnancy became woven into the net of the man's abusive behaviour and was used as another means of controlling the woman. Alma's husband made her have an abortion, saying that the baby was not his. Then he said that it was obviously true that it was not his baby because she had got rid of the evidence of her infidelity.

Some women find that violence during pregnancy is totally focused on the pregnancy itself. Threatening to induce or actually inducing miscarriage was part of the pattern of abuse used by the partners of ten of the women.

> He said, 'I could make you miscarry it'. And he was like sort of punching me in the stomach, dragging me over the bed and you know I was panicking then because I really didn't want to lose it. (Amanda)

One woman described how her partner tried to force her to have an abortion right up until she was five months pregnant. Another man, when told his partner was pregnant, immediately called his friend to drive her to hospital to have an abortion. Later, she says,

> he just wanted to boot the baby out of me. (Marianne)

In another family, the man was unhappy with the woman's second pregnancy. The woman had a threatened miscarriage and was hospitalised for a week due to the man's beatings. Women were sometimes placed in a completely no-win situation where they were beaten for being pregnant, then threatened or beaten if they then had a threatened or actual miscarriage.

> Even when I was pregnant with Rod he threw me against the door so hard and I sat there all night until he went to bed because I was just too scared to move in case he hit me again or in case I lost him [the baby]. I was frightened of moving because I was six or seven months pregnant at the time, and he had threatened me with that as well, he said if I had a miscarriage and blamed him for it he would actually kill me. (Alma)

Some women had very premature babies and they felt it was due to the violence they had experienced during pregnancy. In other instances, although the violence first started when the woman was pregnant, blows to the abdomen were avoided.

> He would never go near me stomach when I was pregnant, he never touched me in me stomach when I was pregnant, he would avoid that, it would be like me legs or me arms more than anything. The back of me head. But he never ever tried to touch me stomach. (Jacinta)

Twelve women had already been experiencing violence before becoming pregnant and found that the violence continued despite the pregnancy.

Being pregnant did not protect women from sexual violence either. Two women were raped by their partners while they were pregnant. Deirdre was eight and half months pregnant when her partner raped her:

> He pushed me on the floor in the bedroom, shut the children out, forced himself on me in the bedroom, and I was eight and a half months pregnant. And I remember just laying there, just thinking nothing, you just go completely numb, and then I remember he got off, and I went into the shower and I must have sat in that shower for two hours. I just felt so dirty, especially because I [was pregnant] as well and I remember just sitting there rocking and then he came up as if nothing had happened. (Deirdre)

Camilla went into labour because her partner raped her. Her partner raped her again as soon as she returned from the hospital after giving birth.

Only three women said that the physical violence stopped while they were pregnant. However, these women pointed out that although the physical violence stopped, the emotional abuse continued or even worsened.

Some men seemed to resent the pregnancy and the woman's consequent contact with health professionals as an area that was harder for them to control. Thus, men prevented their partners accessing health care while pregnant. In one case the man refused to get medical help for the woman and she subsequently miscarried.

Marianne's partner caused a scene in the hospital after the baby was born because she could not leave when he wanted.

> Then when I did give birth to her, he came to pick me up because I was only staying in for six hours and they wouldn't let her home because they wanted to keep a check on her. And when he called for me to go home, I said, 'I can't go'. I pretended that I had to stay in as well. He went berserk, he hated the baby. Wish it had died, it was keeping me away from going home. (Marianne)

This example is chillingly reminiscent of violent men's behaviour noted by Reder, Duncan and Gray (1993) in a review of reports of thirty-five inquiries into child deaths. They reported that the fathers of Heidi Koseda (in this case a stepfather), Shirley Woodcock, Simon Peacock and Charlene Salt all created disturbances in the maternity unit. They interpret this behaviour as evidence that the violent man 'was desperate for them to return home to within his ambit of control' (Reder *et al.* 1993, p.45). Clearly, pregnancy is a time when women may have greater contact with professionals and, as the examples illustrate, there may be indications of domestic violence. However, as O'Hara (1994) points out, the implications of the man's behaviour for the woman and child are too frequently overlooked, in some instances with tragic results.

Mother trying to reassure the children

The attempts of mothers to reassure and protect the children even while they themselves were being assaulted is an important issue emerging from the interviews. When Leila was brutally assaulted by her partner on the street, throughout the attack her main concern was keeping her daughter safe.

> This particular occasion he broke my nose, in the street, of kicking me until my nose broke. And she [my daughter] seen that and all I could do was hold her into the railings to stop her going into the road. The more I was holding her, not holding her, but keeping her back from the road, the more he was kicking me. So I know she was aware, she seen that. (Leila)

Another mother endured a rape by her ex-partner in near silence so as not to waken and terrify her children. Other mothers referred to talking to the children during the assault, trying to reassure them:

> he came up the stairs, had me pinned up against the bed, of course the children were crying their eyes out. I'm just saying to them, 'Don't worry, don't worry, like, you know. (Amanda)

Involving the child in the abuse of the mother

In many situations the violence to the mother was clearly unconnected to the child in any way. However, in other examples that women gave, their children were involved in some way:

> because they [the children] were my weak spot – they were my number one – but it's only now that I look back and I know, that's, that was what he used. Even when I left him and I had a secret hiding place and he hired a private detective, he found me. He even said then, because if I saw him so many nights a week he would leave the kids alone, he wouldn't let the kids know that he was about. Otherwise if I didn't he would follow [my daughter] to work, [he said] 'I could have quite easily got her raped...'. The thing was there, the threat was there, so [I said] 'Yeah all right I will meet you,' anything to keep him away from them. (Marianne)

Kelly (1994) refers to this as a 'double level of intentionality' which she defines thus: 'That an act directed against one individual is at the same time intended to affect another or others' (p.47). Hester and Pearson (1998) also provide examples where the abuse of the woman and the children by the same man was so closely interconnected that they describe them as simultaneous expressions of both domestic violence and child abuse. In the present study, mothers most frequently talked about intervening to protect the child and then being beaten themselves.

> Yeah, because he took everything out on her, everything was always her fault, I always sided with her, [I got] constant beatings, most of it was all about Mona [my daughter]. Because he would treat her in a way, and I would intervene and say no, and then he would start on me, but at least it took the heat off her. (June)

In one case the man was violent to the mother when she intervened to protect the child and then he told the child that it was all his fault that his mother was hurt.

Hester and Radford (1996) found that some violent men forced the children to be physically abusive to their mothers. In the present study, some mothers discussed how the children began to emulate the abuser's behaviour and how hurtful they felt it was to suffer abuse from their children. In addition, although children may not be directly involved in the physical violence to the mother, a number of women interviewed reported that their partner had involved the child in degrading or humiliating their mother. For example, the abusive men had involved the children in making up derogatory songs or drawing caricatures of their mothers. These behaviours led to intense guilt among the children, who very often believed that they were to blame for the man's violence. It also forced the children to become involved in the violence by making them take sides (not necessarily of their choosing). In other cases, the abuser deliberately tried to turn the children against their mother. One woman, whose first husband and father of the children had died, described how her abusive second husband told the children that she had killed their father.

Women frequently discussed how their partners would threaten to harm or take the children in order to control the woman. Threats of taking the children away from their mothers worked very effectively to keep women in violent relationships. One man always took one of the children with him whenever he left the house because he knew that the woman would be unable to leave without all the children. A similar tactic was reported in studies by Hester and Radford (1996) and Malos and Hague (1993). Threats to kidnap the children were not unusual and in some cases these threats were carried out. Women described their feelings of absolute helplessness as they waited for the safe return of their children (in some cases, not for several months). Often they felt let down by the police, who were hampered by the fact that the children were with their father and no court orders (e.g. residence order) were in place. One woman who had left several times and always been found, felt that she had no choice but to have her baby adopted, in order to protect her from the violent man.

One woman was told that if she wanted to leave she must leave one of the children with him, as she did not deserve to have both children. She had to choose which child to leave behind. He threatened to kill her if she did not write a note giving him custody. The woman did leave and the second child was returned to her care a week later.

In other situations when women had left, their ex-partners threatened to harm the children. In all of these scenarios, threats to remove or harm the children worked to force the women to return to the violent relationship. The mother's desperate attempts to flee the violence could not withstand the stronger need to protect her children. As Morley and Mullender (1994) point out, for some time now the evidence has highlighted that women are most at risk from their violent partners around the time of leaving. What has not really been acknowledged but was suggested by some of the experiences described in this study is that the risk to children may also be increased at this point as their father threatens their safety as a way of forcing their mother to stay in or return to the relationship. Mothers may find themselves in a no-win situation as it is often concern about the safety of their children which spurs them to leave in the first place. However, the increased risk to their children may force them back into the situation from which they had been trying to protect them. It is very important that service providers recognise this increased risk to both women and children who are trying to escape domestic violence so that an appropriate response can be planned and delivered in a manner which ensures women's and children's safety.

Impact of violence on women

Women tried to cope with the violence on a daily basis in a variety of ways. The most frequently used strategies were those which aimed to protect the children, usually by trying to minimise the children's awareness of the violence. One of the most common impacts of domestic violence was on the women's health, both in the short term and the long term. The stress of living, and trying to cope, with the man's violence was the most commonly cited cause for these health problems.

Not surprisingly, women reported a number of psychological impacts of the violence, including depression, fear, loss of self-esteem and self-confidence as well as loss of trust in others. These psychological impacts, particularly the loss of self-esteem, in turn made it more difficult for many women to find sources of help, particularly when initial efforts to seek support had been rebuffed.

While in the violent relationship, mothers felt that it affected their relationship with the children, particularly in terms of making them more irritable. After leaving the violent man, however, most mothers felt that they had in fact become closer to their children because of everything they had been through together. At the time women felt somewhat emotionally distanced from their children and consequently felt guilty that they had been so focused on day-to-day survival that they had not been as able to attend to the children's emotional needs as much as they would have liked. Abrahams (1994) found that mothers in her study also reported this emotional distance from their children when they were trying to cope with the domestic violence. The relationship between mothers and children at times also became strained as the children became violent to their mother or women found the children's behavioural problems very difficult to deal with. On the other hand, some women also said that their children became very protective of and loving towards them.

It is not just women's relationship with their children which is affected by the domestic violence but also their relationships with family and friends. Isolating the woman from her family and friends was a deliberate tactic used by the violent man as part of the abusive control. Re-establishing the links with family and friends can be difficult for the woman, particularly if she has to move away to escape the violence. In addition the erosion of the woman's self-esteem and self-confidence meant that it was not very easy for her to make new friendships.

Types of violence experienced by children

As Chapter 1 illustrated, a number of studies have concluded that when domestic violence is present the children in the family may also be at risk of harm. In the present study, children were not directly asked about abuse they had experienced. Therefore, the information in this section comes from details volunteered by children, young people or their mothers. Thus, the rates of abuse reported are dependent on children and young people choosing to disclose the information in interviews and mothers being aware of any abuse suffered by their children and discussing it with the interviewer. The types of abuse are summarised in Figure 2.1

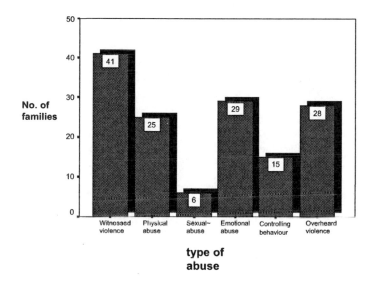

Figure 2.1 Types of abuse experienced by children

Emotional abuse

Emotional abuse of the children was present in twenty-nine families (60%). This describes a range of behaviours directed at the children themselves and separate from any emotional abuse they may have suffered by witnessing the abuse of their mothers. Repeatedly, mothers referred to the emotional abuse experienced by the children as having a more profound and long-term effect than any physical abuse.

The most frequently mentioned emotionally abusive behaviour was calling the child names:

> he used to call me 'a little slut', and that because I would have my friends round and when I was about 13 I had couple of boys round, and he was saying, 'Oh I bet she's doing this that and the other with them', and all that. And then when I came down he was saying, 'Oh you little slag Hannah, you are a little slut'. And I was thinking, hold on, I shouldn't have to stand here and take this from him. (Hannah, aged 15)

Humiliating the child and constantly putting the child down was also a feature of the emotional abuse:

> And he made me go to school in what I had on the night before to clean up in. But Mrs Smith [my teacher] 'cause she knew about it by this stage, I was all right. I went straight into the office and she phoned him up…and I said, 'Don't do anything, don't do anything 'cause you'll get me in trouble' and she just phoned up and said, 'I'm sorry but Mona can't come in these clothes.' And when I got in he was laughing at the fact that he thought he'd humiliated me because I'd had to go to school in my own clothes. (Mona, aged 17)

Mona's mother provided another example of the emotional abuse her daughter was subjected to:

> when she first started her periods he did things like, chase her round the house, and he said, 'Dirty little girl'. (Larissa)

In some cases, mothers referred to their ex-partners making fun of the child's learning difficulty or disability.

In addition, trying to involve the children in the emotional abuse of the mother was experienced as abusive by the children themselves. For example, one mother (Kim) talked about how her 5-year-old son would say that he just couldn't stand any more of listening to his father constantly berating his mother.

A clearer picture of how the children were emotionally abused emerges when looking at the specific examples that mothers and children gave. The following examples illustrate how the abuser's behaviour in each case is designed to have the most hurtful impact.

Specific forms of emotional abuse

- Told child she 'should have been an abortion', that her mother had not wanted her and the only reason her mum and dad had married was because her mum was pregnant with her.

- Was cruel to the child's pet.

- Deliberately broke the children's toys.

- Locked mother out of the house then told the children that she had left because she did not care for them or want them to live with her.

- If child wanted to do something he did not agree with he would say that she did not love him and would say that he was ill and dying. In this case he would also stare at her, nag her and pick on her.

- Gave blatant preferential treatment to his own child.

- Told child her grandmother did not really like her when her grandmother was her main source of support.

- Told the children that their mother's disability would get better if they came to live with him.

- Ripped up a report detailing children's achievement at school and posted the pieces to them.

- Threatened to send child away so he can no longer live with his mother and father because he was having problems at school.

- Told child that mother is an unfit mother and he is going to get custody and that child has to stand up in court and say 'terrible things' about mother.

- Threatened to child to burn the house down.

- Threatened to burn children's bikes if mother left, and told child 'you haven't got a daddy any more'.

- Deprived children of sleep and would not allow them to play so that they had to spend all their time praying.

- Told child that mother was having an affair, that she was taking drugs and that she had AIDS and was going to die – all untrue.

Physical abuse

Previous research identified that children living with domestic violence may be physically abused by the violent man. Abrahams (1994) reported a figure of 27 per cent while Epstein and Keep (1995) cited a higher figure of 38 per cent based on calls to ChildLine from children experiencing domestic violence. The present research found that a variety of physically abusive behaviours against children were reported by both the mothers and the children. In all cases the perpetrator was the mother's violent partner. These physically abusive behaviours directed at the children ranged from severe physical assaults to cases where the mother was concerned that the physical 'discipline' used on the child was too harsh or she feared that the man would lose control. In one case the man hit the child with an iron bar. Some form of physical abuse was reported in twenty-five families (52%). This figure may actually reflect a higher rate than the previous studies or be attributable to the fact that a broader definition was used to include behaviours that caused concern rather than those actions that could narrowly be defined as violence. In all cases, the impact was similar, that is, producing feelings of intimidation.

In nineteen families the concerns centred on the children being hit. A number of mothers appeared to struggle with the notion of physical punishment of children as normative parental behaviour and their own experiences of physical violence from the perpetrator. One mother said:

> but it was still only smacking, you know; it wasn't, there weren't any... no belts or anything. But I know how hard he hits 'cause I've felt it. (Sheila)

And the point was also made by her child:

> He'd get really cross with me and he was really rough really. He didn't know his own strength and sometimes like he'd smack us and he'd only think it was a little tap but we'd end up with ... really red wherever he'd hit us. (Regina, aged 9)

This fear of the perpetrator's possible loss of control, or the feeling that he was not acting within acceptable codes of behaviour, meant that children always had to be alert. Children recognised the power of the abuser particularly in relation to themselves and their mother. He appeared omnipotent and they could see how little power their mother had in relation to him.

> Most people if they get drunk they like laugh and be funny and joke but he didn't. He would like beat Mummy up. And he keeps on smacking me and [my brother] round the head. Mummy tells him not to because she says, you'll give them brain damage, that can happen, and he kept on doing it. He didn't listen to Mummy. (Sabrina, aged 10)

In some cases where a child was not the man's own child, the young person could be subjected to harsher physical abuse than other children in the family. In other cases where the man was not the father, the child in a sense received better treatment as the disciplining of the child was seen to be totally the mother's responsibility. In the majority of cases no pattern was identifiable. Further research examining the differential treatment of siblings by the violent man would be useful in identifying factors that may increase or decrease risk for children living with domestic violence; in addition it would be useful to explore what the long-term impacts of this differential treatment are for sibling relationships.

The next most common concern regarding physical abuse of the children by the violent man was throwing the child. This was reported by nine families. In one case a 1-year-old was thrown, narrowly missing an area of concrete. In another family a small boy was thrown down the stairs. In these situations the child was usually trying to protect the mother during an assault and was thrown out of the way or the child was thrown because of some perceived misdemeanour.

In addition, the violent men threw things such as darts or plates at the children. One young boy raised his hand to defend himself as his father threw a plate at him. The plate broke and the boy was injured. A mother described an incident where her partner threw a large cabinet on top of the baby, who was in a bouncy chair on the floor. Luckily, the fabric of the chair split and the baby fell on to the floor while the frame of the chair supported the weight of the cabinet.

In four families the children were pushed by the man, again very often pushing them out of the way. A further three mothers talked specifically about the children being hurt during an assault on the mother. For example, one man threw a boiling kettle at the mother and the boiling water caught the child also. In these situations, while the primary intention may not have been to hurt the child, the man was certainly reckless as to the child's safety. Other physically abusive behaviours reported were:

- making a child eat raw onions and raw liver
- slamming a door hard on a child, just missing her fingers
- shoving a child's head in a dirty dishwasher
- strapping a child to the bed with a belt
- shaking a 4-week old baby
- dragging a child down the stairs and 'accidentally' squashing his head in a sliding door
- running a young person over with the car
- dangling a child over the stairs or out of a window
- twisting children's ears
- spitting at a young person.

Controlling children's behaviour

Fifteen families interviewed (31%) referred to how the violent man totally controlled the children's behaviour, often using techniques we know, from practice and research, are used to control their partners. The techniques used to control children's behaviour were generally arbitrary, based on what would have most meaning for that child. However, some common patterns could be seen and are described below.

Not allowing children to play

This was an aspect of the man's behaviour that was mentioned by five families. One mother said that the violence towards the children started with the man putting their toys away where they could not reach them and it escalated from there. Others would deliberately break the children's toys or make the children watch, as one by one he would throw their toys in the bin. Children's play was also restricted when they were outside the home by not allowing them to take part in activities at school or nursery; for example, giving instructions to the nursery that the little boy could not play on the climbing frame like the other children. Kara described how she was not allowed to play, but was made to do chores all the time. She explained how she was coerced by the abuser.

> He said, 'If you don't do them, I'll hit your mum', and when he said 'Otherwise I'll hit your mum', I felt scared so I thought I had better do them. (Kara, aged 10)

Controlling children's movements within the home

An unexpected finding, but one which five families spontaneously discussed, was that children's movements within the home were restricted. Usually, this took the form of not allowing children in certain rooms of the house, generally the sitting room, or the room where the family would normally gather together. Other children were made to stay in their bedrooms all the time, being allowed out only to eat. Ralph talked about how he was made to stay in his bedroom and how he was not allowed to sit on his bed or his bedroom floor and at times would not even be allowed to go to the toilet.

> I wasn't very happy and we [my sister and I] wasn't allowed down in the front room at all, we had to stay in our bedrooms. We had to stay, the only time we could come out was when we eat. (Ralph, aged 9)

Another young girl described what a treat it was to go to her granny's house where she was allowed to help with the cooking and washing up because she was not even allowed inside the kitchen at home. Other children referred to being locked in rooms and being very frightened and one brother and sister used to be padlocked into their room at night.

Other behaviours that children and mothers described fell into two general categories: methods used to control totally or regiment children's behaviour and methods by which the man intimidated the children.

Methods of regimenting children's behaviour

Examples of behaviours used to control and dominate the children were given by both mothers and children. Mothers described how the children were not allowed to make any noise, how the children became very quiet and controlled around their father, how they were afraid to ask questions. One mother also talked about how her ex-partner would call the children in from playing to change the television station for him. Another mother referred to how her ex-partner would control whether or not the children were allowed to talk to her. Controlling the children's food intake was used by the violent men in two families, so that they would decide whether or not the children could even have a drink of water if they were thirsty.

Methods of intimidating children

Forms of intimidation that children were exposed to include:

- constantly staring at them
- making a 16-year-old feel so uncomfortable that she left home
- involving children's friends in arguments so they could not bring friends round
- not allowing children to have friends around
- holding child and mother hostage in the house
- damaging furniture in response to child's behaviour and in this way terrifying the child
- depriving children of sleep
- answering the telephone and telling friends not to phone to speak to the young person
- manipulating things said to the children by outside agencies to back up his wishes

- punishing a child repeatedly for being naughty
- stalking children.

Sexual abuse

None of the mothers and children were specifically asked about sexual abuse, and as sexual abuse, more than any other form of abuse to children, may be hidden, the information received about sexual abuse should be understood as very likely to be an underestimate in terms of prevalence. The information regarding sexual abuse was spontaneously volunteered by those taking part. Six children (11%) had been sexually abused by the violent man. Three of the men were the children's father and three were stepfathers. Five of the children abused were girls and one was a boy.

In five families there had been a child protection investigation carried out. In three cases it was decided not to go ahead with a prosecution due to lack of evidence. Two of these decisions were made by the Crown Prosecution Service and one by social services and the police. In the latter case the woman made the man leave the home and social services told her that if she allowed him to return they would remove her daughter. She felt that it was the correct approach to take. At the time of the interview, one woman and her daughter were waiting to learn the court date for the case. In the final case the prosecution went ahead and the man was found guilty and imprisoned.

Fiona referred to how her father emotionally as well as sexually abused her and how this made it all the more difficult to tell anyone about the sexual abuse.

> He used to touch me like when I was in bed. He used to always sort of sit down and go on about how we didn't love him and things and he was going to die and stuff like that. (Fiona, aged 15)

One man told the young girl that her mother had asked him to abuse her sexually and that if she told anyone he would kill her mother, she would be put in a children's home and no one would believe her. He backed up his threats by holding a knife to her throat.

The children were all aware of the violence to their mothers so knew what the violent man was capable of. Goddard and Hiller (1993) emphasise how domestic violence may serve to prevent children disclosing the sexual abuse: 'The existence of other forms of violence, and the victimisation of others by violence will present a major obstacle to the disclosure of abuse' (p.27). In the present study, it took the children a long time to say anything about the sexual abuse they were experiencing, although all of them were 'acting out' their distress behaviourally, for example with nightmares. The little boy who had been abused had come to the attention of the authorities because of his sexualised behaviour, but at that point it was interpreted as being behaviour he had picked up from other children, so nothing happened. Children spoke of their fear of not being believed as inhibiting them from saying anything. As Fiona said:

> So sometimes I'd maybe think it wasn't worth talking to anybody 'cause they might not believe me. (Fiona, aged 15)

Not surprisingly children found it very difficult to disclose the details of the abuse and in the following example it took Shirley two hours before she was able to describe what had happened to her even though she felt the professional's response was sympathetic.

> And they asked me, well to tell them what was going on and they said that I could either speak to them about it or I could write it down. I wrote it down because I had to go into a lot of details and draw diagrams and things and it was really embarrassing but I did it all... They were really nice to me. They made me feel like there was no pressure and I could tell them any way I wanted, the way that would make me feel best. They were both female, that was all right. I think personally they were good with me. (Shirley, aged 16)

Children and their mothers felt very let down when the decision not to prosecute was taken. Mothers felt that as hard as it was for them to accept, it was much harder for the children because they felt, first, that they had not been believed, and second, that the man had not been punished for what he had done.

Summary

It is clear from women's descriptions that the man's violence was around his desire to control the woman and children and was not in response to predictable triggers. Every aspect of women's lives was controlled by their violent partners and the most frequent form of this control was to isolate the woman from family and friends. The most common pattern seemed to be a gradual onset of the violence beginning early on in the relationship or after some form of commitment was made. This finding was also reported by Hester and Radford (1992), Kelly (1988) and Pahl (1985). The gradual onset made it very hard for women to recognise that what was happening was domestic violence.

The emotional and psychological abuse that women experienced meant that women and children lived in a constant state of anticipation, wondering what he was going to do next. Many women said that it was harder to 'get over' the emotional and psychological abuse than the physical violence. Most (83%) of the women experienced physical violence, at times life threatening. Women were commonly attacked while holding small children, which added a further dimension of threat to the violence.

Fifteen women (31%) spontaneously said they had experienced sexual violence from their ex-partners and as women were not specifically asked about the prevalence of sexual violence, it is possible that the true prevalence is higher than this. As with other forms of violence to the mother, children were also involved in the sexual violence in a number of ways. First, children were conceived as a result of rape by the violent man; second, women were raped during pregnancy, sometimes inducing labour with subsequent health risks for both the woman and the child; third, children tried to stop their fathers raping their mothers by physically intervening; fourth, mothers feared that their violent partners would also rape their daughters which then became another way of controlling the women and ensuring that they stayed in the relationship.

Only nine women said that their partners were violent to people outside the family unit and in most of these cases the targets were the women's extended family and friends. Thus, there was no indication that these men were violent generally.

As has been reported by Hoff (1990) and Mezey and Bewley (1997), this study found that becoming pregnant does not mean an end to the violence for many women; in fact the violence may start or increase during pregnancy. Women who were being abused before they became pregnant often reported that the violence continued. When the physical violence did stop in pregnancy the emotional and psychological abuse increased.

Children were involved in the violence in a number of ways; perhaps the most obvious way was when mothers intervened to protect the children and were then beaten themselves. In addition threats to harm or abduct the children kept women in violent relationships or made them return to the violent man once they had left.

Children experienced a range of abusive behaviour from the violent man. Nearly two-thirds of children experienced emotional abuse. Mothers felt that this emotional abuse had more profound and long-term effects than physical abuse. Some form of physical abuse to children was reported in over half of the families and in nearly one-third the violent men totally controlled the children's lives in a similar fashion to that in which they controlled the women. Six children had been sexually abused by the violent man. These figures indicate that when there is domestic violence there is a strong possibility that any children in the household may also be abused by the violent man, as well as suffering from the effects of witnessing the violence. Domestic violence should be perceived then, as a possible indicator of risk to children and the source of that risk is the violent man.

CHAPTER THREE

Forms of Violence
Witnessed By Children

Children witnessing the abuse of their mother

In forty-one families (85%) children were physically present while their mothers were being abused in some way. What exactly does it mean for children to witness domestic violence? Similar to the findings of Abrahams (1994: 73%), in the majority of the families involved in this research thirty-four children (71%) saw their mothers being physically assaulted.

> Daddy punched my mum. My mum just didn't do nothing back and then he started punching her even harder. (Paul, aged 6)

In two of the families the children had seen their mothers knocked unconscious on several occasions. Another child had seen her mother beaten and kicked until her nose was broken. One man had beaten the woman unconscious and then went out leaving the two toddlers alone in the flat with their unconscious mother.

Glenda remembered a number of violent incidents that she had witnessed.

> Well, I remember seeing him get toast and scratch it across her face in the kitchen and then he told us to get out and was shouting at us. And another time, he pushed her ... he pulled her up by her bra and shouted at her and then pushed her down the stairs in my old house and I can't remember what it was over. (Glenda, aged 9)

Children witnessed their mothers being slapped, punched and kicked and hit with objects, often on a regular basis. Hannah said that on one occasion it just became too much for her, she describes herself as having 'freaked out' and how even the violent man's threats could not stop her.

I really, really freaked out about it because he had Mum on the floor by her throat. And he said to me, 'You had better shut up or it will be you as well'. And he came up, I was sat on top of the stairs and he came up to me with his fist in my face and said, 'I'm going to hit you if you don't be quiet', and I carried on screaming by which time Mum had actually phoned the police. So he went back down and then he took, that particular time he took her into the bathroom and started beating her in there, banging her against the wall and stuff. (Hannah, aged 15)

Eleven women had experienced their partners trying to suffocate or strangle them in front of the children. One mother recalled how she had been sitting with her young son on her knee when his father tried to strangle her with her dressing gown cord. The boy's arm had become caught in the cord and as the man was pulling it tighter the child was also hurt.

Three men threatened to kill their partners in front of the children.

He used to always say that he was going to kill my mum, he used to always say that he was going to kill all my family and if like, and he really sounded serious like he really would do it. Well, I'm not saying he would have, but he sounded like that was it. (Mona, aged 17)

In eleven families the children had consistently seen their fathers break things in the house. Furniture was smashed to pieces, doors and windows kicked or punched until they broke. Sometimes children's toys or other possessions were broken systematically. As well as being dangerous for children to be present when things, sometimes heavy furniture, were being thrown about, it was terrifying for them to witness such destruction. It left no doubt as to the extent of the man's strength and power, especially in relation to a small child. If he could throw a heavy table against a wall, a small body would obviously be no problem. Possessions that children needed or loved were broken and often there was no money or the woman was not allowed to replace them. On going to interview one family the little boy immediately pointed out a hole in the living room wall saying, 'My daddy did that'. (Peter, aged 7)

Although children in seven families were not present when the damage was caused, the outcomes of damage to possessions or the home were witnessed by these children. Damaging possessions left visible reminders – holes, marks or telling absences – of the force it took to break them.

In addition to seeing their mother being hit and things being broken, children from nine families saw things being thrown at their mother, at times narrowly missing themselves.

> He'd throw stuff around, throws bottles at Mummy. (Adrian, aged 7)

Children and mothers from eight families described times where the children may not actually have seen their mother being beaten but they saw her being pushed around or being pinned down by the man. There are physical risks to the children in this situation, for example, as mothers are pushed over on top of small children.

Five men threatened the women with weapons in front of the children. Knives were the most common weapons mentioned. Women had knives held to their throats or knives thrown at them. One young boy intervened when his father threatened his mother with a knife, begging him not to hurt her. Another man tried to hit the woman with a broken bottle while she was holding the baby. Ralph recalled how his stepfather tried to snatch Ralph's younger sister and threatened his mother with a gun. His older sister ran for help.

> He threatened Mum that he had a shotgun and he was going to shoot her and kill her and all this. She [my sister] ran over to the phone box to call the police. (Ralph, aged 9)

In five families (10%, the same figure found by Abrahams 1994), the violent men raped the women in front of their children, sometimes on many occasions. The men did not seem to care that the children were there. Sometimes children would intervene, attempting to pull their father away and stop the assault.

Children commonly were present when their mothers were being verbally abused and indeed were often drawn into the abuse.

> I mean I had experienced verbal things he was saying to [my younger sister] like 'Call your mum a slut. Your mum's a f****** c***'. I witnessed all that, but not actually any violence towards her. (Hannah, aged 15)

They saw the facial expressions, the sneers that accompanied the abuse and of course they witnessed the impact that the man's words had. Children in thirteen families (27%) had often been present during the verbal abuse that their mothers experienced. One mother described how she would try to pretend to her two young sons that their father was only joking. She was unable to convince them. It was clear to the children that things were being said to wound, not to amuse.

Four men deliberately hurt themselves in front of the children. Two of these men attempted suicide: one took an overdose and the other jumped out of a high window seriously injuring himself. In one family the children saw the man put his fist through a window and another young boy witnessed his father deliberately cut himself deeply with a knife.

Other forms of abusive behaviour used by the man and witnessed by the children were sleep deprivation, trying to prevent the woman getting emergency medical help, holding the woman and children hostage and controlling contact with family or friends.

Children overhearing the violence

In twenty-eight families (58%), the children overheard the violence to their mothers. In these situations, the children would be in bed and wake up because of the violence or would have been sent out of the room.

> 'Cause when I wake up in the night there was always fighting, sometimes I hear Mummy crying and sometimes I hear her getting smacked and John shouting at her. So I start screaming myself. (Sabrina, aged 10)

Sabrina referred to her absolute terror that her mother would be killed, a justifiable fear as she had witnessed her mother beaten unconscious on numerous occasions.

Sian explained how her older sister would take her out of the room when her father was violent. But she did not want to go with her sister; she wanted to stay with her mother.

> Question: Can you remember why you wanted to stay with your mum [during an assault]?
>
> Answer: Because I wanted to stay with her to make sure she was all right. (Sian, aged 8)

A number of children said that they thought that hearing the violence and their mother's distress was worse than actually seeing it happening. What was evident from these children's accounts was that by hearing the violence but not knowing what was actually happening, their own feelings of powerlessness were increased. From these children's interviews there was the suggestion that they may have been holding on to the belief that if they were able to see what was happening they would have been galvanised into action to help their mother. Interestingly, one young woman found that even some time after the violent man was no longer living with them, it was overhearing the violence that stayed in her memory more than actually seeing it.

> What I remember is being in bed and hearing it all the time. I know I saw it but I can't remember seeing it, can't explain it, it's really weird, just blocked it out, put it to the back of my mind. (Jackie, aged 19)

When children did not physically see the assaults on their mother or if the violence mainly took other forms, mothers often believed that by not talking to the children about it they were protecting them from knowledge about the domestic violence. As this and other research (e.g. Jaffe *et al.* 1990; McWilliams and McKiernan 1993) has so clearly illustrated, children do not have to be physically present during an assault to be aware of domestic violence.

Deirdre talked about how she felt her children could 'sense' it when she was being beaten and how she tried to protect them.

> They probably heard it because I can remember a few incidents if the abuse had stopped at 3 o'clock in the morning and I would go and check on the boys, and they'd both be wide awake. Padraig would be under the bed, Peter would be in the corner of the bed, they wouldn't cry. And I would go in and I'd rock them to sleep and that and you could guarantee that both of them the next day would wet the beds the next morning. They didn't actually see it but obviously they heard it, and they knew what was going on, they could sense it … I'd be like oh my God, stop myself from crying because of the children and that was it. I just stopped crying, he could hit me, beat me to a pulp, I wouldn't even cry, because they can sense it. (Deirdre)

As children pointed out again and again, they could hear the violence and they were able to work out for themselves that something was very wrong:

> we could hear it all the time, like upstairs when we were in bed. We used to hear it all the time so if you say to her [my mother], 'What went on last night?' She'd say, 'Nothing, nothing don't worry about it'. I used to say to her, 'You know I'm not stupid'. (Karina, aged 16)

> Yes, because he'd throw the table, I think you could hear that! He'd broken lots of our tables where he threw them at my mum and things so we knew it was going on. (Marilyn, aged 15)

Children witnessing the outcome of the violence

In addition to being physically present when their mothers were being abused, children witnessed the outcomes of the violence. Cuts and bruising to the mother were seen by children in thirteen families (27%) and children would try to comfort their mothers when they saw their injuries. From children's accounts it was evident that even if they did not actually see their mother being assaulted, they were still affected by witnessing the outcomes.

> What I heard was a lot of shouting and screaming and the shouting was mostly my dad because he did have, he's got quite a loud voice and my mum was screaming. And when she came downstairs next day and she had a big bruise and it really hurt and she had some scratches as well. And I kept on asking her if she was OK and she wasn't. (Regina, aged 9)

In eight families children had seen their mother's distress because of the violence and were quite clear about the cause, even when their mothers tried to dismiss or hide their feelings.

Summary

In 85 per cent of families children were present when their mothers were being abused in some way and in 71 per cent of these families children witnessed their mothers being physically assaulted. In 58 per cent of families, children overheard the violence to their mothers and from children's accounts it would seem that hearing the violence but not seeing what was happening or knowing what to do about it has the potential to increase children's feelings of powerlessness and trauma. In 27 per cent of families children overheard the verbal abuse of their mothers and they experienced this as abusive themselves. In a further 27 per cent of families children witnessed the outcome of the violence, particularly cuts and bruising to their mothers or damage to property. Clearly children were aware of the abuse of their mothers. If they were not physically present during an assault, they witnessed the verbal abuse and the outcomes of the man's violence. Not talking to children about domestic violence did not protect them from it: they were already very much aware that it was happening; instead the silence just reinforced the idea that this was a shameful family secret.

PART THREE

Impacts of Domestic Violence

CHAPTER FOUR

Effect of Domestic Violence on Children

Introduction

For some years now, research has highlighted the fact that domestic violence can have a negative impact on children. Evason (1982) found that 72 per cent of the mothers in her study felt that their children had experienced negative emotional impacts because of the domestic violence. Of the mothers in Abrahams' (1994) study, 91 per cent felt that their children suffered negative effects and 86 per cent said that these effects continued in the long term into children's adolescence. Mama's (1996) study of 100 black women experiencing domestic violence reported that all of the women felt that the violence had detrimental effects on their children. In Clifton *et al.*'s (1996) study mothers were also concerned about the impact of the domestic violence on their children and for many of the mothers 'this was the trigger which led to them leaving' (p. 32).

In the present study, children and mothers both reported a wide range of effects of domestic violence on the children including fear, powerlessness, depression or sadness, impaired social relations, impacts on the child's identity, impacts on extended family relationships and their relationship with their mother, effects on educational achievement and anger, very often displayed as aggressive behaviour. The child's relationship with the father or father figure is also clearly affected by the violence to the mother.

Early research in this area attempted to quantify children's distress and correlate it with evidence of direct abuse to the child in addition to that of witnessing the abuse of their mother (Davis and Carlson 1987; Hughes 1988). Fantuzzo *et al.* (1991) reported that children who witnessed both physical and verbal abuse of their mothers displayed more behavioural problems than children witnessing verbal abuse alone. Hughes (1992) also found that children's difficulties increased as they were exposed to more forms of violence. Attempting to quantify either the violence or levels of children's distress is not helpful in recognising the uniqueness of individual children's responses to violence or the development of a cohesive approach to domestic violence. As Kelly (1994) points out, a range of factors both personal and external influence how children react to domestic violence. An important point to highlight is that children are affected by *all* forms of domestic violence, not just the physical violence. Children and mothers in this study highlighted the impact of living with fear and intimidation on a daily basis rather than the effects of specific physical assaults.

Listening to the emotional abuse of their mother was very distressing for children; for example, Kim described how her 8-year-old son was reacting to being exposed to the emotional abuse of his mother:

> He just said to me last night, he said, 'Mum, my brain feels like a volcano as though all the lava's going to erupt' and he said, 'I've only got a little brain, Mummy, why's he doing this to me? Why is he saying all these things?' (Kim)

Fear

Children who were interviewed discussed how witnessing the abuse of their mother made them feel. The majority of children felt several emotions concurrently; however, by far the most commonly mentioned impact of the domestic violence was fear. Children and mothers reported that children and young people had a general fear as well as very specific fears around the man's violence. In terms of a 'general' fear, children reported being frightened of the violent man or of what he might do. In other words, a fear of the unknown, of what was going to happen next.

Other children reported very specific fears related to the man's violence. The most frequently mentioned of these specific fears was that the children themselves would be hurt by the man. One young boy explained that he had seen his brother being hurt and therefore feared for his own safety.

> Shouting and hitting and stuff, he threw my brother on the bed and against the wall. (Padraig, aged 5)

Some children said that they were afraid, not just of being hurt, but that their violent fathers would kill them. In some instances, children had actually received such threats.

> Well, he told me that if I ever told anybody he would kill me. And he probably would have. (Shirley, aged 16)

In addition, the effect of seeing their mothers assaulted reinforced children's feelings of vulnerability in the face of such damaging aggression.

In relation to their mothers, children reported similar anxieties to those they felt for their own safety. For some children their fears centred specifically on their mothers being hit, whereas others frequently stated that their biggest fear was that the violent man would actually kill their mothers.

> Scared, because sometimes I thought he might kill her the way he beated Mummy up. (Sabrina, aged 10)

Similarly, when asked what his fears were, Seamus responded:

> Question: What were you frightened of?
>
> Answer: My dad actually killing my mum. (Seamus, aged 10)

Children's fears manifested themselves in a number of ways, most commonly as behavioural problems or aggressive behaviour and nightmares.

> Well one [nightmare] was that when I was asleep he [my father] got a knife and stabbed me, that was the other one that I had. I had some more but I've forgotten them. (Gerrard, aged 5)

Bedwetting was also frequently mentioned, specifically in relation to boys. Other symptoms of fear displayed by children were developing a nervous twitch, sleepwalking, stuttering and becoming clumsy when near the abuser. Three children had run away from home. One young girl was left with a fear of the dark because the abusive man used to lock her and her brother in their bedroom at night.

Long-term effects of fear

It is clear from what children and mothers said that this fear engendered by the violent man affected how safe the children felt, even when they were no longer living with the perpetrator. Children's fears of being hurt by their father may become generalised so that they fear any man may hit them. In a number of cases, mothers discussed their anxiety that their children's generalised fear of men did not appear to be lessening with time once they were no longer living with the abusive man. Some children would ask other men to beat their fathers up as a way of punishing them for their violence. The next most common fear reported by children was the fear that once they had escaped from the abuser that he would find them again.

> I'm worried because he might find out where we are, and I am happy because I am away from him. (Kara, aged 10)

One young boy, who witnessed the violent man breaking into their new home and assaulting his mother, lived in fear that he would break in again and abduct the two youngest children. Thus, as for their mothers, children's fears of what the violent man may do were not necessarily erased as soon as they were away from the situation. Feeling more secure and less threatened is a process that takes time for many children and it is important to recognise that these fears are not unfounded as women and children are frequently followed once they have left the violent man.

For many weeks and months after leaving the abusive man, children lived with the fear that he would find them and their mothers and they would be forced to return. One mother related how her 5-year-old son, when playing with a doll's house in the refuge playroom, carefully barricaded all the doors and windows. He then explained to the child worker that it was his mummy's new house and he had blocked the doors and windows so that his daddy could not get in.

The experience of repeatedly leaving and being found by the violent man and having to return home increased children's feelings of powerlessness and hopelessness.

> I just felt so angry that I couldn't help her. All I wanted to do was just get a suitcase, put her clothes in the suitcase, tell her to come with me and all the kids, and just go to a refuge or like some place for like women and children. But we just couldn't get away from him. Wherever we used to go, he used to find out where we were and all our phone numbers of wherever we lived, even he found out where we lived here and every time my mum used to take him back, I couldn't understand why. (Jackie, aged 19)

A 17-year-old discussed how when she was 11 the abuser used to threaten to kill her mother and all the family. She said it made her feel:

> constantly on edge. Never free, never safe. It was like, there was no safe [place] ... being at home wasn't safe at all, it was just that's the place where you are and you're constantly alert. You don't sleep properly, you just sit there and wait for something to happen. (Mona, aged 17)

Even now, she says, the fear stays with her:

> and he, he portrayed himself as invincible. I still think he's invincible, and he used to always say to me, he was going to come outside the school and get his friends to throw acid in my face if I don't do this, and all that kind of thing. And I, like walking down the road you always walk and look see if any cars [like his] are driving past. (Mona, aged 17)

Sadness

After fear children were most frequently 'upset' by the violence against their mother. Children described themselves as feeling:

> Sad. (Francis, aged 6)

> Awful, it made me cry. (Adrian, aged 7)

Children also talked about being with their siblings and all of them being upset and unable to comfort each other.

> All of us [children] went upstairs and there was crying. (Paul, aged 6)

> Upset, and Paul and Tracy were crying and I was … we was all crying, because, we could just hear our mum crying and screaming. And our dad shouting at her. (Glenda, aged 9)

Some children responded to the feelings generated by witnessing the domestic violence by self-harming, in particular cutting themselves. In addition, children experienced suicidal thoughts. Depression and suicidal ideation may be believed to be part of the range of symptoms exhibited by adolescents and teenagers who witness domestic violence. However, this study identified that much younger children are also at risk for suicidal thoughts. For example, one mother relayed how shocked she had been to realise that the violence was making her 7-year-old daughter suicidal. In this case the little girl wrote to her parents saying that she would kill herself if the violence did not stop. Other examples given were a young boy attempting to step out in front of moving traffic, stating that his intention was to kill himself, and another young boy attempting to throw himself from a high window.

Kara carefully described how both her feelings and her behaviour had changed because of the violence.

> When he first hit me mum I felt scared, before that I were happy because me mum were happy, until he started hitting me mum ... Well when I found out and he went, it changed me behaviour a bit, because then I were happy and a bit nice, and now I am more happy and more nice. (Kara, aged 10)

Anger

Children displaying their anger as aggressive behaviour is not unusual following domestic violence.

> I started being naughty because I was always, I started swearing at him and everything. I got really bad, but it got sorted out when I was in the refuge because there was strict rules – shut me up! And that changed it all. That's how my behaviour changed, just started getting a big mouth, and that's all changed ... Yeah – because when I was living with John I used to bang on the walls and shout at him and tell him to stop it, then I used to be scared to do it then and that was when my anger started coming out, and then I could talk about that with all the other kids, and they would say how they were angry and how they were feeling, I didn't feel out of place. (Marilyn, aged 15)

Children frequently reported their desire to seek their revenge on their father or mother's partner, by physically hurting him.

> I would have thrown something at him, that's what I think, I would do that. (Adrian, aged 7)

Both boys and girls were displaying aggressive behaviour. However, some differences were evident in the targets of their aggression. Boys were slightly more often reported as being aggressive to their mother, other children or sometimes, specifically to girls. On the other hand, girls' aggression appears to be very much more directed at boys or men. Several mothers described how their teenage daughters had physically lashed out at boys for their sexist remarks or inappropriate sexual behaviour. At times this behaviour had meant that they had been threatened with expulsion from school.

Young girls' anger at the violence inflicted on their mother and their determination not to be victimised by male violence themselves appeared to be expressing itself as aggression towards males. Children and young people have many emotions concerning the violence to their mothers. They need support in working through these emotions.

Teenagers described their anger building up over time so that eventually all they could think about was to attack the violent man.

> I got to the point where I was starting to think that I was going to kill him if he touches her again. (Hannah, aged 15)

Jackie described how she 'just flipped' after years of her mother being abused and nobody talking about it.

> I went out into the street, trying to find him [my mum's partner] because I was so angry, I just flipped because I couldn't handle him being like that to my mum again, just had enough for years of him being violent towards her. So I rushed up the road trying to find him. I found him, he was driving his car and he run me over in his car. I got up and I was punching him and kicking him and screaming at him. It was in the middle of the night and there was people looking out of the houses and I was really, really, really angry, and I kicked all the lights in his car, just so angry. (Jackie, aged 15)

Girls' fears for their future and their present feelings of vulnerability from boys also need addressing. There is a clear need for assertiveness training with these young people so that they can learn to feel less vulnerable without having to resort to violence. As Sheena said, being aggressive was the only way she knew how to start letting her feelings out.

> Well sometimes, I just lashed, I'd just ... well no, I wouldn't lash out but I'd just get, I'd just have a shouting thing and just let everything out. And sometimes I'd go into my room and I'd just cry and just let it out. (Sheena, aged 12)

Tracy described how the domestic violence had made her feel that she needed to stand up for herself.

> Yeah, I feel different and I've changed a lot as well. Like I used to be really soft and everything, like other people and that, people used to boss me around and that. But now everything's happened, I've got a lot rougher with everyone else, outside or in school and that if someone starts on me I just lash out on them. (Tracy, aged 15)

Powerlessness

Children repeatedly talked in the interviews about their feelings of powerlessness in relation to the abuser.

> Well, I couldn't do nothing because he wouldn't let me in the room. He'd just tell me to go upstairs or if he was upstairs he'd tell me to go downstairs, or just tell me to go somewhere else. (Glenda, aged 9)

At times children conveyed the sense of desperation they felt in wanting to stop the violence but not knowing what to do.

> And I was scared because like he wouldn't take any notice of me and I was like what on earth am I supposed to do if he won't stop screaming at her and stuff? (Fiona, aged 15)

Children often discussed how their feelings of powerlessness increased their distress.

> I felt upset because I couldn't help her and all I wanted to do, sometimes just get a knife and kill him, sometimes, but I knew that I would get into trouble for it. But I just couldn't. There was no helpline or anything we could phone at the time, like there is now, but I just felt so angry all the time. I used to cry myself to sleep and think about a hundred ways how I could kill him, poison him and stab him and stuff. But it's silly really isn't it? But I felt so angry. I just cried all the time for her, I just felt so sorry for her, that I couldn't help her. (Jackie, aged 19)

Children described how they really wanted to be able to do something to help their mother, to stop the man's violence and how they were paralysed by fear.

> And every time he hit my mum I felt like just getting up and whacking him one, but my mum just kept kicking him away. I felt really angry so I just ran upstairs in my room and I'd lock the door. And I just stayed up until 11 o'clock or 1 o'clock in the morning and watched my TV. (Damian, aged 9)

Children were, at times, able to stop an assault on their mother, as in the following example:

> I got in the way and pushed my dad. My dad just walked out then. (Seamus, aged 10)

However, more commonly children were reduced to fantasies of revenge. One 8-year-old boy started his interview saying that he wanted to beat his dad's head in.

Children very frequently said that hearing the violence was worse than actually seeing the assaults because when they could not see what was happening to their mother, they believed that she was being killed.

> It was horrible [when my mum was being assaulted] and what could have made it better was that if my dad hadn't, he would have just, like at least we knew that nothing bad was happening if he had just, like, left the door open or told us that it's OK or something but no one did so he just made it worse. (Regina, aged 9)

Children's feelings of powerlessness can increase their trauma, particularly if nobody is talking to them about the domestic violence or giving them an outlet for their intense emotions. Safety planning with children can be a contentious issue, with opponents feeling that if children are taught safety planning and then are unable to protect either themselves or their mothers, their feelings of guilt will be intensified. However, what children are saying is that they want to be able to do something, they feel guilty at not acting at all; as Jackie pointed out, in the end the only thing she could think of to end the violence was to kill the abuser.

> He was quite a big man; he was much, much taller than me, built like really big. There was nothing I could do, apart from getting a knife and stabbing him, but that's not going to improve anything is it? (Jackie, aged 19)

Children's feelings of powerlessness were not simply confined to the times when their mothers were being assaulted, although they were more intense at that point. Children referred to being aware constantly of how little power they had to stop the violence.

> My best friend at the time, I used to go on holiday with her every year to another country; that used to be quite relaxing to get away from him for two weeks. But I used to, when I would be sunbathing or whatever, I used to be thinking about what he was doing to Mum all the time and knowing that I couldn't do anything about it. (Jackie, aged 19)

Effect on children's identity

Several children referred to the fact that they felt stigmatised by the domestic violence. Even very young children were aware of the stigma surrounding domestic violence. Children said they felt humiliated and degraded by the violence and it clearly affected their identity.

> I was a very private person, like my business is my business, I don't feel no one else has to know. It's degrading and humiliating everyone else knowing what's going on. I just found it degrading just knowing that everyone else was going home and they'd come into school and they'd sit down and say, 'Oh my dad won't let me wear this top,' and I'd think, 'Yeah that's all you lot are worrying about'. (Mona, aged 17)

Children also discussed how important it was for them to realise that they were not the only people experiencing domestic violence. Knowing that it happens to others may lessen the sense of shame a child feels.

Related to the issue of children's identity, two women (one white and one mixed race) talked about how they struggled to protect their black children from racism and to make them proud of their identity, despite the stigma of having experienced domestic violence. Hester *et al.* (1999) recognised the influence of institutional racism on women and children seeking help for domestic violence. They also acknowledged that 'for children from mixed race relationships, trying to understand their experiences might be made more difficult by not knowing with which parent to identify' (p.55).

Girls said that because of the domestic violence they lacked self-confidence and self-esteem and that they were nervous and timid. Mothers referred to both boys and girls, but particularly girls, being withdrawn. One young girl felt that she had had to grow up too quickly because of the domestic violence and another boy felt that he and his siblings had missed out on a lot of things when they were growing up because of the domestic violence.

Effect of domestic violence on children's health

Mothers mentioned a number of health problems their children had suffered and which they felt were directly related to the domestic violence. These included asthma, eczema, eating disorders, headaches, stomach pains, disturbed sleep, babies having feeding problems, delayed development, in one case delayed speech and in another instance, severe general developmental delays. Hague *et al.* (1996) also reported delayed development of children as a result of domestic violence.

Effect on children's education

> When I went to school it affected me a lot because all day I was thinking about what would happen when I would go home. So at school my work level dropped for quite a bit. So it affected me not just at home but at school. And then there were like, in the mornings when they started arguing and I'd go into school crying and people would ask me why I was crying and I couldn't tell them. When I get told off at school, not just because lots of kids when they get told off they start crying, but I cry because then it's also added on to my plate of other problems. (Regina, aged 9)

As has already been highlighted in the section on children's anger regarding domestic violence, children often bring many problems into school because of the man's violence at home. As we have seen, one of these effects of the domestic violence was aggression, which spilled over into school. For example, one 5-year-old boy had been suspended from school twice for violence to teachers and children. Jackie described how the domestic violence had affected her younger siblings at school.

> At the time I felt sorry for Terry and Karina because they were younger, they couldn't get out of it. All they could hear was the arguing. Obviously they grew up with the violence all the time so they used to go and beat the kids up at school 'cause they thought that was the right thing to do because they had grown up with it. But now, they're all right now, they're lovely now. (Jackie, aged 19)

A mother whose 5-year-old son has special educational needs talked about her guilt. She felt that his educational problems spring from the fact that she was never allowed to play games with him or read to him when he was small. In order to protect him from the violence she had to do as her ex-partner said.

Domestic violence affected children's educational achievement in three main ways:

- aggression in school
- lack of concentration
- school refusal.

Several children were reported as being unable to concentrate while at school so that their work suffered significantly. At least two teenagers were unable to go on to tertiary-level education as planned because they had fallen behind so much with their work. Children and young people pointed out that they were totally unable to concentrate on their schoolwork because they were so worried about what might be presently happening or going to happen at home.

> When I was at the middle school, when I was about 10, then that's when the teacher started to notice something was wrong. And if [Dad] beat Mum up I would be at school thinking, 'What if he's come back?' or 'What if I go home and Mum isn't there?' 'What if something has happened?' So I was always a nervous wreck and then like I just wouldn't do any of my work, really defiant and that, because I was just worrying what the situation in the home environment would be when I got home from school. (Hannah, aged 15)

Jackie discussed what it had been like for her:

> Yeah, my school work really went downhill and my exams, 'cause at the time I was taking my exams when all the fighting and arguing was going on and I couldn't study because of the arguing, I could hear constant arguing all the time. And I failed all my exams because of it and I blame him for it, I didn't try at all, I just couldn't be bothered any more, I just gave up. Also I was quite rebellious at school, not as bad as some people, but just wouldn't do the work. And I would keep getting letters coming home saying that I hadn't done the coursework and it was all just down to him really, I just couldn't be bothered to do it. So I failed all my exams and that was it, left school without any qualifications, got a good job now though, well sort of a good job. And all the arguing at home used to make my coursework, I couldn't be bothered to do it, I used to just sit there and cry and shake because I couldn't do my homework. And sometimes I just felt like going downstairs and slapping them both saying, 'Shut up, I'm trying to do my work'. But as I say there was nothing I could do about it. All my friends at school were comforting me and saying that it was all right and they were helping me do my work, like giving me their notes to copy and stuff. I used to copy them down like word for word what they wrote. But as I say all my work, failed all my exams, I put it down to him what had happened at home. (Jackie, aged 19)

Consistent with the findings of Jaffe *et al.* (1990), some children felt that they could not attend school because they were simply too frightened to leave their mother on her own. Children described how they just could not shut out the images of their mother being beaten, making it impossible for them to remain in school.

I'd think about my mum being hit and then I just would walk out of school and come home and then not go in for another three days and then go back again and walk out. I didn't like the thought of her being on her own with him, so I stayed at home all the time. And that's really what started it off, and now I usually stay at home even though she's not getting beaten up. I'm used to it. (Marilyn, aged 15)

This young girl's mother described how she would send her daughter to school but she would sneak in the back door and hide in her room so her mother did not even realise that she was in the house.

Karina pointed out that incidents in school could trigger memories of the violence, leaving her feeling vulnerable.

[I] failed all my exams, I put it down to him, what had happened at home. The atmosphere at school, the atmosphere at home was exactly the same, and whenever I heard the teacher shouting at a child, I just used to cover my ears 'cause I don't want to hear no one shouting. It's like, every time I heard someone shouting, it was like bells ringing in my head. I just don't want no more shouting, I used to just want to run out of the room and burst out crying because I don't want to hear no more shouting. (Karina, aged 16)

School can serve as a place of refuge for children, giving them some respite from the violence, although they can feel torn between not wanting to go home after school and needing to see their mother and be reassured that she was all right. Some children would attempt to spend as much time at school as possible, getting there very early in the morning and leaving very late, even if it meant getting into trouble in order to do so.

And I used to make myself have detention so I could stay later, so I would miss the last bus. (Jackie, aged 19)

Sleep deprivation was a tactic often used by violent men and it affected the children as well as the women. One little boy kept falling asleep in class because his father used sleep deprivation on the woman and child as part of the abuse.

A teenager describes how the violent man would destroy anything that meant a lot to her and this included her schoolbooks.

I had books from infant school that I really wanted to keep and give to, show to my kids. 'Oh look what I've got.' I loved school, so they were really important to me, they meant more than anything. And that was my work, that was stuff that I got really good marks on that I could show. All gone. All of it. But I used to be terrible, I used to really leave early for school and then get ... come in as late as I could possibly come in. (Mona, aged 17)

Mona also described how difficult it was moving constantly and having to change schools all the time.

There was one particular high school that I really, really wanted to go to and I got in and I was all excited and everyone was all excited 'cause this was the school that I'd spent most of my time at and all my friends were there and I was all excited to go to this new high school. And then we moved. That was awful, that was really awful and then I had to go to a high school where, it's bad enough having to go into high school because it's really scary going into high school in the first place, you know you're the youngest there, and then didn't know anybody. Or I'd always start terms halfway through and I'm used to being the new person now anyway. (Mona, aged 17)

Effects on children's relationship with their mother

Not surprisingly children's relationship with their mother was affected by the domestic violence. In some cases, children (usually boys) appeared to imitate the aggressor's behaviour and become violent to their mother. Mothers discussed how hurt they were by their sons seeming to turn against them. Other children copied the way the man spoke to their mother and as a result the mother–child relationship became strained. Glenda explained how difficult it was to stop her young brother being violent to their mother.

Paul copies like when he saw my dad beating up my mum, Paul copies it and he always hits my mum and everything as well.

Question: How do you feel when Paul hits your mum?

Answer: Well, I think it's not his fault, he's just copying the bigger person. He doesn't listen. We tell him he's going to get in trouble but he says, 'How comes Daddy didn't?' And then we tell him because my mum would try to talk... I'd tell him because my mum would try talk to him but he wouldn't listen...my dad wouldn't listen, so that's why he still got away with it. (Glenda, aged 9)

Other children were verbally abusive following contact with their fathers, a finding also reported in Hester and Radford's (1996) study of contact following domestic violence.

On the other hand some children became very protective of their mother's physical and emotional well-being. Small children may become very clingy with their mother, needing to keep her in sight at all times, although it was not unusual for children then to avoid their mother when their father was around. In this way small children attempted to protect themselves by not demonstrating a close alliance with their mother in front of their father, a strategy also noted by Hilton (1992).

On the whole young people either felt that because of their experiences of violence, their relationship with their mother had improved or on the other hand they blamed their mother in some way. Sometimes children were conscious that they were being irrational in apportioning the blame to their mother but could not help how they felt. Children blamed their mother for making their father leave, for splitting up the family and for 'taking' the violence for so long.

> Well, I were angry with him and in one way I were angry with me mum for choosing him. (Kara, aged 10)

In one family the teenage girl was very angry that her mother had not informed her that her stepfather had a conviction for child sexual abuse. She consequently blamed her mother when he sexually abused her younger brother.

Another young person described how the abuser used to get her into trouble and then her mother would blame her. She felt that it has left them with the legacy of being unable to communicate, leaving them impatient and frustrated with each other. One teenage girl was being sexually abused by her father. She believed that her mother knew but was not doing anything to stop him. Their relationship became strained until they could start talking to each other about what had happened.

Communication appeared to be the key in differentiating those young people who blamed their mother and those who felt that their shared experiences of violence had brought them closer. Those who felt that their relationship with their mother had improved stressed how they were able to communicate very well with each other about current issues in their lives as well as the domestic violence. Children and young people referred to how being able to talk to their mother about the domestic violence enabled them to understand better the dynamics of what had been happening.

> I think it actually improved it [our relationship]. It made me realise how much she really did care about me, even though she had always been moody. (Shirley, aged 16)

> Well, as I said it probably got us closer together but I think it definitely did affect our relationship. I felt that we weren't a family, we were just people living together, and that but I mean, that's because I didn't really know what was around the corner, whether it was going to be a thump in my face or Mum's. I just felt as though I was living a walking, talking hell really. (Hannah, aged 15)

Children need to express how they feel about the violence but they also need to hear their mother's perspective in order to make sense of what happened. How to talk to their children about the domestic violence was, as will be discussed later, an issue that mothers really struggled with.

Learning a new way of being together

Having left the violent man, mothers and children often had to learn a new way of being together. This usually involved a much more relaxed, violence-free life. Children initially had to learn where the boundaries lay in this new existence and a number of mothers reported that their children had at first struggled with issues such as who was now the 'boss' or what was 'right' or 'wrong' in terms of their behaviour. Marianne described how liberating it was for the children as well as herself when they went to a refuge.

> I was taking the mickey out of Ian [my son], and he turned round and said, 'I've never seen you laugh like that!', but he hadn't, because I had never laughed like it. (Marianne)

Martine described how her little girl had been too frightened even to play before because the violent man had not allowed them to make any noise at all. She used to spend her time just sitting quietly, not doing anything, just sitting there. Since moving to their new home, the little girl happily played with her toys. Her brother, who had always wet the bed, had stopped as soon as they had moved away from the violent man.

Effects on children's relationship with their father

It is hardly surprising that experiencing domestic violence had significant impacts on children's relationship with their father or father figure. Of all the impacts identified, being 'scared', 'nervous', 'nervy' or 'frightened' of the abuser were the ones most frequently mentioned.

> Can't stand him. Can't stand him at all. I'm scared though because, he's, he's everywhere. (Mona, aged 17)

Ralph talked about how he had felt frightened of his father but could not work out why. He said he had blocked the memories of what had happened. Later when he was no longer living with his father he remembered.

> And when I first moved in with grandma I was wondering why I was scared of him and I had forgotten most of the things what had happened. And when I was coming on about 7, I remembered all this stuff and all this stuff was coming to me and I felt really scared. (Ralph, aged 9)

In addition to children being frightened of the violent man, children were described as 'wary' of him. Children did their best to avoid being in the same room as their father and when they had to be near him, they were edgy and watchful.

Another commonly reported impact of the violence was that the children's relationship with the man changed once the child had witnessed the violence to the mother. Where children had been close to the man beforehand, after witnessing the violence they no longer felt the same about him.

> Complete pig ... And I just, I don't even want to be in the same country as him, I think he is a complete psycho. (Hannah, aged 15)

> I didn't talk to him that much after that [witnessing my father's violence]. I felt he weren't worth talking to. (Tracy, aged 15)

Allied to this change in the relationship following the child witnessing the man's violence, in seven families the children or their mothers specifically raised the issue of the children no longer wanting contact with their father post-separation because of what he had done to the woman. Children were reported as being angry with the perpetrator because of how he had treated their mother. A number of mothers explained how their children felt betrayed and let down by their fathers.

Children described feeling angry at, ashamed of or let down by their father. In one family the children described how they were embarrassed by their father because of his violent behaviour. The 9-year-old girl in this family said that she was angry at him, ashamed of him and disappointed in him. She concluded by saying:

> I don't like him that much. (Glenda, aged 9)

Her 13-year-old brother said:

> I was ashamed that he was my dad ... I hated him, at the time I did. ... It was like I couldn't even trust my own dad. (Aaron, aged 13)

One mother described how her little boy was very angry with his father and talked a lot about getting his revenge on him when he grows up.

> And he just said to me, 'If I get my weights when I grow up,' he said, 'I'm going to go round and I'm going to beat him'. I said, 'It's not the answer, love, it isn't, that's all there is to it'. (Kim)

Some children coped with these feelings of anger toward their father by confronting him with what he did. Other children went out of their way to shun their fathers actively, not only refusing to have contact with them, but also refusing to speak to or acknowledge them in any way. For children who felt like this toward their father, it was often a relief when he was no longer living with them.

> And when they came back, I'd asked my mum where Dad is and she said, 'He's left,' and I said, 'Yes!' So Mum said, 'Why are you saying yeah?' And I said, 'Because there'll be no more arguing and I won't feel so upset and stuff'. (Regina, aged 9)

For many children though, their feelings regarding their fathers were not so clear-cut and they experienced a conflict of emotions in relation to them. Numerous mothers talked at length about how torn their children felt between wanting to continue seeing their father but not wanting their father to continue abusing their mother. The conflict for children appeared to arise from the fact that they liked or loved their father but detested his violence. Children were clearly struggling with trying to understand how someone they loved could behave so horribly. Conflict was also created for children by the abuser trying to turn them against their mother, or take sides against her.

An interesting feature of the relationship between the violent man and the children in the household was that siblings were treated differently by him. Over and over both mothers and children referred to the man clearly favouring one child over another. In the majority of cases, this involved favouring a boy over a girl. In no case was a girl reported as receiving more favourable treatment than a boy. The children were obviously aware of this differential treatment and were very hurt by it.

> I didn't like it ... it just felt like I wasn't there at all ... I don't know why but he wasn't really interested in anything I done good. Whereas Oliver [my

brother] he would have a lot of interest in and I think it's probably because he was a boy. When we weren't seeing him, I didn't feel that I actually missed him a lot, because he didn't show much appreciation of anything I did or show that he loved me or that he cared or anything like that. So I didn't really actually miss him. (Regina, aged 9)

Children from five families were described as having very close relationships with their father. These children emphasised that they missed their father. In one family, although the four children had witnessed their father's violence, they continued to deny that he had been violent. Their mother described her ex-partner as very loving towards the children but unable to set boundaries for them. She highlighted that the children were very close to their father. Her daughter described how she felt that her father had always tried to see the children's point of view.

Yeah, well sometimes when I'd done something wrong, Mum would probably have a go at me and Dad would try and say, 'Look, stop having a go at her,' because he'd normally stick up for me I suppose. (Sheena, aged 12)

Three mothers felt that their children had a better relationship with their fathers after their mother and father had separated. There appeared to be two reasons for this; first, the children were no longer witnessing the abuse of their mother, and second, after separation, their fathers put more effort into spending time with the children.

It was very difficult for the mother–child relationship when children tried to cope with their feelings of loss of their father by blaming their mother either for the violence or splitting the family up. One of the difficulties frequently discussed by mothers was that following separation from the violent man, mothers and children faced a traumatic time trying to cope with their feelings and the impact of the violence. They each had many emotional needs. In addition they may have had many material needs, having to learn to survive on the reduced income of a single parent. Mothers were also in the position of being totally responsible for the care of the children and that included disciplining them. Fathers, on the other hand, would see the children periodically and invest energy and money in making sure that the children had a good time. In some cases mothers did not feel that the father giving the child treats or presents was a deliberate ploy to win the child's affection but were aware of how it influenced the child's perceptions of both parents. These mothers referred to the fact that in the children's eyes the one who could give them material things, that is, their father, was the better parent.

More frequently mothers (and sometimes children) referred to the violent man using money as a way of controlling the children. For example, one woman described how her ex-partner had never contributed anything to their son's upkeep but then would spend several hundred pounds on a birthday or Christmas present. Another woman said that her ex-partner used his greater financial resources to try to turn their children against her and had clearly stated to her that this was his intention. In another family both the children and their mother described how the father would promise the children material things and then use it to manipulate their behaviour. These men were constantly promising and withdrawing treats, making one child feel guilty for depriving the other siblings of a promised treat because of an apparent misdemeanour by that particular child.

Karina talked about how she felt that her stepfather had tried to buy the children with money and presents. At one point she said he bribed her younger brother with sweets to get him to open the door and let him back into the house. A 7-year-old girl was very aware of the violent man providing treats for her immediately after he had been violent to her mother.

> After the fight he used to bring us magazines and some sweets and stuff. (Shauna, aged 7)

Three of the mothers said that their ex-partners had not been interested in the children and had not given them any attention. One woman pointed out:

> He didn't even want me to have them in the first place. (Marina)

She described how, when she had been hospitalised for long periods, her sister had looked after the children and their father had not visited them. A further three mothers discussed how their ex-partners were inconsistent with the children so the children never knew where they stood.

There were particular issues for children who had been sexually abused by the violent man. A young girl who had been sexually abused by her stepfather was very angry that he did not go to jail:

> but I would have liked them [the police and social services] to have done something with him. I don't think it was right that he just stayed at home while everything happened and that he's still free basically. (Shirley, aged 16)

In most families where the violent man was not the children's birth father, the children had initially accepted their new father figure. However, three children described how they had not got on with their stepfather from the beginning, even before the violence started.

> But he used to shout at me and I used to walk off. I put it across that I didn't like him at all from the first minute I saw him. And he knew that I didn't like him so we didn't really used to talk to each other apart from when we would argue and I used to tell him to leave Mum alone all the time. He used to turn around and sometimes push me, that was the only violence, just push me out of the way. He used to tell me to go away to go up to my room or something, just so he could get on with beating my mum up all the time. (Jackie, aged 19)

Effects on children's relationships with extended family

A small number of children discussed the effect of the domestic violence on their relationships with extended family. In one family, after the woman married a new partner who then became violent, he stopped the children having contact with both their father and their paternal grandmother. The children missed this contact very much.

Adrian had tried to tell his grandmother about the violence and felt very let down when she would not believe him.

> I told Nanny Susan what he did. That was his mum. And she said, 'Don't be horrible'. (Adrian, aged 7)

Another family were harassed by the paternal grandfather after they had left the abuser, and were very hurt by this.

> Oh God that was really scary because he would like make phone calls and then we would pick up the phone and then it would just go, breathing and then it would go dead. Or it would be late at night and we would hear this banging on the door and we'd go down to open the door and there would be no one there, really scary and also it was really upsetting because it was my own grandparents. (Zara, aged 12)

Mona highlighted how important extended family can be in providing a sense of security.

> I got on really well with my family. He didn't like that at all. I used to spend most of my time at my nan's, I used to, every time I could. And I wouldn't have a bath in my house, I don't even know why. 'Cause I just

didn't feel comfortable, it just didn't feel like it was my house. I wouldn't have a bath in there and I wouldn't eat in there. I'd eat when I went to school and I'd have a bath when I went to my nan's. That's what I used to be like and it was never, I'd never class it as home. (Mona, aged 17)

Effect on children's friendships

Domestic violence can have significant impacts on children's social development. Most strikingly, their ability to form and maintain friendships was curtailed both directly and indirectly by the domestic violence, thereby increasing children's isolation. Children were frequently not allowed by the violent man to have friends come to the house. Other young people said that even if they were allowed to bring friends home, they would not have done it anyway in case their friends saw the man being violent.

> Yeah, I didn't feel comfortable people coming round. Because like they would say, 'Oh I'll call for you tonight,' and I would say, 'No it's all right, I'll come out and meet you,' because I mean, I think I would feel really, really embarrassed. Embarrassment was my main fear if someone came round and saw someone hit my mum or me. It's not the sort of usual thing that happens. (Hannah, aged 15)

Mona said that her friends would not phone or call to the house because they did not want to have to deal with the man's violence either.

> But my friends won't come to my house. 'Mona I won't knock for you, we'll wait down the bottom of the road at about 8 o'clock yeah, so you can come out.' Nobody would knock, nobody would phone me because they didn't know if it was a good time to phone or a bad time to phone. (Mona, aged 17)

Some children would have friends round to the house only when they were sure the violent man would not be there.

> Because he wanted to hit me mum even if they were there and I didn't want them to see him doing it. (Kara, aged 10)

Young people described feeling too uncomfortable to have friends in the house when the man was there. One young girl said that her friends would visit but it meant that she was constantly on edge in case her father was violent to her mother. Conversely, another girl reported that she would take a friend home to stay the night as a way of protecting herself from her father's violence.

As well as not being allowed to have friends round to their house, young people talked about how they were also not allowed to go out to meet their friends. Mona described how not only did she feel she could not bring friends home, but also her father would manipulate the situation by sending her on errands, to prevent her meeting her friends outside the house as well. Children's and young people's friendships were further hampered by the abuser deliberately embarrassing the young person in front of their friends, as in the following examples.

> He used to throw them [my friends] out. Because he had to go to bed he just told them to go. It made me feel bad and embarrassed, and usually upset. (Marilyn, aged 15)

> So he'd embarrass me, like my friends would knock on the door and he'd either say, 'Go away,' or he'd let them in but he'd do something. He'd either shout at my mum in front of them or he'd push me about or he'd, he'd, say things in front of them that wasn't necessary. And there was no point in having friends round 'cause ... I mean I remember one time at 12.30 my friend Cindy come round, couldn't believe it. She stayed over the night and he hit my mum when she was there, he wouldn't let us out of the house. All three of us had to sit in the house, couldn't go nowhere, it was awful. (Mona, aged 17)

All of the above factors made it very difficult for children to make and maintain friendships, a crucially important aspect of their development. Children all need to feel that they belong to their peer group and resent any difference that may set them apart. By drawing their friends into the abuse the abuser extends his power outside the home and makes it so much more difficult for children to fight the stigmatisation of domestic violence. In addition to the direct effects of the man's violence on their friendships, young people also referred to the indirect effects that made it difficult to establish a social life. One of these more indirect effects highlighted was that children's self-esteem suffered because of the violence. They then found it difficult to form friendships.

> I wasn't very confident in myself and I was really nervous kind of thing and like my self-esteem wasn't very high so I would be like ready to put myself down all the time. So like if people treated me badly or whatever or they ignored me then I would like take it like it was supposed to happen. (Fiona, aged 15)

Other young people felt that they were always holding things back (i.e. the reality of the violence at home) from others so they never got really close. These effects can continue for some time, as one young person pointed out. Even some years after they had left the abuser, she feels that she cannot get too close to people or tell them too much about herself in case any information gets back to the violent man and he finds them. Another impact of the violence on children's social development is that repeated moves to escape the violence mean that it is very difficult to maintain friendships.

Particular effects were mentioned in relation to teenage girls; these included alcohol abuse, promiscuity and aggressiveness. Naomi described her behaviour as a teenager:

> I became really resentful then. I became even more aggressive than I already was. I didn't want to know anybody. As far as I was concerned everybody else was a piece of shit. I started hanging around with a bunch of lads from the village; half of them had been in prison, God knows how many times now. I must have picked the worst bunch in the entire village. We'd sit at the bus stop drinking cider or drinking Thunderbird or drinking sherry or whatever was the cheapest going, and I used to go home and father used to give me a bollocking. Sometimes he'd give me a wallop. (Naomi, aged 24)

In addition, in several families, although the teenage girls wanted to be involved in heterosexual relationships, the fear of male violence prevented these young women from continuing their relationships. As the relationships became more serious, the young women clearly felt that the only way to protect themselves was to withdraw, either by ending the relationship or distancing themselves emotionally. Unfortunately, this study does not include a similar group of young men so that issues regarding young men's heterosexual relationships following domestic violence could not be explored. This is an area that clearly needs to be addressed by further research involving young people. Kelly (1994) and Hester et al. (1999) have identified the need to look at the impact of gender in responses to domestic violence without resorting to assumptions regarding stereotypical behaviour patterns. With regard to young people's relationships following domestic violence, any research must be set within the current social construction of young people's relationships and domestic violence recognised as one factor but not the only influencing factor.

Summary

It is very important to recognise that children are affected by all forms of domestic violence, not just physical violence. Fear was the most commonly reported impact of the domestic violence and this fear had both short-term and long-term effects. This fear does not automatically disappear once the children are no longer living with the violent man: the fear of being found by him and of further violence persists for some time.

Children were also 'upset' by the violence and were at times depressed to the point of considering suicide. Children as young as 7 were reported as being suicidal. Anger was another effect of living with violence and this anger was often displayed as aggressive behaviour, particularly to other children. Not surprisingly, children felt very powerless in the face of the man's violence and from their accounts it is apparent that these feelings of powerlessness and hopelessness increased their distress.

Children reported that the domestic violence made them feel ashamed and stigmatised with consequent effects on their self-esteem and identity. Living with violence also had impacts on their health and education such that children suffered a number of stress-related health problems, for example asthma. The effect on children's education was most noticeable in terms of school refusal, lack of concentration and aggression in school. School can be stressful for children who experience domestic violence but it can also be used as a place of refuge.

Children's relationships within and outside the family were clearly affected by domestic violence. Children could, at times, copy the abuser's behaviour to their mother and this strained their relationship with her. Overall, though, most children in the study felt that they had become closer to their mother because of everything they had been through together. Although it is very difficult to talk about the violence, the key to a good relationship between children and their mothers seemed to be a commitment to communicating about the domestic violence.

Domestic violence, in the main, had a negative impact on children's relationship with their abusive fathers. Children said that they were frightened of him, angry with him and felt betrayed by, embarrassed by and ashamed of their father. It was not unusual for siblings to be treated very differently by the abusive man, particularly in terms of his own children being treated differently from the woman's children or boys receiving better treatment than girls. The long-term effect of this on the children's relationships is an area that would benefit from further research.

Children's relationships with extended family were affected by the strain of having to keep the secret of the violence or not being allowed to have much contact with extended family. Friendships were also difficult to maintain because of the domestic violence. Children reported four main effects on their ability to make and maintain friendships: being too uncomfortable to bring friends home; not being allowed out; their father deliberately embarrassing them in front of their friends; constant moves to escape the violence making it difficult to maintain friendships. The study picked up that there were particular effects on teenage girls, particularly in terms of forming relationships with boys. As the study does not include a similar group of teenage boys, it is not possible to provide a comprehensive picture of the effects of domestic violence on young people's socialisation and relationships. This is also an area that should be explored fully by future research.

CHAPTER FIVE

How Children Understand and Cope with Domestic Violence

Children's awareness and memories of the violence

Repeatedly in interviews mothers talked about how, when they were living with the perpetrator, they had been unaware that the children had witnessed their father's physical violence. For many mothers it was only when they had left that they realised the full extent of their children's awareness of the domestic violence. For some mothers this realisation came when their children actually spoke to them about their memories of the violence.

> She said, 'I could hear you Mum, I could hear you crying, I could hear you screaming. I actually went once or twice into the hallway and saw him beating you on the stairs.' Because we'd open plan staircase and I didn't even know she'd seen it. She even told my ex-husband. She said, 'I saw what you did to my mum'. (Denise)

Other women discussed how, having left the perpetrator, they no longer needed to deny the violence either to themselves or others and how they were now very aware of incidents which indicated that their children had known what was happening.

> I thought maybe they were safe from it all, but like I said it's not until you leave that you realise that they were actually experiencing it as well. I just used to think, oh I'll keep quiet, they won't know. They knew because they used to walk along to the school and I used to put my head down and Padraig used to go, 'Mum where did you get your black eye from?', and I used to [say] 'Oh I was rubbing it too much, I had something in my eye', and he used to go, 'Oh all right'. Just the look on his face! He wouldn't say anything else, but he'd be ashamed for me, I could see on his little face. Like, as I was going into his school, I'd put my head down and put my hair over it. And I could see him, he'd go, 'Leave me here Mum, I'm all right today. You go off, I'll go into class by myself'. And I used to walk off and

think to myself, he's 5 years old and he knows, and I used to just walk off and keep my head down. And then he would be the first one out of class, rather than the last one strolling out with his books, he'd be the first one, 'Come Mum, come then,' and we'd jump in the car. ... Ah bless him. Like I said you don't realise until you actually leave, and them little things hit you. (Deirdre)

In the interviews, mothers expressed particular surprise at the level of awareness that very young children had regarding the violence and how the memories had remained.

She was only one when we left. What I didn't realise was she understood a lot more than I knew. We were sat here one night and right out of the blue she said to me, 'My dad used to make you cry. My dad used to hurt you'. And I said, 'Well how do you know?' 'I saw him.' And that was at 3 years old and she's 4 now, it's a long time ago since she said it. But she must have known, she must remember. (Jacinta)

Hester and Pearson (1998) provided instances of children recounting episodes of abuse that had occurred when they were as young as 2 or 3.

Having managed to leave the violent relationship, mothers frequently became aware of how witnessing the domestic violence had actually affected the child. While living with the violence, a number of mothers had believed that the children were too young to be aware of what was happening, or if they were aware, that the painful memories would fade as they got older without leaving any negative impacts.

Me hoping that they would forget about it, but they didn't. Kids have got long memories I'm afraid! (Dawn)

Another way that mothers tried to protect the children was to deny or minimise the violence, for example telling children that their father was only play fighting or that they were hurt accidentally. Children were clearly not fooled by these excuses.

Mothers talking to children about the domestic violence

The majority of mothers said that while it was happening, they had not initiated discussions with the children about the violence. Usually, they felt that the children were not old enough to understand and they did not want to upset them.

> But I don't really want to talk about it because I don't want them to remember it, to be honest. I mean as they're older if they can remember things, fine, I'll be happy to sit down and talk to them about it. But now I don't want to dredge it all up for them. Because I think I just want them to get on with their life and enjoy it, you know. They're too little to be worrying about things like that really. (Marina)

Mothers often reported that they would explain to their children when they felt they were old enough to understand, and this had in fact been the case in many families. Mothers had not talked to the children about it when it was happening but at the time of the interviews most said that they now talked very openly about the violence.

Mothers generally were clear that they would always answer the children's questions about the domestic violence as far as they could.

> We started talking about things and she asked me certain things; if she asked me did [my ex-partner] do this or that I would tell her. But if I think some things are too bad to tell her I don't tell her. I might say he might have done, I can't remember and she never pushes it; if I'm being evasive she never pushes it. But if she asks a question I answer her. (Bernice)

It is a sad irony that so many women stayed in the relationship believing it to be the best thing for the children, yet when they did manage to leave they discovered not only that the children were aware all along but also that they were experiencing negative effects.

> I tried to keep a lot of it to myself. I didn't want to, I don't know, burden them with things that was worrying me or whatever, I tried to keep their life as happy as I could. Which all came out after I did actually leave. (Rita)

Mothers who had talked to the children about the domestic violence usually said they did so for two main reasons. First, they wanted the children to realise that domestic violence is unacceptable, and second, they felt that the psychological impact on the children would be lessened by discussing it. Other mothers found that the children started asking questions about what was happening so they began talking about it in that way. One mother described how she tried to 'cover up' the domestic violence at first but that her daughter would not accept her excuses. However, she found that her son was not able to discuss the violence and her daughter could not talk about the more extreme incidents of violence.

Knowing what to say, how much to say, how to say it and when to say it were prominent concerns for mothers who have experienced domestic violence. One woman said that she had always been open about the domestic violence with her 7-year-old daughter but worried that it was too much for her to cope with. Mothers feared that their children would be overwhelmed if they knew the truth about the domestic violence and on the other hand felt the children deserved to know, or at the very least not be lied to. They were also mindful that the violent man was the child's father (or father figure) and that the child had a different relationship to him from the woman. Women did not want to add to the children's trauma by saying 'nasty' things about their father (even when they were the facts). Thus, women commonly felt that they did not know what to do for the best.

> I don't know if it's right to say nothing to her, whether I should, say, discuss things and get her to see it in a more … get her to see it for what it was. Whether she's too young to be doing that with her, I don't know. … I'd like to know how it would affect her and to know what I can do. I don't even know how to talk to her about it, because I don't know whether talking to her would be the right or the wrong thing to do, because I don't want to lead her in to anything. Thinking about things she hadn't thought about maybe and going too far. (Danielle)

In their interviews children referred to their confusion about the violence, especially when they were younger, and their inability to understand why it was happening.

> I didn't quite understand it when I was so young, because … I just got used to it, when he used to hit me and my little brother and then my mum. I just got used to it. (Marilyn, aged 15)

Young children particularly seemed to search for the cause of their father's violence, often examining their own or their mother's behaviour in an attempt to find a 'trigger' for the violence. Older children were clearer that their father's behaviour was not rational or predictable.

Rosita used her brother as an example to explain how younger children do not understand domestic violence.

> Question: So Ryan didn't know, he didn't understand what was happening?
>
> Answer: No he just thought, 'Oh they are just having a little fight,' because we fight, we fight and that …
>
> Question: You and Ryan?

Answer: Yeah. And he thinks it's just a thing like that, and it isn't. It's like because Ryan can say, 'No we've finished it now. I don't wanna …' and I just say, 'Fair enough,' and we make up. But that isn't like it and Mummy can't say, 'Oh I've finished now, it's OK. Do you wanna make up?' It's not like that, and well, what I know about what's happened is, he was very violent and he was horrible, and I really hated him and I couldn't wait until we moved, when it was happening. (Rosita, aged 8)

Not knowing whether to talk to the children about the domestic violence was, as we have seen, also linked to the hope that children were either unaware of or unaffected by the violence. However, most children were very aware of the violence and it does not follow that they should not be allowed to talk about it. Domestic violence had been their actual experience: talking about it did not create the trauma, experiencing their father's violence did that. Talking about their experiences, or at least knowing that they could talk about them, was very important for children. They may not have wanted to discuss what happened in detail, but acknowledging that it happened was important. A minority of mothers interviewed said that they had tried to talk to the children about it but the children had made it clear that they did not want to talk. These mothers felt that children did not want to talk about it because it raised painful emotions or because they felt that they were protecting their mother by not discussing it.

It is important that any discussions of the violence are led by the child's pace and needs, and that children feel that they can broach the subject when it is the right time for them. Acknowledging that the violence happened and that the child can talk to his or her mother is the crucial first step.

Children's awareness of the atmosphere in the home

Children and mothers from fourteen families felt that the children were aware of the atmosphere that the violence created in the home. The word 'tense' was used over and over again to describe what things were like within the house or, as one young girl said, 'stressing'. Mothers felt that even very small babies were aware of the atmosphere and would be fractious or hard to settle.

There was always an atmosphere, you know, you could cut it with a knife sometimes. Even as babies they can sense, sense it. 'Cause I always thought it was colic to be honest and I'm giving them Infacol and took 'em to the doctor's and the doctor's saying, 'No, there's nothing wrong with them.' And I thought, 'Well why the hell do they scream then, you know?' And they just used to scream as if they were in pain. (Marina)

Mothers and children both referred to the constant anticipation, always waiting for the next abusive episode. Women and children spent considerable time and energy in trying to second-guess what the man's mood would be like so they could try to make things better.

> It was like everyone had to do everything he says, otherwise he goes mad. (Aaron, aged 13)

Frequently, mothers and young people referred to being able to 'cut the atmosphere with a knife', constantly scared of doing something 'wrong' which could be used as an excuse to trigger an assault.

> Well, it was quite bad. Always worrying ... when he was in bed you had to be silent and we used to always stay out in the back garden just in case we made a noise. We used to be scared in case we did. So the atmosphere used to be really horrible. (Marilyn, aged 15)

Two mothers spoke about how obviously relieved their children were to escape the tense atmosphere when they managed to leave the violent relationship. Sheila painted a very vivid picture of her children's reactions when she told them that their father would not be coming back.

> Oliver asked me where his dad was, and I said he wasn't here. And he said, 'Is he coming back?' and I said no, and he jumped up and down and ran, ran jumping up and down going, 'Yes! Yes!' And then Regina, when she'd come home in the evening had said, first words were, 'Did you have a nice time while Daddy was out?' because that was the only time we'd have a nice time and I said, 'Yes, and Daddy's not actually coming back'. And she was in here and she ran up and down going, 'Yes! Yes! My atmosphere's going to be so different'. (Sheila)

Other mothers described how children's behavioural problems such as chronic nail biting or bedwetting stopped immediately when they were no longer living with the violent man.

Children's coping strategies

Children described using both physical and psychological strategies to enable them to cope with the violence. The two main types of physical strategies that they used were physically intervening to try to stop the violence and developing safety strategies to protect themselves, their siblings and their mother.

Mothers and children discussed a number of ways in which children had intervened to try to protect their mother. Children tried to intervene both in crisis situations and in proactive ways to try to stop the violence on a more long-term basis.

Children's crisis interventions

Children would scream at the man to stop hitting their mother. They would hit him and try to pull him away.

> I got in the way and pushed my dad. My dad just walked out then. (Seamus, aged 10)

> I tried to stop him and he pushed me away. (Paul, aged 6)

One mother described how her young daughter bit, scratched and jumped on her father in an attempt to stop him assaulting her mother. Another young girl would go and pack as soon as she heard her father shouting.

> She would hear John start and she would go and pack our bags ready to go. Once he'd threatened to burn the house down and I'd calmed him down and talked to him downstairs and when I'd gone up[stairs], she was only young then, and she'd packed all her toys and what she could. And all her little bags were all full up in the bedroom, she was crying. It was heartbreaking. (Tamsin)

Two young girls interviewed had tried to stop their fathers raping their mothers. One would physically try to pull the man off while he was raping her mother. The other young girl, who was then aged 4 or 5, walked into the bedroom while her father was raping her mother. She shouted at him to stop and then climbed into the bed, trying to protect her mother with her own physical presence. Hester and Radford (1996) also pointed out that children try to protect their mothers by their physical presence.

Knowledge of their own powerlessness in this situation can lead children to contemplate desperate measures. For example, a teenage girl wanted to buy rat poison and poison her mother's partner. Another teenage girl described how she went looking for the man after a vicious attack on her mother.

> [He] threatened to kill us all. And he said to me mum, when he left, he said, 'You better lock all your doors and windows because I will be back to get you'. Then after that I went out into the street, trying to find him because I was so angry, I just flipped because I couldn't handle him being like that

to my mum again. Just had enough for years of him being violent towards her. (Jackie, aged 19)

Sabrina would try to protect her mother by claiming responsibility for things that went wrong. A young boy said he would come downstairs in the night, pretending he needed the toilet. He hoped his appearance would stop the violence.

As well as trying to help their mother themselves, children would try to get outside help, most commonly running to neighbours or calling an ambulance or the police.

> The first time I tried to phone them [the police], he pressed the thingy button to the cut line off and then the second time I tried, he took the receiver off me and put it down so I couldn't phone them. (Kara, aged 10)

In three families children had climbed out of a bedroom window and ran until they found a phone that they could use to call the police.

Another way that children try to cope with domestic violence is to become very protective of and concerned for their mother's welfare, at times assuming a parenting role. A woman who developed an eating disorder described how the children would try to persuade her to eat. A teenage girl described how she would focus on her mother during the violence, trying to stay calm so she could look after her mother.

> Because she [my mother] was sort of like too fragile kind of thing. So I had to look after her. (Fiona, aged 15)

In addition, children would try to comfort their mother after an attack. One woman suffered many blows to the head and her daughter would frequently try to keep her conscious until the ambulance would arrive. She would talk to her and wipe her face with cold flannels. The little girl was no more than 9 years old at the time.

Older children talked about trying to protect younger siblings from knowledge of the violence. They did this by not talking about it in front of the younger child, turning music or the television up to cover sounds, taking the child out of the room and trying to reassure them or convince them that everything was all right.

> He was shouting. I knew that he was hurting my mum and I knew that my mum was going to stick up for herself and that, and that she would win, and I was going on the couch, 'Mummy's gonna win, Mummy's gonna win'. And I was in tears, and Paul was like, 'What's the matter? and I would

go, 'Nothing, it's OK. It's OK, yeah my eyes were just watering. What do you want to play?', because I didn't want him to know I was crying. (Rosita, aged 8)

Children's long-term strategies

In addition to trying to intervene in the crisis of an attack on their mother, children developed strategies to try to deal with the violence in a more long-term way. One woman told her mother that her injuries were accidental. Her daughter waited until she was alone with her grandparents and then told them the truth.

> She actually told her Grandma when we took the children and left them and came away and she told her Grandma that Daddy hit her Mummy and it weren't an accident and then they like intervened. (Trudy)

A teenage girl described how she went to bed with her clothes on and drank lots of coffee to stay alert so that she could quickly get help or escape.

> And then I'd drink loads and loads of coffee, keep my clothes on so I didn't have to rush to get, didn't have to get ready in the night or go … 'cause I ran out of the gate in my nightie once and that was embarrassing and I thought, 'If I stay in my clothes, then I'll be all right'. (Mona, aged 17)

Naomi recalled how her younger brother had kept an air rifle under his bed in case he felt he needed to use it to protect their mother.

> He [my brother] had his air rifle, and he would be trembling that much I wouldn't have been surprised if one day he actually finally shot him, you know what I mean. Good job it wasn't anything more than an air rifle. (Naomi, aged 24)

Children's safety strategies

Children devise a number of physical strategies in an attempt to stay safe on a daily basis. Most commonly, children and young people would try to stay out of the violent man's way, particularly if they felt the atmosphere was tense. Children spent a lot of time in their bedrooms or if they were older they would become involved in activities outside the home or visit friends a lot.

It was just bad, I just used to go out on purpose just to get away from him. Just to go round friends on purpose and me and my boyfriend would go out for walks and listen to my music really loud so I wouldn't listen to the arguing all the time and the fighting. And then just, that was it really, a really bad atmosphere ... used to stay round their houses a lot and their mums, their parents used to be quite comforting and I used to talk to their parents all the time. (Jackie, aged 19)

This was obviously easier for young people than small children who were unable to leave the house by themselves. However, small children would try to leave the room or hide.

As was mentioned earlier, school was frequently used as an escape from the violence. In addition, children and teenagers had, at times, moved out of the home either to friends, extended family or bedsits to escape the violence. A number of children considered running away from home and in some cases they did attempt to run away. One mother recounted how her daughter would always say to her that they had to leave and how in the end, it was her daughter's determination that meant they left for good. Her daughter said in the interview:

We had to get away but we were scared 'cause when we left, we was up the road, and Mummy said, 'Come on we'll leave tomorrow'. But I said, 'No, let's carry on because if we leave tomorrow he'll know won't he? And then he'll lock all the doors and then we won't be able to go, that's why.' (Sabrina, aged 10)

Another strategy, used particularly by younger children, was to ally themselves with their fathers to protect themselves. Although they were 'clingy' with their mother when alone with her, they would physically avoid her when their father was around. Children also tried to avert the violence by trying to control their behaviour so as not to provoke an assault on their mother. This meant that they were always trying to be good, doing exactly what they were told, never being cheeky or 'answering back' and, particularly for small children, keeping very quiet.

Children also thought of ways of behaving which they hoped would protect their mother, not just themselves. For example one little boy would try to persuade his mother to be submissive in an attempt to avert his father's violence. He also suggested that he go to live with his father in an attempt to stop him harassing his mother during contact arrangements.

Naomi described how she and her siblings had planned with their mother to help her leave.

> We decided amongst ourselves, I was 18 at the time, Julie 17, and the boys 16. And we said to her, 'Right, Tuesday morning, you cash your benefits first. Don't go and buy food, don't do this and that. We'll manage for the week. Just take the money, buy a train ticket, go up to your folks, and don't come back.' Because she tried women's refuges and stuff and he'd always find them and kick the door in, so that was just it, just wasn't working. (Naomi, aged 24)

Children's psychological coping

Children found a number of ways to cope psychologically with the violence to their mother. The main ways that children described were expressing their feelings about the violence in a way that felt safe, denying the reality of what was happening and conversely, needing to be aware of exactly what was happening in terms of the violence. When describing their distress, children often referred to how they had learned to cope with the feelings generated by the violence. Frequently that coping involved trying to deny what was happening.

> Yeah, sometimes when I'm feeling a bit down and I think about it, it does make me cry, but otherwise it just doesn't because I just kind of try to blank it out really. (Zara, aged 12)

> Try and get over it as much as you can, and just try to stop thinking about it. (Ray, aged 10)

> I tried to block it out, like I put the [bed] covers over my head, but even then I kept hearing it. There was nothing I could do about it but I felt unhappy for my mum 'cause don't know, just didn't like her being unhappy and being beaten up. (Karina, aged 16)

Others tried to find some distraction.

> Half the time I was happy like reading a book, the other time I was really down. (Marshal, aged 8)

Sheena described how she tried to cope by keeping her feelings bottled up.

> I was maybe upset inside, I don't know. But I never showed it if I was. (Sheena, aged 12)

Unfortunately her distress showed in episodes of self-harm and the development of an eating disorder.

Expressing their thoughts and feelings about the domestic violence was also an important way that children learned to cope with it. Children said that they talked to siblings or friends about what was happening and, as Fiona said, she used every opportunity she could to say how she felt about her father.

> If I had a chance, if anybody like said something about my dad or whatever, and I had a chance to say something nasty about him, I'd say it and it made me feel better. (Fiona, aged 15)

However, it is not just other people that children talk to. Toys and pets provided comfort also, as this girl described:

Yeah, but sometimes I talk to me teddies.

Question: Does that help?

Answer: Yeah, because they keep secrets because they can't talk. (Kara, aged 10)

A boy turned to his dog for comfort.

> But at least I had one person who cuddled me and that was my big dog that I used to love ... I'd say something [to my dog] like thank goodness that we've got someone who is going to care for me and not fight all the time. (Ray, aged 10)

Thus, toys and pets can play an important role in helping children cope with domestic violence, yet many children have to leave them behind when they flee the violence.

The ways that children learn to cope with domestic violence can become an established pattern of behaviour or way of viewing the world, which may be seen by others to be 'maladaptive', for example, children deliberately getting a detention to avoid going home in the evening. However, these behaviours have a perceived or actual role in protecting the child and as such they will not be surrendered until the child feels secure. When working with children who have experienced domestic violence, it is important to explore with them what certain behaviours or views mean to them. The fears underlying children's patterns of coping not only are based in their actual past experiences, but also reflect the reality that leaving the abuser does not necessarily mean that the threatened or actual violence is left behind.

For example, a young woman described how she lived in a constant state of readiness to flee from the violent man, even some years after they had escaped from him.

> I've got a certain section of stuff that I know if I have to move quickly, that's what I'll take. I used to basically live in a bag. I used to leave everything that I need at my nan's house and, like, that was stuff that I like, really, really liked. And live from a bag basically. Just the stuff I needed for school and that was it. Nothing ... I made sure nothing mattered to me so if he came in here and he decided he wanted to smash that, he could smash it, because it didn't matter any more. So then therefore nothing was valuable. (Mona, aged 17)

She was not being paranoid. Her father had already found her mother and at the time of the interviews this young woman had her own baby to protect.

A number of children discussed at length their need to know what was happening to their mother during an assault:

> Just tell me things and not shut the door so that I don't know [what's happening]. He could have stuck a knife in her for all I know, with the door shut. And the worst thing for me was actually not knowing what was going to happen next, not knowing what was happening then and not knowing what was going to happen next. That was the most frightening thing for me. (Regina, aged 9)

For these children the fear of the unknown seemed worse than actually seeing the injuries to their mother. What the children appeared to be highlighting was how they were being further traumatised by their absolute loss of control over the situation. They did not know what was happening to their mother, they did not know how to stop it, they did not know what to do, and they did not know how far the man would go. It was not unreasonable for the children to fear that their mother might be killed. Teaching children safety planning may mean that they *feel* they have more control in the situation or at least enable them to protect themselves.

The idea of safety planning with children experiencing domestic violence is a somewhat contentious one. Safety planning involves telling children how to protect themselves and possibly how to get help when their mother is being hurt. Opponents feel that it puts too much responsibility on the child to stop the violence or call help. This is especially so if the situation worsens due to something the child has done in trying to help. From what the children in this study said, it seems that there is a need for safety planning. We know that loss of control contributes to feelings of trauma and children clearly said that not knowing what was happening or what to do, that is, not having any control, made them feel more distressed. Children who are taught safety skills relating to domestic violence may or may not be able to act on them, their actions may improve or worsen the situation or have no effect. However, by providing them with the resources to try to make some decisions in violent situations, their loss of control will not be as great. We cannot assume that guilt engendered by acting in a way which inadvertently increases the negative consequences of a violent attack on their mother is any worse than the guilt children feel hearing their mother being beaten time after time, and not being able to do anything at all. The most central aspect of safety planning is the message to children first and foremost that they must protect themselves. In this way children's sense of responsibility for the outcome of the violence may be lessened as they are given 'permission' to protect themselves.

Children's powerlessness

Children seemed very aware of their lack of power in situations of violence and spoke about their need to believe they had some form of control over what was happening to their mother and themselves. As we have seen, given their resources, children tried to cope in a variety of ways and as previously discussed, there were a number of interviews where references were made to children trying to protect women by their physical presence. In some cases it did actually inhibit the man's violence at that point. Children also referred to things they would have liked to do but were too frightened, for example phone for help. One child said:

> Once when he was drinking sort of thing I was going to throw his drink away 'cause he was being nasty to Mummy but I was too scared to do it. (Sabrina, aged 10)

Children described their frustration at not knowing how or when to seek help.

> They were fighting and I didn't know what to do and my little brother was by the phone and he kept on saying that he was going to phone 999 and things. And I said, 'Don't 'cause we might get into trouble'. And then he started crying and I had to calm him down and he kept on going upstairs and our dad kept on telling us to go downstairs and we didn't know what to do, so I just ended up crying with him. It was horrible. (Regina, aged 9)

Children often feel that they are in a no-win situation. They are scared of what will happen if they do not get help for their mother and they are scared of what will happen if they do try to get help.

One young boy had, out of the blue, apologised to his mother for not protecting her from the violence. He was 9 when he spoke to his mother about the violence but 5 or 6 when it was happening. He is a poignant reminder of how responsible (and guilty) children can feel with regard to protecting their mother.

> About a fortnight ago he got in bed early with me one morning, and he woke me up. And all of a sudden he said, 'Mummy, I am really sorry I didn't stand up for you when Daddy used to hit you but I was only little and I was afraid'. And I said, 'Oh that's all right, I didn't expect you to'. And he said, 'If he did it now I would smack the bastard one'. (Alma)

Some children said that they just wanted to forget about the domestic violence. Interestingly all these children were open in their discussions about their experiences. Perhaps what is important is that children can choose whether to think about what happened as opposed to being disturbed by unwelcome reminders such as nightmares or flashbacks. Children were often very much focused on looking forward rather than dwelling on the trauma of the violence. For example, when one young boy was asked what advice he would give to other children in this situation he said:

> To just forget about the bad stuff and just forget about the past and just think of the future really, best thing to do. (Francis, aged 8)

Summary

Children, even very small children, appeared very aware of the domestic violence. In their interviews a number of mothers expressed their shock at how aware their small children had been of the violence and how accurately they had retained those memories. At the time mothers often believed that they were protecting the children from the violence and were unaware that the children frequently witnessed assaults. Once they had left the violent man, mothers could clearly see the effects on their children. Talking to the children about the violence was obviously very difficult for mothers. They did not want to upset their children and they had many worries about what to say and how to say it. Most mothers talked to the children about the violence once they had left and this was particularly so in response to the children's questions. From the children's point of view, it was very important for them to be able to discuss the violence in order to make sense of what happened and how they felt about it.

On witnessing the assaults on their mothers children felt sad, confused, angry, fearful and guilty for not protecting their mothers. Regardless of age, children were very aware of the tense atmosphere in the home and lived in constant anticipation of trouble. Children learned to cope with the violence using both physical and psychological strategies. The main physical strategies they used were physically intervening in both the short and the long term to try to stop the violence and developing safety strategies such as trying to stay out of the man's way. The psychological strategies that they used included talking about their feelings, denial, and needing to know details of the violence. In learning to cope with the violence, children may display behaviour which might be seen to be problematic; however, this behaviour may represent a strategy developed by the child in order to cope with the father's violence.

Children felt very powerless in the face of their fathers' violence and they frequently thought of things that they wanted to do to protect their mothers but were too frightened to be able to act. Safety planning with children may serve to decrease their feelings of powerlessness and subsequent trauma.

PART FOUR

Agency Responses to Domestic Violence

Agencies

Women and children will have contact with a number of agencies while they are experiencing domestic violence and particularly as they seek help. As the following chapters outline, help-seeking is a process and women generally will have to approach a number of agencies, often many times, before they get the support they need. Homer, Leonard and Taylor's (1984) study of eighty women attempting to leave violent partners found that over half contacted between six and eight agencies and 13 per cent had contacted between nine and eleven agencies. Hanmer and Saunders (1993) reported that on average women contacted eleven agencies before getting appropriate help. They also found that black women may experience more difficulty in accessing help than other women, with black women in the study reporting an average of seventeen agency contacts before receiving support. Bowstead, Lall and Rashid (1995), Imam (1994) and Mama (1996) have all highlighted the difficulties faced by black and Asian women and children in seeking help for domestic violence. As the sample in the present study is predominantly white, it must be acknowledged that the experiences outlined in the following chapters are mainly a reflection of the agency responses received by white women and children. The kinds of agencies involved are summarised in Figure 6.1

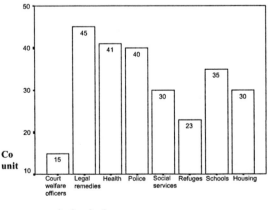

agencies involved

Figure 6.1 Agencies involved

CHAPTER SIX

Social Services' Responses to Domestic Violence

Introduction

Social workers have a statutory duty for the protection of children, and in terms of domestic violence there has traditionally been a split between provision for women (usually refuge based) and social work services for children. In 1995 *Child Protection: Messages from Research* (Department of Health (DoH) and Dartington Social Research Unit 1995) was published. This represented the result of a programme of research commissioned by the DoH into child protection. Not surprisingly, a number of these studies found domestic violence to be a factor in child protection work (Brandon and Lewis 1996; Farmer and Owen 1995; Gibbons, Conroy and Bell 1995). This accumulated research emphasised the need to move away from an investigative social work practice base to one that emphasised family support. 'The stress upon child protection investigations and not enquiries and the failure to follow through interventions with much needed family support prevented professionals from meeting the needs of children and families' (DoH and Dartington Social Research Unit 1995, p.55). Since the mid-1990s there have been some moves to partnership working between statutory agencies and voluntary groups and a growing recognition that 'woman protection is frequently the most effective form of child protection' (Kelly 1994, p.53). Hester *et al.* (1999) and Mullender (1996) offer detailed suggestions and examples of good social work practice in relation to domestic violence.

Findings

Thirty families had contact with social services. Of these, ten were happy with the response they received, fourteen felt that they had received a negative response and for six families the response had been mixed.

In thirteen cases it was the woman herself who had initiated the contact. In four instances the violent man contacted social services and in thirteen cases the contact was made by somebody else, usually a professional such as police, health visitors, refuge staff and medical personnel. Two women reported that extended family contacted social services and a further two said that the contact was made by their neighbours. There were six malicious allegations out of these calls and these included the two calls from neighbours.

Reasons why contact was made with social services were as follows:

- Concerns regarding the safety of the woman and children were the reason in twelve cases. Two of these cases involved the violent man snatching the children and in the rest of the cases the threat of the man's violence was identified as the concern.

- Ten women contacted social services because they needed support, usually in coping with the impacts of domestic violence on the children or themselves. Two women requested respite care for the children: one of these women had a disability and the other was physically unwell in addition to coping with the impact of domestic violence.

- Children's disclosure regarding child sexual abuse prompted contact with social services in four families.

Violent men involving social services as part of the abuse

When the women's ex-partners contacted social services it appeared to represent an attempt to continue to control and further intimidate the women once they had separated. In one case the woman's ex-partner phoned social services and said that she was physically abusing the children. A social worker then phoned the woman, who explained about the domestic violence and the social services did not visit or take it any further.

Similarly, another man made allegations to social services about the woman's care of the children. Social services carried out some checks and the woman said,

They decided that I am the ideal mother now. (Camilla)

One man, who was himself using drugs, went to social services after the woman and children left, saying (falsely) that the woman was taking drugs and working as a prostitute to buy drugs. In another family, the man snatched the children after the woman had left. She was unable to get any help from social services. After the children were returned to her, a social worker began to visit. Some months later, the social worker told the woman that the reason she had been visiting was because the children's father had alleged that the woman was abusing the children and they were checking it out.

Involvement with social services was also identified as leading to an escalation in the man's violence as he saw his total control over the woman being eroded by the support she received from the social worker. Jem described how difficult it was for her, because she really needed her social worker's support but had to 'pay' for it in terms of more frequent assaults.

> I was getting beaten practically every day because I had someone giving me attention, which was the social worker. She'd come and she'd take me out to places, show me places that I'd never even seen before that are just down the road basically. And just for me to spend time away from my husband and to have some time to myself and it [the violence] just got worse. (Jem)

Fear of children being removed

Over and over again women referred to how they had been frightened that if social services came to know about the domestic violence, they would remove the children. We shall see later how this fear acted as a barrier to women seeking help. In addition, some violent men deliberately manipulated this fear in order to control the women further, especially to ensure that they did not tell anyone about the domestic violence or try to leave the relationship. Danielle explained how her partner would spend hours convincing her that the only thing stopping professionals removing the children was the fact that she was with him.

> I don't know why I believed him, I don't know why. Just, maybe it was just drummed into me for so long that I was a bad mother, I believed what he said, because I thought they [professionals] must be saying this. And he'd get me cowering in the corner, he'd have me like two or three hours and sometimes have it nights in a row you know. And he'd wait 'til he'd really broken me down and I'm just like sitting in the corner with my hands over my face and he'd say, 'Oh but I'm here, I won't let them do it. You've got me, there's nobody else but you've got me. Don't forget that.' (Danielle)

Judith described how her partner used this threat against her from the time her son was born:

I came home with Francis when he was a few days old. He was born on the Tuesday and we were home on the Friday. I'd been indoors half an hour, there was a row, I can't remember what about, but he [my partner] threatened to call social services to say I was an unfit mother. In fact picked up the phone and pretended to dial the number, pretended he was speaking to somebody and was saying I was an unfit mother. And I had been home half an hour, I had been a mum less than a week. (Judith)

Positive social services response

Ten children and adults interviewed said that they had received a positive response from social services. This was because they felt they were taken seriously and appropriate action taken or support given. Women referred to how the support of their social worker enabled them to leave the violent relationship and reinforced their belief that separating from the violent man was the best thing not only for themselves, but for their children as well. An ongoing supportive relationship with a social worker was an important factor in deterring women from returning to the violent man after they had left. Women referred to being able to talk to their social worker when they were feeling depressed or finding it difficult to cope and thinking of going back. Having someone to talk to and encourage them meant that they found the strength to continue building a new life for themselves and the children. A supportive social work response was also seen by mothers as offering more protection for their children because there was someone else concerned with the children's best interests apart from themselves.

Often the key to successful social work involvement was the effort the social worker put in to building the relationship with the woman and her children. Deirdre talked at length about her first meeting with her social worker.

I had no money, no social money, and he [the social worker] came up to see me the next day, and he was absolutely marvellous. He walked in and Padraig [my son] stopped at the door, turned around and walked back out, so he [the social worker] got on his knees, and he had loads of toys and sweets and that, he was laughing with me and Paul [my son]. And then Padraig slowly started walking in the door, and then he [the social worker] completely ignored Padraig and carried on playing with the others and then eventually Padraig sat down with him. And then he just carried on playing as if Padraig had been there all the time. And then Padraig just kept looking at him a bit strange and then he went, 'Are you going to hit me? You're a man, are you going to hit me?' and [the social worker] said, 'No! I won't hit you,' and carried on playing. 'My dad hit me, my dad threw me up the wall and banged my head,' 'Did he? He's a naughty man isn't he Padraig? Not all men are like that.' And he just carried on playing again, and he'd say things like, 'I wasn't allowed to cry, 'cause if I cry, I'm a wimp,' and he [the social worker] said, 'I cry, I cry all the time,' and then he carried on playing again. But he was absolutely brilliant, and he gave me some money, and he took the children out to McDonald's. And now when the children see him, Padraig cries at the door when he goes. He literally cries. (Deirdre)

Deirdre describes her social worker as 'an absolute diamond' and says that she wishes that she had known years ago that a social worker could be like this. She described herself as

very, very satisfied with social services. (Deirdre)

Learning to trust and stay involved with social services could be very difficult for women who were still in the violent relationship and having to deal with their partner's opposition to any social work involvement. Lucy highlighted how difficult it was for her when social services first became involved:

Chris [my partner] was totally against them, totally against social services, so I was stuck between the two of them, you know, trying to stay involved with them but at the same time trying not to go against Chris's wishes as well. It was a very difficult position to be in. (Lucy)

Lucy herself admitted that because of her partner's influence, she 'worked against' social services. However, despite a very difficult start she appreciated the effort that her social worker made in overcoming her reluctance and felt that social services were supportive.

The social worker I had for seven years spent an awful long time getting to know me and working me out. A real long time, gaining my trust and confidence and we felt more like friends, so I was very sorry for her to leave. (Lucy)

Negative social services response

Fourteen families were unhappy with the response they received from social services. As outlined below, there were a number of themes identifiable in this dissatisfaction.

Domestic violence not acknowledged

The most common reason for women's dissatisfaction with social services was that social workers did not acknowledge the domestic violence or take it seriously. As one woman said:

> The social workers they give me at the time seemed to be trainees and they didn't really seem to know. It was as if they didn't really take me seriously and when I asked for help to back me up on things, they used to back down, well now we can't do this and we can't do that. (Rita)

Some women questioned their social worker's qualifications and believed that they demonstrated a lack of awareness regarding the dynamics of domestic violence. For example one woman expressed her concerns that her social worker did not understand how certain areas were not safe for her to go to because of the possibility of being found by her ex-partner. In other situations where social services were involved because of the children's difficulties, although the social workers were aware of the domestic violence they did not relate it to the children's distress and so did not work to address the issue. Women described their desperation at trying to find therapeutic help for their children but not being able to get it through social services.

In some cases once the woman had left with the children the violent man snatched the children as a way of forcing the woman back into the relationship. Social services were not always sympathetic in this situation.

> I went to social services and I'm saying that I'm at the end of my tether and I can't cope, and they were so horrible to me I couldn't believe it, and they said, 'Well, he's the father.' (June)

Marianne's story represents an extreme example of domestic violence not being acknowledged as a key social work issue. Marianne had a baby unbeknown to her violent partner and had the baby adopted because it was the only way she could see to protect the baby from the violence. Social services knew the reason that Marianne was having the baby adopted was because of her partner's violence but she said they did not help her. Marianne said that regarding the adoption, social services 'done their bit' and 'were marvellous' but at no point was she offered help around the key issue, which was her partner's violence. Indeed the domestic violence was not acknowledged at all. Social services seemed to define their role narrowly and addressed only those aspects of Marianne's experience that they saw as an unambiguous social work issue, that is, the adoption.

Women who had contact with social workers working in the area of mental health were dismayed at the lack of recognition of the implications of the domestic violence both for themselves and their children. One woman who was hospitalised because of mental health problems she developed as a result of the domestic violence was upset that once she was discharged from the psychiatric hospital, social work involvement ceased. She could not understand why she was unable to get help for her son, as she was very concerned about the psychological impact of the domestic violence on him.

Cheryl believed that she was labelled an unfit mother because she suffered mental health problems as a consequence of the domestic violence. Her ex-partner had locked her out of the home and kept the children. Cheryl spent three years fighting to have the children returned to her care. Eventually it was discovered that the children were being abused and they were removed from their father's care. Cheryl had told social services about the domestic violence but felt that they did not really listen to what she was saying about it. She felt very much that they were biased against her.

> I think they still saw me as a very uncoping person. Obviously my spell under the psychiatrist didn't help. I think at that point, they said it on numerous occasions, that they would place the children with me as an emergency as there was nowhere for them to go besides put them out with complete strangers. But they were only with me pending fostering. (Cheryl)

The impacts of the domestic violence and the enforced separation from her children were overlooked and the crucial issue seen to be Cheryl's perceived mental instability.

> The guardian *ad litem*'s [GAL] reports referred to me as being mentally unstable and having had mental problems, which I was lucky enough to track down the psychiatrist I had been under and he'd sent a lovely letter to court saying that I am as sane as they come. But we had to go for psychiatric assessments as well because of that. She [the GAL] felt my lifestyle wasn't suitable because I didn't work, which I'd actually given up work when the children came back. Just generally I'd been labelled as being unsuitable and that they wanted them placed with a nice family, a nice two-parent family somewhere. (Cheryl)

Women may develop mental health problems because of the domestic violence; however, the experience of women in this study was that although they had contact with a number of professionals, the focus remained totally on their perceived mental health problems. The women were viewed in isolation from their life situation; their problems regarded as internal psychological processes rather than a reaction to daily violence and intimidation. Humphreys (2000) also found that professionals often did not make the connection between women's mental health problems and the domestic violence they were experiencing.

The child protection register and social work support

Women were critical of the fact that even when children were placed on the child protection register, no social work support was forthcoming.

> When kids are on child protection like, you're supposed to get help and support from them and I got none, and it ain't just for me eldest one, I mean I can see his future ending up in prison. Because he thinks that if he can do, he can do it. That's what he's been doing, I think it's bang out of order the way that my social worker hasn't even bothered helping us, and he's taking glue and everything, never used to. That's what hurts. (Janice)

Some women were resentful that their children had been placed on the child protection register, seeing it as a negative judgement about their care of and ability to protect their children. They felt that there was no recognition of the lengths to which they had gone to protect the children from the violence. For example, Camilla's children were placed on the child protection register when she disclosed the domestic violence in the course of an access dispute (pre Children Act 1989). She felt that putting the children on the register was a reflection on her and she was not happy about it. Some time later, in a new relationship, when other children were born they were automatically registered.

> The only thing I didn't like was that the children were put on to the 'At Risk Register'. I didn't mind them being put on it because of the father, but it makes me look bad as well, which I didn't like. I'd gone through everything I've gone through now and lost everything again to make sure my children are safe, and yet they were on the 'At Risk Register'. (Camilla)

Years later Camilla found out by accident that the children were still on the register. She had thought that when their names were placed on the register they would automatically be removed after a short while. In the intervening years the family had no contact with social services.

A common perception of social services was that they would respond only reactively rather than proactively, as this woman verbalised:

> You see, I can't get help from the social services unless I attack the children and then I'm regarded as an abusive mother. Then they go on the 'At Risk Register'. Then we get help. (Bea)

Some women welcomed or even requested that their children be placed on the child protection register. They saw it as a way of further protecting the children. Following the discovery that her partner had sexually abused their son, Jacinta attended a case conference and asked that her children's names be placed on the child protection register. She felt that if that happened, it would enable her to break her partner's 'hold' on her. She also thought that if he snatched them, social services would be able to remove them from him. The children were put on the register.

Marianne also asked that her child be placed on the child protection register as a way of preventing her ex-partner snatching the child. Social services said that they would not do that because Marianne was protecting her daughter.

> I wouldn't have minded, there is no way them children are in any threat from me, so it didn't bother me. I mean I know it's very nice for them [social services] to think that [I could protect them] but as far as I was concerned it was just something to save them, to help them, but they wouldn't do it. All right, it's very nice to think that they [believed I could protect them], but at the same time I wasn't strong enough to protect them from him, because I kept going back to him or bothering with him. Whereas if they had been on the 'At Risk Register', I could have used that. (Marianne)

The common perception was that children who were registered would get support that they might not otherwise get. However, as the examples illustrate, this was not necessarily true. Placing children's names on the child protection register could be a difficult decision for mothers to understand as it felt as if they were being judged as incapable of protecting their children. Or they felt that others perceived the mother as the one posing the threat to the children. In other situations, mothers viewed the child protection register as a tool to protect both the children and themselves. They saw it as giving a clear message that the man's violence was wrong and the mother would be supported in taking action to protect the children. What is concerning is the lack of follow-up, once it had been agreed that children were at risk.

Perceived mishandling of and lack of support concerning
child sexual abuse investigations

Being involved in an investigation into alleged child sexual abuse is obviously a sensitive time for children and their carers. Mothers voiced a number of concerns regarding the handling of such investigations. Two of the mothers who contacted social services because their daughters had disclosed sexual abuse were distressed by the fact that a male social worker came to interview the girls. They felt it should have been a woman. One of the girls refused to talk to a man and a female social worker came to see her. However, the female social worker was very unsympathetic.

> They sent a social worker, he was a man. She wasn't going to talk to any men, after what had just happened. We said we'd try her with a woman. A woman came, and she says, she was a very nasty woman, I can't even remember her name. She said something like, 'I don't know what you're all sitting around moping for, he only tried to rape her; he didn't actually succeed.' So we told her to get out of the house, and we've never spoken about it since. (Martine)

Martine was then scared to approach social services regarding the domestic violence in case the children were removed. She said she did not think they could help. Overall she feels let down by social services.

Leila said that, ironically, she had not contacted social services for help while living with the violent man because she feared they would become overinvolved, that is, remove her daughter. After her daughter's disclosure of sexual abuse, Leila and her daughter went to a refuge. They had no money and Leila asked her social worker for financial assistance but her request was refused. Later Leila asked for help in coping with her daughter's behaviour following the disclosure but she was told that her daughter was not a priority.

Stephanie's son Terry disclosed that his father had sexually abused him and an investigation was undertaken. Stephanie was very unhappy with the way the investigation was handled. Neither she nor Terry had any warning about Terry being interviewed so Stephanie had no opportunity to prepare him. Instead he was taken out of school and interviewed by a policeman and a social worker with no familiar person present. Terry was very distressed and unable to talk about his abuse. As a result the case was dropped. Stephanie feels that the police officer and social worker should have come to meet Terry first before the interview or at least have given her enough time to prepare him.

Cheryl was also unhappy at the way her children's investigation was handled. Like Stephanie, she felt that more time should have been spent on planning.

> They barged in like a bull into a china shop really and I don't think they handled it well at all. I saw the social worker at 5 o'clock one evening. I had a message at 10 o'clock that night to be at Shirley's school by 9 the following morning at which point a different social worker and a WPC [woman police constable] went in to interview. Now they told me at that time if she didn't disclose at that interview she would have to go back to her stepfather's house, and he would have to be told about the accusations that had been made. Now she was 9 years old, 10 years old, very frightened. It took two hours before she actually did disclose and they were just on the verge of giving up. And I know if she'd have gone back into that house at that point he would have killed her. She'd been abused for three years. I didn't see that waiting a couple more days and planning it carefully was going to make that much difference. He had the capacity to kill and I think he would have done. I mean luckily she did at that last minute disclose and a place of safety order was drawn up and they were out. (Cheryl)

Mothers felt that they needed support in coming to terms with the knowledge that their child had been sexually abused, as Jacinta explained:

> I didn't know if I was a victim, I didn't know what I was, but nobody actually said to me, 'Well Jacinta, this is the position and we're here for you and we'll help you understand all this.' I didn't understand it all, but I didn't get any help to understand anything. I mean I went through two years of being really, really angry with him [my ex-partner], with social services and with me because I had no support at all. (Jacinta)

Mixed response from social services

Six women said that they had received a mixed response from social services. For these women the response they got varied from social worker to social worker. The crucial factors in determining what type of response they got were the social worker's awareness of domestic violence and its impact on the woman and children and the social worker's ability to provide practical advice or services. For example, two women in the study had contact with social services after witnessing a woman being stabbed to death by her ex-partner when he broke into a refuge. Both women described the social workers as 'lovely women' and 'very nice', but both of them felt that they did not get the support they needed for themselves or for their children, who had also witnessed the murder.

Cheryl had a very difficult relationship with social services over a number of years. However, she felt that she was very lucky in that she was eventually allocated a social worker who was new to the team and they built up a very good relationship. The new social worker recognised that Cheryl had done everything she could to protect her children and was clear about the impact of the domestic violence on both Cheryl and her children. Cheryl perceived her support as invaluable.

> She was very, very good, very supportive and she still is. But without her I don't know how we would have got through it, no. (Cheryl)

Children's perceptions of social services

Lack of information

Children's and young people's dissatisfaction with social services seemed to focus on the lack of information they were given, particularly with regard to the process when they were involved in a child abuse investigation:

> I don't think I had any security, any knowledge of what was going on. I needed to be told everything. I didn't realise that there was a chance that I might have been taken away. But I think I should have been told a bit later [after the investigative interview] by somebody what was going to happen with my dad. But my mum was really the only person who told me that. (Shirley, aged 16)

Jackie was very dissatisfied with the response her family received from social services. She knew that she and her siblings had been put on the child protection register because her stepfather had a conviction for sexual abuse but she said that the social worker did not talk to them or explain what was happening. Jackie wished that the social worker had talked to them and explained more, particularly as her stepfather later sexually abused her younger brother.

> Nobody told us anything, we just got sent to this case conference and that was it really. And we didn't hear anything else after that. (Jackie, aged 19)

Lack of contact

Very few children reported that they were unhappy with their contact with social services. It should be noted, though, that children's own actual contact with social workers appeared to be minimal even where there was an allocated social worker. Social workers may have visited the home but not necessarily spent time with the children, even when the children were the sole reason for social services involvement. One very clear example of this was given by Stephanie. There were concerns about her 5-year-old son, Terry, as he was displaying sexualised behaviour. A social worker came to visit but did not speak directly to Terry; instead the social worker discussed his behaviour with his parents in Terry's hearing. The matter was not taken further. After Stephanie had left the violent relationship, Terry disclosed that his father had sexually abused him. Stephanie speculated that if the social worker had spoken directly to Terry when the concerns were first raised, Terry might have been able to say what was happening, thus further abuse could have been prevented.

Positive social services response

Children who were given information and felt that their views were taken seriously by the social worker were very positive about the intervention. As with mothers, children were very appreciative of a social work approach which concentrated on building a positive relationship and worked at the child's pace.

One young girl had been interviewed regarding possible sexual abuse. She said that she felt embarrassed while talking to the social worker but that there was nothing the social worker could have done to make it better.

A young boy described his social worker in terms of being the one who rescued him from the violent situation. He said that he found it easy to talk to her about the violence because she understood. A number of children stressed how important it was for them that they felt it was easy to talk to the social worker about their experiences. One young person explained how she had not wanted to meet the social worker. She said she did not see the point. However, she wrote to him expressing her wishes and he wrote back to her. She felt that her views were taken seriously.

Another social worker had spent time preparing the children in a particular family for the possibility of them being accommodated by the local authority for a week to give their mother a break. When it did actually happen, the children were very positive about it.

> She said that we might have to go away for a while, that's what she kept saying to us, but we didn't really think about it. But when it did come, it was all right, when we did have to go, it was good. (Tracy, aged 15)

Fiona had been sexually abused by her father. In her interview, Fiona stressed how the social worker concentrated on building a relationship with her thus enabling Fiona to trust her.

> I think with the social worker and them, like they talk about stuff, other things at first so I grow to trust them and then we would start talking about stuff like that [the sexual abuse]. (Fiona, aged 15)

Summary

Of the thirty families who had contact with social services, most were unhappy with the response they received. A positive social services response was one where the domestic violence was taken seriously and the social worker put a lot of effort into building a relationship with the woman and children. A negative social services response was one in which the domestic violence was not taken seriously or there was a general lack of awareness regarding domestic violence.

Women's fear of their children being removed by social services if they knew of the domestic violence was the main factor inhibiting women seeking formal help. This fear was then deliberately manipulated by the violent man as a way of keeping the woman in the relationship. Some violent men also made allegations of child abuse against the woman as a way of continuing to control and intimidate her once she had left him. Women also reported that if they were involved with social services while still living with their violent partners, then they experienced more violence, as the men perceived the involvement of social services as undermining their control over the women and children. A number of issues emerged regarding the child protection register and social work support. Mothers whose children were on the child protection register perceived a lack of social work support despite their children being on the register. On the other hand mothers whose children were not on the register thought that they would get more support if they were on the register. Some women felt that they were being negatively judged by having their children placed on the child protection register, whereas others saw it as a means of further protecting their children. Mothers whose children had been involved in child abuse investigations generally felt that the investigations had not been handled sensitively.

Although there was a lack of direct contact between social workers and children, children were generally positive about their contact with social services. They valued an approach which made them feel that they were being taken seriously, that worked at their own pace and they appreciated the effort made by the social worker to build a relationship with them. On the negative side, children felt that they should have been given more information, particularly if they were involved in an investigation into alleged child abuse.

CHAPTER SEVEN

Police Responses to Domestic Violence

Introduction

The main pieces of legislation that the police can use to respond to situations of domestic violence are the Offences Against the Person Act 1861, the Police and Criminal Evidence Act 1984 and the Protection from Harassment Act 1997.

Hester *et al.* (1999) concede:

> Many aspects of domestic violence are difficult to define as crimes, nor do they fit readily into common categories of 'assault' under criminal law. The criminal law and the courts perceive harm in terms of physical abuse. (Hester *et al.* 1999, p.83)

This 'incident-focused' system, they argue, ignores many aspects of the controlling and intimidating behaviour that is women's common experience. However, the authors point out that in the late 1990s case law has defined 'actual bodily harm' to include shock and nervous conditions, thus recognising the psychological impacts of abuse.

Findings

In total, forty families had contact with the police. Of these, eight were happy with the police response, sixteen were dissatisfied and sixteen had received a mixed response. In thirty out of the forty cases it was the woman herself who called the police. In nine instances someone else, most commonly a neighbour, was the one to make the call. Children in two families phoned the police (in one of these cases at different points the mother had also phoned).

Issues with regard to women contacting the police

There were a number of issues which women raised in relation to contacting the police. One of these related to barriers to calling the police in the first place. Some women believed that the police simply would not get involved in domestic violence.

> I mean I didn't think the police would be interested. I've got to be honest; I was totally gobsmacked [shocked] at their reaction. I couldn't believe it. (Kim)

She, like many other women interviewed, was unaware of how the police could help in this situation. Some women appeared to have internalised the message that domestic violence is accepted and did not realise that their partners were in fact committing a crime.

> While we were living together I didn't think he were breaking law, I didn't think he could break the law against me if we were living together, I thought they might laugh at me. I didn't know it were illegal, it's very weird what you think when you're actually going through it. (Bernice)

Other women said that they had been afraid to call the police. For one woman this fear arose from her immigration status. Her partner had deliberately given her false information regarding her status in order to ensure that she did not call the police. When the police were called, he told them that she was an illegal immigrant (she was not). However, the police did not get involved in his allegations.

Calling the police might stop a particular assault but women also reported that in the long run it could make matters worse because their partners saw that they 'got off with it' and would then punish the woman for calling the police.

> I mean if they appear when you've just been severely beaten they'll take him away. Sometimes they keep him in overnight, sometimes it's just for a couple of hours. But you know what's going to happen the minute he walks back through that door. Which most of the time isn't worth it so you don't bother calling the police anyway. (Camilla)

In relation to calling the police, it is interesting that a number of violent men threatened to tell the police that the woman was 'mad' so that they would dismiss any allegations of violence.

> He'd be saying things like, 'You daren't call the police because I will tell them that you are having a nervous breakdown.' (Marcia)

The idea that they could be perceived as having mental health problems fuelled women's fears that they might lose their children.

Women at times found it emotionally difficult to call the police, particularly when their partner was the father of their children. Women described feeling guilty for calling the police to their children's father and in some cases dropped the charges against the violent man because of this guilt. Women who returned to the relationship or dropped the charges against their violent partners then also struggled with their guilt at 'letting the police down'. The reason women generally gave for not continuing with a prosecution was fear either of their ex-partners or fear of having to go through the court process. Women were left feeling guilty for wasting police time and in some cases felt that individual police officers tried to exploit this guilt in order to convince the woman to continue with the case. For example, Maisie phoned the police after an assault and they came very quickly. She did not realise that by making a statement she was agreeing to press charges. She did not want to press charges. The police kept her partner overnight and she phoned up to see when he would be released. She felt that they were being 'very evasive'. While on the phone to the police she said that she did not want to press charges and she heard someone in the background making disparaging remarks.

> So I says I don't want to press charges or anything like that and I heard someone saying in the background, it was said that I could hear but not obviously to me, 'Oh do you hear the silly woman? Now she doesn't want to press charges, she knows we'd be back around there in a week.' You know, it was said so I could hear it you know and someone said, 'Oh wasting police time, you know.' (Maisie)

Maisie was understandably angry with the police for their comments and felt that they did not understand how threatened she felt. If women's fears regarding prosecution of their partners are not addressed, they are extremely unlikely to prosecute. Instead their guilt will only be intensified and inhibit them from seeking police help in the future.

Three women discussed wanting the decision to prosecute a man for violence against his partner to rest with the police not with the woman. The reason they gave for this was to protect women from further violence as the man attempted to intimidate her into dropping the charges against him.

> I would have liked for the police to have come into my home and intervened and said, 'Whether you're going to prosecute him or not, we're

taking him away, we're going to prosecute him.' And in that way he couldn't have blamed me. (Margo)

Another issue which women highlighted in relation to contacting the police was that their ex-partners tried to involve the police in their abuse of the women, for example, by making allegations of child abuse against the woman.

Positive police response

Eight women reported that they were pleased with the police response. Generally this was because the women felt that the police were taking the domestic violence seriously and supporting them.

> Fantastic. I think if I'd realised how much help and support there was ... because I know at one time if they got called to a domestic they just used to sort of quieten you down didn't they? Not that I knew that from experience, it's like other people. I think you think to yourself, what's the point of involving them. Well I didn't even know there was a domestic violence unit, I didn't even know they existed, I didn't have a clue. (Kim)

The following quote from Jem highlights a number of aspects of police response to domestic violence which were rated positively by women in the study. Jem called the police even though she did not know what they would do. She found their response very quick and very efficient. The police made her partner, Simon, leave the house because that is what Jem said she wanted.

> They said they'd hang around for a bit, they'd patrol the area and that they'd put an alert out so that if a 999 call comes through or a call to a local police station they would realise and come back quite quickly, which I thought was really good. They were concerned for my emotional welfare; they wanted to know if I wanted to go to the hospital or whatever, am I okay? Am I sure I'm okay? Are the children all right? I didn't know they'd be so intense with regard to my children as well. I said, yes I'm fine etc., and then the domestic violence unit called me up a couple of days later. (Jem)

Thus, women valued a police response that combined the following elements:

- a quick response
- officers taking the domestic violence seriously
- officers concerned for both the women's and the children's welfare
- follow-up, particularly from the domestic violence unit
- referral to other appropriate agencies such as refuges, solicitors or local support groups.

Negative police response

Sixteen women said that they were unhappy with the response they received from the police. Generally they felt that the police were not taking the domestic violence seriously. Women reporting a negative police response were more likely to be describing experiences from several years previously, although some women's recent contact with the police was also perceived by them to be negative. Four women said that the police response to them was to treat the call as a 'domestic', that is, to say that they did not get involved in domestic violence.

> Or even the police, once when I rang the service, they said they don't get involved in domestic violence cases and I think legislation must have caused them to look at it more seriously over the last couple of years but previously they weren't really interested. (Davina)

Similarly Denise had also contacted the police several years previously and was told that there was nothing the police could do.

> I called them once when he really beat me, one night, when I managed to grab the phone and they came and at that time I was pretty disgusted because they said, 'You're man and wife, there is nothing we can do.' He had actually broken my nose. That frightened me. I never trusted after that. I didn't trust anyone in authority after that either. I think that's why I was so frightened when I had to go to court to apply for custody, because the only authority people I had asked for help was the police and I just felt like they'd kicked me in the teeth really! But now, the police do get involved now, don't they? From what I've heard. But at the time, no. They wouldn't get involved because it was domestic. (Denise)

She was told by the police that even if she pressed charges, 'it wouldn't get there', and she got an even worse beating when the police left. Some time later her husband assaulted her and left her for dead rolled up in a carpet at the side of the road. A motorist found her unconscious and badly injured and she said that the police 'still didn't want to know'.

Denise was not the only woman dissuaded by the police from pursuing criminal charges against her ex-partner: there were a number of women interviewed who reported this experience. For example, at the advice of a police officer Danielle decided to bring charges against her ex-partner and went to the police station. She was told that she needed to go to the police station in another town. Danielle went there and was informed that she needed to go to another town three miles away to be photographed. She went to the police station as directed and was told: 'It's the wrong time of night to make a report.' She was also advised that she needed to make the report in the town in which she was living. On her fourth visit to a police station Danielle managed to see a policewoman, who dissuaded her against bringing charges.

> And she [the policewoman] sort of basically said, he could have a good solicitor and you know did I realise that he'd probably get away with it by having a good solicitor. And he'd say he was justified, he could say he was justified because he was trying to get her [my daughter] away from me and he was justified in using the force he had against me. So I had to realise that I was going to go through all that procedure and it would mean people standing up in court saying things about me. And I gave up really, thinking well if they don't think it's justifiable then perhaps I've got nothing to complain about. I mean I thought, you know, if the police had said, 'Oh yeah definitely,' I'd have thought they thought I had something to complain about. But if they didn't then I obviously didn't have anything to complain about, I suppose. (Danielle)

While individual police officers may feel that they are protecting women from the trauma of a difficult court case, they need to be mindful of the fact that they may be giving abused women and violent men the message that domestic violence is not serious enough to warrant the full intervention of the criminal justice system.

Women were critical of a police response that treated the domestic violence as a 'disturbance' and did not offer information regarding sources of support such as contact numbers for the local refuge or domestic violence unit.

In more than one case the police said that they were unable to do anything because the woman was not physically marked. Women feel helpless and frustrated in the face of an uninterested police response and the knowledge that phoning the police might not make any difference. For example, one man told the woman that if she phoned the police, he would just say that he was not there and he would get witnesses to support his statement.

Frequently women reported that when the police were called to the home they would remove the man and tell the woman that they would keep him overnight. Instead they kept him for only a few hours or just drove him somewhere else. Instead of having some time to recover from the assault or decide what they wanted to do, women were then unexpectedly faced with the return of their now very angry, violent partner.

Women also called the police when their ex-partners snatched the children. In most cases the police were hampered by the fact that no court orders were in place preventing the man taking the children. Women, however, felt that more could have been done to locate the man and children. In one instance it took six weeks before the police found the man and child. In another family, the man had been charged with alleged child sexual abuse. His children were on the child protection register and there was a court order prohibiting him from taking them. He took one of the boys and the woman called the police. The policewoman who came said that she would not remove the child and said it was the woman's fault for bringing the child into the man's house (she had not).

Mixed police response

Women frequently reported a mixed response from the police, finding that they were treated differently by different officers, different teams and different areas, at different points in time, or even for different aspects of their experiences.

Different officers

The most usual contrast made was between uniformed police and domestic violence unit officers, with domestic violence officers usually being seen as more sympathetic. Women felt very supported when officers from the domestic violence unit would get in touch following uniformed police being called out to a violent incident. Women referred to domestic violence unit officers as being very clear that domestic violence is not acceptable and offering women emotional support and practical information such as refuge or helpline numbers. Vivien described her contact with the domestic violence unit and how supported she felt.

> I'd take in the kids with me, and explain all, and he [the domestic violence officer] said, 'Don't let him get away with it.' And he was talking to the kids about cartoon characters and different things so he made them feel really relaxed and even Beverley [my daughter] came out and she said to my nan, 'That was a really nice man, a really nice man in there, he made us laugh.' But it was really relaxed and very sympathetic; he said, 'I just can't understand how men can do this, no one deserves to be hit.' (Vivien)

On the other hand, uniformed officers were often perceived as being dismissive of domestic violence and as insensitive. For example, Judith called the police following an assault. They asked to see her injuries and she felt that she had to show them her bruises, which were concentrated in the chest area. Afterwards Judith felt humiliated by having to show the male police officers her bruised breasts. She also realised later that her front door had been open and anyone passing by could have seen her. That incident put her off contacting the police again. She said:

> there was no [police] woman there to help me, to talk me through what I could do and what I was entitled to do and what sort of protection I was entitled to from the police. I didn't feel that I got any. (Judith)

However, regarding her contact with the domestic violence unit, Judith said:

> they were absolutely brilliant, they were making sure I was all right virtually all the way through. I had a phone call in the evening; I had a phone call the next morning and [the] sergeant turned up at court for me. I couldn't have wished for a better response other than arresting him and leaving him in jail for the weekend. They took things as far as they could. (Judith)

Women sometimes felt that uniformed police would not take any action against the man other than telling him to leave the house. Women's experience frequently was that once the police left, the man would return and would assault the woman for calling the police. In addition, by not giving the man a clear message that he was wrong, they reinforced women's self-blame. June recounted how at one point a police officer said to her ex-partner, 'My missus gives me a headache as well'. Her experience with the police highlights a number of concerns. June went to a refuge and she arranged a police escort to go back to her home to collect some things. She described what happened:

> I'd left and I'd moved but I went back to try and get some things. I didn't get anything because he was there screaming and shouting, and he had a knife and he was saying to the policeman, 'I'm going to stick it in her throat and rip it out'. And he was telling the policeman what he was going to do to me, and [the policeman] was saying, 'Yeah, all right mate,' and I was like – 'He just said he's going to kill me! You're telling him it's all right mate!' So that really gutted [upset] me. In the end the police said, 'We just think it's best you just leave your things'. So they didn't help me get anything out of there, I left without anything and I reported them for that because I was so upset the [police] man just stood there and listened to how he [my ex-partner] was going to kill me. (June)

June's ex-partner threatened her sister on the street and she had to run into a shop for safety. Her sister reported it to the police, who said it was a 'domestic argument'.

> It's a domestic argument, that's what they told my sister. And she was saying, 'Well no, it's not my man. He has nothing to do with me, he's my sister's,' so he never even actually got a warning for that, nothing. (June)

June had taken injunctions out against her ex-partner but he kept breaking in to her home. She phoned the police but did not receive a supportive response.

> I mean I phoned them seven times in two weeks the last time, and they were saying to me that they were fed up with me calling them. I mean what is the point, what am I supposed to do? Not call them and let him come in the house? (June)

On the other hand she felt that officers from the domestic violence unit 'took it more seriously' than uniformed police. She felt that the uniformed police were scared of the violent man but that this was not the case for the domestic violence officers. She said:

> They made me feel safe and made us feel that I was well in my rights and that he had no right to do what he was doing so that helped me. (June)

Different points in time

Women also reported differing police responses to their situation at different points in time. Camilla had contact with the police in the 1970s and again in the late 1990s. She described the service she received both times as a 'terrible response'. In the 1970s she said it was:

> Oh a terrible response. It really was – 'Oh another domestic ... OK.' And if you called them on the spur of the moment because your life is at risk it does take a while for them to get there, because they see it as another domestic and that is it. (Camilla)

More recently Camilla charged her ex-partner with actual bodily harm. The police agreed to escort him back to get his things. Instead they let him go on his own and he stayed. Camilla moved out and a friend went to the house to collect some things for her. Her ex-partner thought it was Camilla coming in the house and attacked the friend. In the ensuing scuffle Camilla's ex-partner was injured and her friend was subsequently charged with grievous bodily harm. Camilla herself was charged with conspiracy to attempted murder.

> But the worst of it was when the violence was against the man I was with, that was different, that was an attempted murder. And the funniest bit was that whilst I was in the police station and they were trying to interview me, and he accused me of this attempted murder, I was covered in bruises! I had the black eye and the split lip, bruises around my throat, and to me it was self-defence, to them it was attempted murder, but what he did to me was just domestic violence. (Camilla)

The charges against Camilla were dropped. Her ex-partner then broke into her house and tried to burn it. Camilla called the police at 11.00 p.m. but they arrived at 1.25 a.m. They did not interview her ex-partner about the fire; they told her that he would only deny it so there was no point. She asked the police officer what she should do now that her ex-partner knew where she was.

> I was speaking to a DC [detective constable] and he was dealing with my case, and he was dealing with the case of the girl who had just left the refuge; it was a young girl and she'd just been found stabbed to death by her ex[partner]. And he was dealing with the same case, and I said, 'What am I supposed to do now that he is in [town]?' And he said, 'Stay in and keep the door locked!' And that's it! And yet he'd just walked away after identifying the body of a girl who had just been stabbed fifteen times by her ex[partner]. Which to me didn't make sense – not at all. (Camilla)

In contrast Deirdre had contact with the police twice since 1994, and found the response much more positive on the second occasion. On the first occasion an officer referred to the call as 'another domestic' and referred to Deirdre as a 'paranoid woman'. She had to plead with the officers to take her partner away so she could pack her things and leave. They promised to keep him overnight but in the end they drove him a little bit from the house and let him return home again immediately. On the second occasion Deirdre found the police much more sympathetic. They discussed her options with her and made it clear that they would support her in whatever decision she made and organised a refuge place for her.

In other situations women felt that the first time they called the police they had received a positive response but on subsequent occasions they felt that the police attitude was, 'What are you still doing here?'

Different responses to different aspects of their experiences

Some women reported that they received different responses from the police for different aspects of their experiences. Most commonly women reported a very different response to the suspected sexual abuse of their children from the woman's allegation of domestic violence.

One woman found the police very supportive concerning her daughter's allegation of sexual abuse against the woman's ex-partner. In the end the Crown Prosecution Service decided not to go ahead with the prosecution.

> No they were very nice; the WPC she was extremely nice; there was nothing besides the interview, she did come and explain to Shirley [my daughter] why they weren't going to prosecute, which I requested they do because Shirley couldn't see why he wasn't going to be punished. (Cheryl)

Regarding the domestic violence, however, Cheryl's experience was very different. When her partner had threatened her and her baby with a gun her elder daughter had phoned the police. Cheryl said that the police were not interested and in fact told the man where she had gone.

> Ralph [my son] was in his bedroom absolutely petrified, Shirley [my daughter] was running a mile down the road looking for a phone box and it was quite a nasty incident. The police came, weren't interested really, a friend of mine arrived at roughly the same time, piled me and the children into her car, took me to her house. The police then told him where I was staying. He turned up the following day and threatened her, threatened my friend with a shotgun, at which time the police were called again and they did try and take some action that time, and I ended up, there was no criminal prosecution again. I took an injunction out. No they did nothing,

indeed they told him where I'd gone and told him to come and see me tomorrow when I'd calmed down. (Cheryl)

Another woman was very impressed with the response she initially received from the police.

> The police were fantastic, you know, they saw the bruises, they took photos of it. They asked me what happened, I told them. They said first thing is you write the statement, then you go to the hospital and then we will come and see you once you have calmed down and everything is all right. (Lana)

However, they then forgot to send the photographic evidence of her bruising off to the Crown Prosecution Service.

Children's views of the police

Children were very often not aware of their mother's contact with the police. However, they were clear that the police have a very important role to play in giving the message that domestic violence is wrong and the usual way they do this is to arrest the violent perpetrator. Children seemed to be aware that the police's involvement in domestic violence signified that it is a very serious matter. As one young boy described, children often realised that their mothers involve the police as a last resort.

> And she rung up the Old Bill [the police] because she couldn't take no more. (Marshal, aged 8)

Teenagers were quite critical of the police response to domestic violence. One young person remembered her mother phoning the police and the police saying that they would not get involved.

> And I can remember Mum phoning the police once and they wouldn't, they said that they wouldn't actually get involved or anything. (Fiona, aged 15)

Hannah described the police as 'useless'.

> Oh they were useless. I thought, you're here to protect people, what are you doing just stood there saying, 'Oh we can't do this and we can't do that'. So I thought, well you can't do anything. (Hannah, aged 15)

Finally, one teenage girl felt that calling the police actually made things worse.

Usually I wouldn't phone the police because I know that makes it worse. The police just come to the door and then they go and leave him in the house, which means that my mum's getting in more trouble, I'm going to get in trouble. (Mona, aged 17)

Mona did actually phone the police on one occasion and when they came to the house they told the violent man that she had phoned them, thus placing her in grave danger.

I phoned the police, right, and I said to them, I said, 'Oh quickly he's hitting my mum.' I said, 'I've got to go Safeway's, I've got to come back with the stuff.' So the woman said to me, 'Well, you go where he's sent you to go and we'll send the police round.' She said, 'What's your name?' And I said, 'Mona.' So they went back and said, 'Oh Mona phoned. Mona phoned us and told us something's wrong.' So that was it, that was what caused all the problems for me. Well, by the time I got there, they'd gone. I was lucky because my auntie just happened to be passing through and she'd stopped and she goes, 'Quick, get in the car!' And then she quickly got my mum. But the police, if it was for the police, well he'd have probably killed me if I'd have gone in there. (Mona, aged 17)

Mona believes that when the man sees that the police are not interested, it reinforces the violent man's behaviour, as well as increasing the risk for the woman and children.

Summary

Of the forty families who had contact with the police, the majority were not happy with the response they received. The main reason for this was that the domestic violence was not taken seriously and women were not given any information regarding appropriate support agencies. A positive police response was one in which the domestic violence was taken seriously, the police responded quickly and were concerned for the women's and children's physical and emotional well-being. Follow-up, particularly from the domestic violence unit, was also very much appreciated, as were referrals to other agencies. A number of women reported a mixed response from the police, giving the impression that the approach of individual officers very much reflected their own attitudes regarding domestic violence and were not always positive. Overall domestic violence unit officers were perceived as being more sympathetic.

Women discussed a number of barriers to calling the police, including not knowing that the police could or would do anything about the man's violence, fear of making it worse, and guilt. As with social services, some men tried to involve the police in their intimidation of the woman.

Children often had no direct contact with the police when they came to the house. Teenagers, however, were often critical of the police response and generally did not see them as helpful.

Hester *et al.* (1999) state: 'Up until the mid-1980s, the police response to domestic violence was very variable, depending on the attitudes and approach of the individual officer' (p.82). The present study found that many women's experiences indicate that this variable response is very much in evidence. However, it is also clear that practice is improving, particularly with the move towards establishing domestic violence units; their response was perceived as positive by women in this study.

CHAPTER EIGHT

Schools' Responses to Domestic Violence

Thirty-five families had contact with schools or nurseries specifically about the domestic violence. Twenty-four of these families felt that they had received a positive response from the school. Very few mothers or children expressly said that they felt unsupported by the school or nursery, rather they felt that the school should be aware of what was happening in the child's life but they did not actually expect any support concerning the domestic violence. On the other hand, the twenty-four families who felt positive about their contact with the school felt that the school staff had gone beyond the confines of their role as educators to offer emotional support to the children and their mothers. In addition, mothers, in particular, were grateful when the school referred them to another agency for ongoing support either for themselves or the children.

Mothers talking to schools about the domestic violence

In thirteen families the mothers had gone to the school and told the staff about the domestic violence. There seemed to be two main concerns that prompted mothers to tell the school about the domestic violence. First, they felt the school should be aware because of possible effects on the children's behaviour. Second, mothers had concerns regarding the safety of the children; that is they were afraid their ex-partners would try to snatch the children from school.

Mothers commonly said that they turned to the school in desperation; they just did not know whom else to talk to. Recognising the impact of the violence on their children's academic performance was often what drove mothers to confide in their children's teachers.

> I went up to the school in tears, because I didn't know where else to turn. Because her schoolwork was going downhill, she was going around with the wrong crowd. (Vivien)

Vivien described the school's response to her daughter's behaviour problems in school as being:

> marvellous, absolutely brilliant ... they understood why.

By telling school staff about what was happening in the children's home life, mothers hoped to set up support for their children in school. As one young person said, once his teacher had been made aware of what was happening:

> She used to treat me all right because of what had happened. (Stuart, aged 14)

Another young boy said:

> Yeah I spoke to my form tutor 'cause my mum told her what happened and she said that if I needed to talk, to come to her. (Aaron, aged 13)

This support was seen to be important by mothers not just in terms of children's emotional needs but also in relation to teachers' understanding that the reason children had not done their homework or were exhausted in class could indicate that the previous evening or night had been eclipsed by their father's abusive behaviour.

Fears that their ex-partners would snatch the children from school was another reason women gave for talking to the school about the domestic violence, usually after they had left with the children. Women explained to the school about the violence and told them that their ex-partner was not allowed to take the children from school. One mother discussed how pleased she was with the school's response when she discussed her fears of her daughter being snatched. They asked for a photograph of her ex-partner so they would recognise him if he were hanging around the school.

Children talking to teachers about the domestic violence

In fifteen families children had directly told school staff or done something that alerted teachers to the possibility of domestic violence. In four instances, once the children had said something, teachers approached their mothers and offered them support also.

Five of the children who spoke to their teachers about the domestic violence felt supported by the teacher.

For example, one little boy described how he can have a

> special five minutes. (Peter, aged 7)

with his teacher whenever he wants. Another young girl said that she had wanted to talk to her teacher but was too embarrassed.

> I just felt a bit embarrassed really because like not many people get their mums beaten up by their dads. (Zara, aged 12)

In the end she was so upset one day going in to school that she told her teacher everything:

> and she was really good. (Zara, aged 12)

What is concerning is that although the teachers were supportive of individual children, in none of these cases did they speak to the child's mother or make a referral to another agency. One young person felt that a teacher had been very supportive over many years and she really appreciated having someone to talk to. However, there were clear child protection concerns and no action was ever taken by the teacher. Young people frequently wished for more practical support from their teachers, particularly in terms of information about where to get help.

In a further six cases children had spoken to their teachers about the domestic violence but no support at all was offered. Two children had directly asked for help but were told that there was nothing the teachers could do. One mother was shocked to discover that her daughter had asked a teacher for help and was told that they were unable to do anything unless the woman herself asked for help but no one approached her to discuss what her daughter had said. Young people referred to talking to teachers and friends at school about the domestic violence but nobody doing anything about it.

> I used to tell teachers and my friends at school what he was like and they, I could see they believed me but they couldn't do anything about it. (Jackie, aged 19)

One mother was very angry that her daughter had been let down by the school. Her daughter had told them what was happening at home and was told by the teacher that the school would get her some support if her mother agreed. Her mother said yes but then nothing happened. She feels now that her daughter will not open up again because she has been let down. Another mother felt that the teachers did not want to know. Her child's teacher had spoken to her at an open evening about her concerns regarding a poem her son had written. However, the teacher did not try to talk to the boy about his experience or refer him to another agency.

His mother said,

They never bothered. (Marcella)

In six families the child's behaviour alerted school or nursery staff to problems at home. In two cases the staff then spoke to the woman about what was happening and then referred the family to another agency. One teenage girl explained how her teachers would ask her if everything was all right at home because her schoolwork was really suffering. She always told them everything was fine because she blamed herself for what was happening.

I just said no, it was all fine at home because I didn't realise at the time what he was doing. But like if he was shouting at me, I just thought, well, I've done wrong. (Karina, aged 16)

At times teachers were aware of children's behavioural difficulties that mothers did not know about. By approaching the child's mother and discussing their concerns, the problem could then be addressed. For example, Gerrard was experiencing difficulties in contact with his father and consequently his behaviour at school was affected. The school highlighted the problems to his mother. His mother was then able to get help for him.

Positive support from schools

Children and mothers from twenty-four families reported receiving positive support from schools.

My headmaster and my teacher knew about it all, and they were really helpful and my headmaster just said, 'If you ever want to leave the lesson you just come out and you come and see me and you can go home.' (Jade, aged 12)

What was really appreciated by families was a response from school staff that was concerned with the children's emotional welfare as well as academic attainment. It was evident that where families received a positive response from the school, they were taking the domestic violence seriously and understood the dynamics involved. One mother described the response she and her children received from school as 'brilliant'. When she explained what was happening the school said that they would 'keep an eye' on the children and be there if the children wanted to talk about it. Another mother said the school was not 'overly concerned' about her child but it was clear from the child's interview that he felt supported by his teacher.

> She says, 'I'll talk to you at playtime, dinnertime, any time, whenever you want to speak'. (Marshal, aged 8)

Mothers appreciated that teachers were aware of possible impacts on the children and thus were ready to offer help. One mother and her son and daughter had witnessed the killing of another woman by her ex-partner, who had broken into the refuge they were staying in. The woman told the school what had happened. Her son was offered a counsellor by the school but he turned it down; the woman felt that it was too soon for him to be able to use the counsellor appropriately. Her son's headmaster was very supportive:

> [He] took him under his wing a little bit and he used to ask him how he was feeling. (Kathryn)

The headmaster would also phone to see how the woman and her daughter (who did not attend that school) were doing.

Another school was very supportive when one young girl started displaying behavioural problems and then refusing to attend. Again, they were clear about the role of the domestic violence in causing the young girl's problems.

As one mother pointed out, school can be the one constant in children's lives when the violence disrupts their home and social life.

> I managed to keep them in the same school, I wanted to keep them there, they were happy at school. And I think school was the one thing in their lives at the time that was a safe continuity, something stable. The school were aware of everything that happened and they were very understanding and supportive. (Alma)

Thus, schools have a crucial role in emotionally supporting children experiencing domestic violence. Repeated moves to escape the violent man often meant that children were unable to stay at the same school. In one family who took part in the research, the children had attended four different schools in two years. As well as disrupting their academic career, it was not always easy for children to adapt to new schools, particularly when they had to start midway through a term. Feeling that they stand out as the new boy or girl added to children's pressure when they were already struggling with the stigma of domestic violence and the upheaval of having moved to a new area leaving extended family and friends behind. Believing that their teacher understood and was available for them to talk to meant a lot to children in this position.

Three young people reported that they had received a lot of support from their teachers but had wanted more practical help.

One teacher had approached a young girl and asked her if anything was wrong. The young girl had not admitted that anything was wrong as she wanted to keep school and home separate, and not 'overload' the two. But her teacher handled it sensitively and the young girl eventually opened up.

> And one time she said, she ... we sat down and spoke about it and from then on she was all right, because like when I was late for school or when I was a bit distressed, she'd look after me. (Mona, aged 17)

Jackie felt very strongly that her schoolwork had suffered but her teachers noticed and were supportive.

> Well, my coursework and schoolwork collapsed like and teachers obviously picked up on that and they understood why and they just kept telling me, like pushing me saying, 'Hurry up, do your work'. They made allowances for me because of what was happening, like let me have a week or two more than everybody else. (Jackie, aged 19)

However she wanted more practical help.

> Well, not support as such, but they understood and like comforted me, but that wasn't really, it didn't really help me a lot because they didn't really help me to help my mum, because that's all I wanted was to help my mum and the kids, that's all I wanted. I didn't care about myself, I just wanted to help them all the time. But the teachers were all right at the time but now, I think some teachers, they pay for themselves to go get counselling so they know how to treat children who have that in the home, but then they didn't. So it's a lot better now than it was back then. (Jackie, aged 19)

Summary

Thirty-five families had contact with schools in relation to the domestic violence and the majority of these found the school's response to be helpful. These mothers and children felt that the school offered emotional support and were not just concerned with the child's academic performance. One criticism that could be levelled at schools, however, is that there was at times a lack of action on the school's part, especially in relation to making referrals to other agencies.

CHAPTER NINE

Health Professionals'
Responses to Domestic Violence

Doctors

Twenty-nine women and children said they had contact with their doctor about the domestic violence. Fourteen people described their GP (General Practitioner) as supportive and fifteen felt that they were unsupportive.

Supportive response

When women and children referred to their GP's response as supportive, they described an understanding of the dynamics of domestic violence and being offered emotional or practical support. However, only five of the women were offered practical support from their doctors. This support took the form of writing a letter in support of a woman's request to be rehoused away from the violent man, and other women were given information about agencies which could help, particularly refuges. Women said repeatedly that they had not known where to get help, thus this information-sharing role of the GP was very important. Two women were happy that their doctor had referred them to a counsellor or therapist. In one case the woman had phoned the doctor because her daughter had tried to commit suicide. The doctor got them an appointment for family therapy the following day.

Women experiencing domestic violence frequently attended their doctor's surgery because of stress-related complaints. One woman described how she had gone to her GP with a number of different stress-related conditions and her doctor had advised her to call the police for her partner's violence. Two women related how they had been frightened that they had breast cancer but in both cases their problems were a manifestation of the stress caused by the domestic violence.

Three women described their GPs as being very concerned with their well-being and as offering emotional support but not any practical advice. For example, one GP knew from the beginning about the violence that the woman was experiencing. He often advised her to leave, but did not suggest how she could get help to do that. He would see the bruises on her but she would make excuses and say that she had fallen over. He said that if she would not leave he would give her something to help her while she stayed in the relationship and he prescribed Valium for her.

Similarly another doctor noticed a woman's bruises when she went for her six-week check-up after her son was born. The woman initially said she had fallen over but the doctor challenged this and she admitted that her partner was violent. In another case the doctor knew about the violence and kept telling the woman to leave, but as in the other example, he did not tell her where she could get help to do this. After one occasion when the man assaulted the woman, the doctor would then turn up at her home unexpectedly to check that she was all right. When the woman did separate from her partner her GP gave her sleeping tablets and when her 8-year-old son became suicidal he prescribed medication to help him sleep also.

The above examples highlight that doctors may not know what to do when there is domestic violence. Their responses indicated a high level of concern but the advice they gave was not always appropriate in the circumstances. While it is important that professionals clearly give the message that domestic violence is not acceptable, it is not very helpful repeatedly to tell women to leave without giving them practical information about agencies such as the Women's Aid Federation that will facilitate their leaving.

Two young people said that their doctors helped them to cope with the domestic violence because they talked to them about how they were feeling and they listened to them. In one case the doctor realised that the teenage girl's physical symptoms were a manifestation of the distress caused by the domestic violence. He referred her to a psychologist but she felt that she had received more support from her doctor than the psychologist. Fiona felt that, unlike the psychologist, the doctor was taking a 'real interest' in her.

> He asked if there was anything that I was really scared of or that was worrying me and I said that I don't like my dad very much, because, like, he shouts a lot and he's an alcoholic and he gets upset with Mum, like, hits her and things. And then he referred me. (Fiona, aged 15)

Unsupportive responses

An unsupportive response from doctors was one where the GP did not want to know about the domestic violence or made it clear it was not an issue that the doctor felt that he or she needed to address, that is, seeing domestic violence as falling outside the role of a GP.

Judith went to her doctor when her son was a few months old. She did not want her son growing up witnessing his father's violence and she asked her GP for help. She did not know where else to go. The GP responded by saying that he did not want to hear what she had to say about her partner's violence. After this experience she felt that there was nobody to listen or to help. Years later the doctor referred her son to the family psychiatry centre because of his behavioural problems. Judith believes that if the doctor had given her help when she needed it her son would not later have had these problems.

A similar reaction was reported by another woman whose GP's response to hearing about her husband's violence was:

> He just said, 'What do you expect me to do about it?' (Tamsin)

As this woman describes, the impact of this kind of professional attitude greatly compounds the problem for women seeking help.

> I just back-pedalled and felt embarrassed really. Because you don't know what you expect them to do, because you don't know what you expect of anybody. You're just hoping that somehow you're going to solve this problem. (Tamsin)

Another woman talked about her disbelief at her GP's insensitive response. She had initially gone to her doctor to have her injuries recorded and at that point she did not want to discuss the violence. Later her ex-partner raped her and she went back to her doctor very distressed.

> I was just shaking, I couldn't speak, I was crying and that was the stage where I was at. And I told him I'd been raped and whatever and this and I was having difficulty and I couldn't go back to work. And he said, 'What did he do that for?' And I just remember thinking, I mean I just got more appalled by it afterwards that he [said], 'What did he do that for?' And I felt like saying, 'Well you tell me, you're a man. How am I supposed to know? Why are you asking me, why am I responsible for what he did?' (Sheila)

Trying to maintain some kind of normal routine to their lives can be very important for women experiencing domestic violence. This may be particularly true for women employed outside the home. For these women, managing to hold on to their jobs is very important, not just from a financial point of view but also because it may be an area separate from the violence in which a woman feels good about herself. One woman described how she had managed to hold on to her job at all costs despite all the violence she was experiencing. At one point she was very stressed and needed to take time off from work. She went to her doctor for a sickness certificate but she was not very understanding.

> No I never got a supportive response. It started when Seamus was born, I had postnatal depression for two years after having Seamus and unfortunately she was one of those doctors that said, 'Pull your socks up, come on, just get yourself together,' you know? 'You're just being silly, get on with it, you've got a baby you've got responsibilities,' you know? So and it started from there. But on the odd occasion that she would take leave, they used to bring younger GPs in and it was ... I think it was one of the younger GPs that said, 'These are the agencies that are available to you. Come on, you're a young woman, you can do this,' you know. (Kim)

One woman described how she had to go back to her doctor several times before he would help her. Her doctor had known about the domestic violence for some time. When she left her violent partner, her daughter's behaviour became uncontrollable. She asked her doctor for help but he told her, 'There's nothing really we can do.' She then went back to her GP asking him to refer her daughter to someone so she would get help. He did not.

> Then she got so naughty again, and I took her back, and in the end I says to him, 'Look, I want her referring to somebody.' And he didn't want to do it; he said, 'No, because sometimes when children have seen people, like psychologists, it can go the other way, they would have got over it by themselves, and it could make them worse.' (Trudy)

Finally the woman went back and told her doctor that unless she got some help she would be unable to have her daughter live with her any more. Her doctor referred her daughter to the child and adolescent unit.

Other women criticised their doctors for not wanting to know about the violence by, for example, accepting stories of injuries which were plainly untrue. Some doctors would record women's injuries on file but never actually talk to the women about the violence. One woman described how her weight dropped to six stone. Her doctor asked if she was all right and she said that she did not eat very much. That was the end of the matter.

Women talked about going to their doctors and saying that they were depressed and being prescribed antidepressants without any real discussion about the reasons for their depression. Fourteen women had been prescribed sleeping tablets, tranquillisers or antidepressants (or a combination). One woman had been convinced by her violent partner that she suffered from very bad premenstrual syndrome (PMS) and therefore the problem was hers and not related to his violence. She went to see her doctor and was clearly very stressed; while talking to him she was peeling the skin off her hands. She told the doctor that she had PMS. He acknowledged that she was in a 'state' but did not discuss with her what might be causing her stress and prescribed her tranquillisers and sleeping tablets. Thus, almost one-third of women interviewed spontaneously mentioned that they had been prescribed some form of medication for the emotional impact of the domestic violence.

Health visitors

Nineteen families had contact with health visitors while they were experiencing domestic violence. Of these, ten individuals were pleased with the support they received from the health visitor and nine said that the health visitor was unsupportive.

Supportive response

Women often mentioned that they spoke to their health visitor because they did not know whom else to talk to. For example one woman who confided in her health visitor said that she had spoken to her in preference to her doctor:

> Because I don't want pills, I don't need pills. I want some help and I don't know who to go to. (Stephanie)

When Stephanie spoke to the health visitor about her son's behavioural problems, the health visitor spoke to the boy's school and they made a referral to family and child therapy. Stephanie's teenage daughter spoke in her interview about the fact that following the little boy's disclosure of sexual abuse by the violent man, the health visitor was the only professional who visited the family.

In some cases women also said that the health visitors knew about the domestic violence but for some time the women were unable to talk about it.

> He'd gone to work. I couldn't let her [health visitor] in because he'd locked me in. So I had to ring him to come out ... I said to her that he had taken my keys by mistake. I daren't tell her that he was locking me in. She knew there was something; she said she was concerned 'because your weight's just going down rapidly, you're looking very tired.' I think she thought I had postnatal depression. I got where I didn't want to touch [my

baby]. I thought maybe he's a bit jealous of the baby, not giving him enough attention and stuff, I ended up with postnatal depression through it. [The health visitor] came round, and the doctor, and while my husband was there he said I must rest. Within an hour of them going he dragged me out of bed, started hitting me, saying, 'Get this housework done,' but I had nowhere to go, I felt trapped really. (Denise)

In this case the health visitor kept coming back and would talk around the issue of domestic violence. Then one day the health visitor directly asked Denise if her partner was violent. Denise said no and would not let the health visitor back into the home. Denise described how not knowing how the health visitor could help inhibited her from saying anything, highlighting how women need to know what help is available before they can ask for that help.

Another woman described how her health visitor would always ask her how her partner was but the woman pretended everything was fine. Later the woman went to speak to the health visitor and found her very supportive, particularly about getting information about support agencies.

Giving women practical advice about sources of support for themselves or their children was the main thing that women rated as positive in relation to their health visitors. Another important point about health visitors is that by coming into the home they see things that other people are unaware of. For example, one woman said her health visitor knew about the domestic violence and

was pleading for me to leave for ages. (June)

She described how the health visitor would come to the home and see the violent man

in the raw. (June)

The health visitor wrote the woman a letter of support for her request to be rehoused away from the violent man. Following the move, the woman had a new health visitor whom she described as

brilliant. (June)

and who put her in touch with a local support group.

Generally then, as well as providing emotional support, health visitors were valued for providing women with information about how to access help from a variety of professionals and voluntary groups. Unusually, one woman who described her health visitor as supportive said that she advised her not to contact social services. The woman felt that the health visitor thought she could cope better than she could.

Unsupportive response

Of the nine women who were unhappy with their health visitors, the most common criticism was that the health visitor visited only very briefly after the baby was born so they did not feel able to say anything about the violence. Other criticisms focused on the health visitor not being aware of the dynamics of domestic violence. For example, in one family the health visitor knew about the man's violence but would try to counsel both the man and his partner together. As the woman said, the emphasis was on the two of them working it out together, not on helping the woman who was experiencing the violence. Another mother, whose baby had feeding problems, said that she felt the health visitor was judging her as a bad mother and she was frightened that her children would be removed.

> All they can see is I'm this mother who can't feed her children. They're going to think I'm a terrible mother. (Danielle)

She talked about how the health visitor never asked her how she was or asked about the relationship, so she did not feel she could confide in her. As Danielle's story illustrates, women may have similar fears concerning health visitors as they do of social workers, namely that they will remove the children. For a number of women this meant that they were too frightened to reveal the domestic violence, even when the health visitors asked about it directly.

Accident and Emergency departments

Ten women attended Accident and Emergency (A&E) departments because of the injuries caused by their violent partners. Six of these women did not see the response of A&E staff as helpful.

Supportive responses

Four women were happy with the response they had received from A&E staff, and that was because they took the domestic violence seriously and tried to help the woman. When one woman explained to A&E staff how she had received her injuries, they called the police and would not allow her husband in to see her. Another woman had initially been taken to hospital because she had tried to commit suicide. When she was asked why, she said she had financial problems and the staff believed her. Later her partner broke her nose and took her to hospital the following day. Staff knew from her injuries that she had been assaulted and pleaded with her to tell them. The woman felt that there was no point:

> If the police can't help, what can you lot do? (Denise)

She did feel, however, that they were very sympathetic.

Bernice described how she had first been to the hospital when she was pregnant and later when the baby was born. One of the nurses approached her and directly asked whether she was experiencing domestic violence.

> When I went in twice with the baby, the second time she actually sat down and said, 'I've got a fair idea of what's happening but it's up to you to tell me.' And I did actually tell her and she said, 'We can get you help but I have got to have your permission,' but I wouldn't give her permission. Because if I got outside help while I were still in that relationship, it were more grief for me, a lot more trouble for me at home. (Bernice)

When she came back to the hospital again with injuries caused by her partner, she was too ashamed to tell the medical staff how it happened. It was not until she had already involved the police and was back in A&E for a final time that she admitted that her partner caused the injuries.

Unsupportive response

The six women who reported A&E staff as unsupportive did so because they felt that they did not want to know about the domestic violence and thus did not make the woman feel as though she could tell them the real reason for her injuries. Others felt that when they had told, the medical staff just ignored what they had told them.

Camilla described how she had suffered a very serious injury when her partner had punched her in the face and knocked her down the stairs so that she banged her head on a concrete post. At the hospital she and her ex-partner told conflicting stories about her 'fall'. None of the staff tried to find out the truth even though the woman had a handprint on her face.

Camilla's contact with A&E staff illustrates the importance of giving women the opportunity of being seen without their partners present.

> They asked me who had did it and I said it was my husband and he came in with me and they sat there and said, 'You do realise what you have done to your wife.' And he said, 'Yes, and I am very sorry,' and in front of him they asked me if I wanted to take action. If they had asked me without him being there, I would have said yes but when they asked me if I wanted to

take action, they [violent men] sort of look at you and I said, 'No, no.' I daren't. I think that was the worst bit, they could have taken me to one side and said, 'You don't have to go back to him, do you want to take action?' I'd have done it definitely. (Camilla)

This man subsequently hit one of the children with an iron bar and they took the child to A&E. Camilla told them what had happened. They spoke to the man but did not make a referral to social services. Later Camilla was taken to hospital again after an assault and this time she told them that she did want to take action. She described what made the difference for her on the last occasion:

I couldn't see because both my eyes were that puffed up I couldn't even tell if he was there or not. And when they asked me who did it, because I couldn't see whether he was there or not, I didn't care anyway, so I told them! But if I had been able to open my eyes and look at him and he had seen me, I couldn't have told them anything. I think it was just because I couldn't see him if he was there and I said, 'Yes it was him,' and they asked me if I wanted to take action and I said, 'Yes.' (Camilla)

Camilla pointed out that none of the hospital staff offered her advice regarding support agencies except for one nurse who suggested they go to marriage guidance.

Women described how they lied about their injuries because they were never given an opportunity to explain what really happened or they felt staff would not understand.

You just make up some sort of story; it comes off the top of your head as you come in the door. Not once did I get offered any help ... You never felt as though you could, it was just a case of them doing their jobs, stitch your head and then go home. (Deirdre)

Sometimes even when women asked for help, they did not receive any. For example, one woman said that she had been to A&E several times for injuries caused by her partner. Once she had to be given a tetanus injection because he had badly bitten her. She was never asked how she got the injuries. She asked for help but was told that the hospital could only look after her wounds. Not surprisingly, she feels that A&E staff do not bother about domestic violence.

They would say, 'Do you want us to report this to the police or is it a domestic?' And once you say it's a domestic they just don't bother. (June)

It is not just A&E staff who need to be aware of domestic violence. Women and children may have contact with a number of medical personnel who need to recognise that domestic violence may underlie the presenting problems. Danielle described how her baby stopped feeding due to the tensions caused by the domestic violence. Nobody asked the mother how she was or what she thought might be contributing to the baby's feeding difficulties. Instead she felt that she was being judged as an inadequate mother. The baby was eventualiy hospitalised and while there a nurse said to the woman:

> You know it's OK to actually admit you don't like your children. (Danielle)

On a more positive note, one woman with a disability told her consultant about the domestic violence and found him very supportive, particularly with regard to a dispute over the children's residency.

Mental health professionals

Ten families had contact with mental health professionals: five with psychologists, four with psychiatric services and one with child guidance.

Psychologists

Three families who were seeing psychologists saw them as being supportive. One child was seeing an educational psychologist because of his behavioural problems at school. Another family was having family therapy and in the third family the children's father requested that the children see a psychologist because of a dispute over contact. In this case the psychologist agreed with the mother's concerns about the father's contact.

The two families who were unhappy with the response they received from the psychologists highlighted their lack of awareness and understanding. One mother said that the psychologist did not understand the implications of the domestic violence and she also gave the impression that she thought the woman's daughter had fabricated the allegation of child sexual abuse against her father. Not surprisingly in this situation, the daughter herself reported that the psychologist was not at all supportive.

> I found it hard to talk to her, like sometimes I did feel she was like [thinking], 'What on earth are you going on about?' After a while my mum sort of threw my dad out and I was, like, it was just after that had happened and, like, I was really scared that he was going to come back and whatever. And she [the psychologist] said, 'I think you should stop like being so silly and irrational' kind of thing ... [I felt] a bit betrayed really because like you

sort of like expect to be able to trust her and everything. And like you'd expect like that she'd believe in you kind of thing. But like, you just feel like she's against you instead, it just causes more problems. (Fiona, aged 15)

The other family unhappy with the psychologist's response was one of the families who had witnessed the woman being stabbed to death by her ex-partner. The mother felt that the psychologist concentrated on the woman's daughter whereas it was her son who had witnessed the killing. Then the psychologist kept cancelling appointments so they did not go back. The woman referred to the psychologist as a

waste of time. (Marcella)

Her son also felt that the psychologist was interested only in his sister, and he talked at length about how he felt that the psychologist should have been aware that due to the trauma, he was unable to understand what she was saying to him. He needed her to use simpler language.

Like talked more as if I were a lot younger than what I am. Say like be able to explain it easier, because of like build-up of stress it does, you don't take it in properly, you know. And it would have been easier to talk more, not as hard to understand and stuff like that. Easy like talking to younger people and stuff like that, you know you talk not as complicated. (Stuart, aged 14)

Child guidance

At the time of the interviews one child was attending child guidance and the mother and child were happy with the service particularly as the child's behaviour continued to improve.

Adult psychiatric services

Only one woman who had contact with psychiatric services felt that they were supportive. This woman had spent years trying to get her children back from her ex-partner and in the process had 'a nervous breakdown'. She attended group therapy at a psychiatric unit and found it very helpful. In addition to the therapeutic input the staff would role-play court hearings with her so that she was better prepared for the difficulties which arose in the course of contact hearings. Later in the proceedings concerning the children, the report of the guardian *ad litem* referred to the woman as being mentally unstable. The woman contacted the psychiatrist who had treated her and he was very supportive.

> The psychiatrist, when he wrote the letter for the court hearing for the children, said that the only reason I was there [the psychiatric unit] was because of the children, because of what had happened to the children and there was no danger if the children were returned to me. His letter to the court said he'd never met a more competent woman. (Cheryl)

The three women who were unhappy with the psychiatrist's response generally described a lack of commitment on the psychiatrist's part to building a therapeutic relationship so that the issue of domestic violence could be addressed. There was also a criticism of psychiatrists who addressed the presenting problem only, for example, suicidal ideation, and prescribed antidepressants and in-patient treatment without addressing the underlying problem of the domestic violence which was causing these symptoms. Camilla described how, after she had separated from her violent ex-partner, he had pleaded with her for a reconciliation. She said that she would consider returning only if he got help. The GP referred him to a psychiatrist. Camilla described the consultation:

> And he only went once. But I think the psychiatrist was totally crackers anyway. He sat there and he smoked one cigar after another, and had this chair on wheels, and he sort of went from one room to the other and back again, and round and round and you couldn't concentrate. And he just kept saying, 'Well why do you think you do this?' 'I don't know.' 'OK, do you want to do this?' 'Don't care.' 'OK.' You know it didn't do any good whatsoever, and then he suggested we tried marriage guidance. And that was it, off we went, we walked out of there, and my husband said, 'Well that was a load of crap, I ain't going back,' and that was it. So that was the only help that we actually got offered. (Camilla)

Summary

Women and children who experienced domestic violence frequently attended their doctor's surgery because of stress-related complaints. Families were almost equally divided between those who thought that their doctor was supportive and those who did not. Supportive doctors offered emotional and practical support such as telling women about refuges. They also challenged women's explanations for bruising when they were trying to cover up the man's violence. Unsupportive doctors made it clear that they did not want to know about the domestic violence. Of concern is the apparent readiness of doctors to prescribe some form of tranquillisers for women experiencing domestic violence without offering any advice about sources of help. Health visitors were generally seen as being supportive especially as they offered practical advice about what to do and where to go to get help for the domestic violence. At times, though, health visitors were perceived as a threat in that they might play a role in removing the children if they learned of the violence.

Most of the women who had contact with Accident and Emergency staff felt that they were not sympathetic and that they did not want to know about the domestic violence. Excluding child guidance, women and children mostly did not feel that mental health professionals acknowledged the domestic violence and its impact.

Overall then, of all the health professionals whom women and children had contact with, health visitors were seen to be the most supportive.

CHAPTER TEN

Refuges and Counselling Services

Refuges

Twenty-three families had stayed in a refuge at some point. By far the majority of women who stayed in refuges saw it as a very positive experience.

> I mean they're not ideal places, they're not. However, compared to where I'd just come from, it was a godsend you know it was ... I was quite happy there, the women in there were nice. And I mean like I said, I was there for a number of months and they, I mean I saw a lot of women coming and going, and it was a nice friendly place as well. Everybody mucked in, and the kids were happy, there was a playroom there and all. It wasn't ideal, but it was better like I said, than where we'd come from.(Kathryn)

Making the decision to go into a refuge is often viewed by women as a last resort.

> It was just a month of abuse, and then like he bust my nose again in September two years ago, I had two black eyes, both my ears were all black and blue, purple and everything. And that's when I came to the women's refuge because I couldn't take any more of it. (Janice)

Women frequently said that they had received more support from refuge workers than from any other source including family and other professionals. Women referred to the refuge workers as the only people they had to turn to and one woman emphasised that if she had not gone to a refuge she would have ended up going back to her violent partner.

Clearly, emotional support was very important for women living in refuges but women interviewed for the study also highlighted the importance of the practical advice they received from workers. When fleeing from the violence women were faced with having to take a number of practical steps very quickly and were confronted with a baffling array of forms to be filled in. Women appreciated being guided through the formalities of legal proceedings regarding their children or in pursuing a case against their ex-partner, or divorce proceedings, finding a school for the children, finding a family doctor, getting crisis loans, filling out benefit forms and applying for housing.

Sally said that she felt coming to a refuge opened up opportunities for women that they had previously been denied.

> A lot of women, they go through a lot of domestic violence at home but they still have ambitions you know! It's not that they don't want to go out there and do things but because they are suppressed by what's going on around them, it's so hard. So coming to a place like this [a refuge] I just felt all free and I could do what I wanted to do. (Sally)

She hoped to be able to go to college.

Camilla spoke at length about how conditions in refuges had improved greatly over the years. Her first time in a refuge was in the early 1980s. At that time, Camilla said that the refuge offered shelter but no real support and women were sent back home after a couple of months. She said that she was put off from going to a refuge again but in 1994 she returned to a refuge and found it very different.

> 1994 was the second time I went into a refuge and that was completely different. We had backup from social services; they had their own children's counsellor, which was a great help, because then everything didn't come back on me. Most of the time in the refuge I think most of the women felt guilty because of what the children are going through rather than being able to help themselves. So having a children's counsellor helped. (Camilla)

In addition to help from the workers, the support of other domestic violence survivors was seen to be crucial.

> I'd never been to refuge before, but I think if I'd have done that the first few years ago I wouldn't have been in this situation. I would have had my own place by now. Because I think being in here, I think everyone relates to everyone, and everyone talks [about] their own problems here. We sit here at the night-time and we all tell each other different things and it makes you stronger and [you] realise you can't go back to that again. It's only when you hear other people as well and knowing how much it does go on, and there is a life away from that sort of thing and you can cope on your own, that it makes me feel, well I've been here six weeks now but I definitely wouldn't go back again, never in a million years. I know I've got

to wait a long time to get a house, but I am prepared to wait for it. But I think this has done me a world of good coming here, because obviously it's really, really helped us, having the help. (Vivien)

As expected, women reported that refuge life was not entirely without problems and the main difficulty reported was the communal living. Women emphasised that they really appreciated the support in the refuge but living with so many other families in such close proximity and often for quite lengthy periods was not always easy. Another factor that women found hard was being cut off from family and friends.

Two women described their time in two non-Women's Aid Federation refuges and their experiences clearly indicate that although a safe place is crucial, it is not the only issue in helping women and children to escape violent men. Danielle said that the refuge she stayed in was run by a charity and that there was no counselling provided or in fact even any basic awareness of domestic violence. She described the workers as 'just wardens' and outlined their role:

> You always felt this feeling that you were being checked up on and under surveillance was what I felt. Oh I can remember this one really poor girl, she had five children and she was in there and they said they thought she ought to have one of her oldest ones taken away for a while and they actually arranged for this child to go in care. They seemed to have this authority to ring the social worker up and get the child taken into care. (Danielle)

When Danielle's ex-partner traced her to the refuge and came to the door, the workers said to her:

> 'He just wants to talk about your children.' (Danielle)

and encouraged her to see him even though she did not want to.

Bernice described a somewhat similar type of refuge, which had no workers other than a part-time warden who took rent and maintained the building.

> It were like you were on your own, like a roof over your head when I were there. I were grateful for that roof! But that's all it were. You can look back and think it were a horrible place to live but it were safe and then you can think of all these ways that it can be improved. I know a lot of refuges do have child workers though. And support from counsellors that are assigned to refuges but we just had a four-bedroom house with a part-time worker. So it was up to us to like help. (Bernice)

Sadly, three women said that the stigma attached to having to go to a refuge prevented them from seeking help sooner. Women referred to how they were surprised at both the level of service they received in the refuge and how far the reality of refuge life differed from the stereotype.

> The first time I went into the refuge was in the early 1980s, I think that's what actually changed my life. If I had known that they were there, if the services were there, I would have used them, but they weren't advertised, and I think it was the 'battered wives' home' image that put me off. (Camilla)

Children's experiences of refuges

Children generally described themselves and were described by their mothers as being very positive about staying in a refuge.

> It was awkward because you know, you had your own room [at home] and then you move [to the refuge] and you've got to sleep with your mum or maybe even another family, but I thought it was lovely. It was more of a family than it was at home. I really liked it. I used to love it when we used to go in there. (Mona, aged 17)

Over and over again, children emphasised the fact that it was only when they went to stay in a refuge that they had opportunities to discuss their experiences, either with other children or with refuge workers.

> We used to sit down in the kitchen round the table and used to draw, and write down what violence we had been through. (Darren, aged 11)

> I liked it because there was so many people there and everybody was like your relatives and I liked it. It was good because then you knew what they were going through and they knew what you were going through. And you could talk about it; there was some girls and another boy my age and we used to sit down and talk about it and they moved out and so did we … Yes, we do still see them. I cried when I left! I liked it so much I cried! Because when I was living with [the violent man] I used to bang on the walls and shout at him and tell him to stop it. Then I used to be scared to do it then and that was when my anger started coming out, and then I could talk about that with all the other kids, and they would say how they were angry and how they were feeling, I didn't feel out of place. Because when there is no one to talk it makes you feel like I'm the only one. But when I started talking to them I knew there was more, and I just wanted to help my mum more. (Marilyn, aged 15)

Mothers referred to the benefits of direct work with the children in refuges and some mothers reported that their children's behaviour had improved since they had been living in the refuge. Marilyn described how she felt her behaviour had improved.

> But when I moved up here and talking to refuge workers and all the other kids, got me over it quicker, than what it did in the first place. I started being naughty because I was always, I started swearing at him [the violent man] and everything. I got really bad, but it got sorted out when I went, I was in the refuge, because there was strict rules – shut me up! And that changed it all. That's how my behaviour changed, just started getting a big mouth, and that's all changed. (Marilyn, aged 15)

Vivien was very pleased with the programme of group work for children running in the refuge.

> Different things, like they are learning to work through their anger, which you wouldn't get unless you're in a refuge. I mean this is where they do it here. So although you're being helped on one side they [the children] are being helped here. It's brilliant, it's a six-week course and every week they work on something different. All to do with their feelings, how they feel. Because I think a lot of the times kids don't … no one asks them how they feel, how they feel about their parents being separated, how they feel about different things. And obviously you need counselling and also the kids need counselling as well because they're depressed and unhappy, and a lot of time I think the kids get pushed under the carpet. (Vivien)

Going to a refuge meant a big improvement in some children's lives in a variety of ways. One mother said that when they went to live in a refuge, her children had things they never had before, such as toys, because their father used to break their things. She described how individually they were much happier in the refuge and could enjoy things together as a family that they never could before.

Two children who had not lived in a refuge reported positive perceptions of refuges also. One young girl had, for safety reasons, to live separately from her mother, who was staying in a refuge. In relation to her mother being in a refuge she said:

> I felt she were in refuge because [my mother's partner] were hitting her and that she would be better off there than at home. (Kara, aged 10)

Jackie described how for years, her biggest wish had been that she and her siblings and her mother could escape to a refuge.

I just felt so angry that I couldn't help her. All I wanted to do was just get a suitcase, put her clothes in the suitcase, tell her to come with me, and all the kids and just go to a refuge or, like, some place for, like, women and children. But we just couldn't get away from him. Wherever we used to go, he used to find out where we were. (Jackie, aged 19)

Children's only criticism of refuge life was that there should be more facilities for children (not all had contact with a child worker) and as with their mothers, communal living was not always easy for them.

It were OK but sometimes, like, it got a little crowded, couldn't get any privacy. (George, aged 13)

Camilla made an important point regarding follow-up or outreach work once the women and children leave the refuge. She felt strongly that this is a badly needed service but recognised that refuges are not usually able to provide this service because of the lack of funds.

But it is the funding that is the problem. And nobody seems to take any notice. Which is a shame really because I think there should be, how can you put it, some kind of contact after. Because the problems don't go away overnight. I mean you move into your house at 3 o'clock in the afternoon, and 3 o'clock the next morning you're still awake, there's nobody – that's it, you are on your own. And that's the children included. So if they couldn't talk to me they would have nobody. Up until then the services for the children were quite good. (Camilla)

Counselling: support received by women

But I just needed somebody ... a shoulder to cry on really, somebody who I know wasn't just going to stab me in the back or you know, run a mile or whatever. I just needed somebody to be there for me, you know. (Marina)

Women had contact with a wide variety of counselling services, ranging from relationship counselling with their violent partners to group work specifically for survivors of domestic violence. They reported a range of responses from these services, as this section will outline.

Six of the women had gone with their violent partners for counselling during the relationship. All of the six were highly critical of this type of relationship counselling as they felt the dynamics of domestic violence were not recognised at all. Additionally one woman said:

But I don't think [the agency] is sensitive enough to issues around ethnicity and gender at all. And so, I mean what is the point in it really? 'Cause if I'm not going to feel comfortable and they're not going to think about it, then it's not helpful. (Sheila)

During the relationship women had also phoned helplines, usually very distressed and at times even suicidal. They reported a mixed response from these helplines. Even accessing this kind of help can be difficult for women experiencing violence.

I phoned the Samaritans on numerous occasions but I couldn't actually get to their office. They kept making me appointments but of course I couldn't get out of the house at that point without a good reason of where I was going. So it tended to be nights that I could ring them once he'd fallen into a drunken stupor. And at which point they would say there was nobody there. I'd have to come to them during the day, which was impossible for me at that time. (Cheryl)

Ten women had gone for individual counselling during or after the relationship and others had attended groups for women experiencing domestic violence. However, being able to utilise this kind of support is problematic while in the relationship because women's movements and contacts are generally so controlled by their violent partners. One woman described how she would lie and say she was going to an evening class so she could go to a domestic violence support group. Marina described how following an abortion (which she had been forced to have by her partner), a counsellor from the hospital came to see her but she was unable to say anything.

A counsellor from the hospital come out and talked to me and he [my partner] would sit on the stairs and make sure I didn't say anything ... so he would have been able to hear everything anyway. And I was supposed to be sitting there saying how I felt and everything and oh God, I couldn't talk. Just couldn't talk, you know I said that I was fine and I was getting over it and really I was really broken up inside, I was in pieces you know. And I had to ring ... he made me ring her up one day and said, 'Look you stop her from coming here or else.' So I had to ring her up and say, 'You know I don't need you to come any more, I'm doing all right.' But inside I was, 'What am I going to do? How the hell am I going to go on?' And I nearly committed suicide about four or five times since I've been with him. (Marina)

Two women did not find counselling as helpful as it should have been. One of these women had been hospitalised for depression and although the counsellor knew about the domestic violence, she did not help the woman in terms of practical advice on how to get out of the situation. The other woman saw two different counsellors, and a therapist. The first counsellor made her feel that she was blaming her violent partner and

It probably wasn't his fault. (Dawn)

Because of this reaction, she was then unable to tell the second counsellor about the domestic violence and he wanted her to return to her husband. When the woman later saw a therapist, the man's violence was raised but not discussed; therefore she did not find it useful, as the core problem was not addressed.

The other women were attending specialist domestic violence support projects and were very positive about the support they received from these agencies. Women were particularly enthusiastic about the support groups run by these projects.

I think somebody to talk to like the [project is] absolutely fantastic, I'd be lost without them, to be absolutely honest and I don't miss a week. It's just being able to go and talk and knowing that there's women there in the same boat and that know exactly where you're coming from. You know, it makes a whole heap of difference knowing you're not on your own. And things that you feel and you experience and emotions that you have and you think that you're the only person that has them. When you actually speak to other women and they, you know, they know what you're talking about. (Amanda)

I think the women's support group is one of the best things; at the time it was just like my life line really. They were there for me, they really give me the emotional support that I needed, I think … Well, I think if I didn't stumble on the women's support group, and I think a lot of women who go there would say the same, I don't even know if I would be here now. (Maisie)

Counselling: support received by children

Children in twelve of the families had received some counselling support from agencies because of the domestic violence. Two children had been in touch with a national helpline. One child tried for three days to get through to the helpline. However, his mother felt that when he did get through to a counsellor it was very useful for him.

I actually got through for him. But he was on there for about twenty, twenty-five minutes and when he put the phone down, you could see it in his face he actually felt better that he'd spoken to somebody really. (Kim)

In another family the violent man found the helpline number when going through the young girl's things and it made matters worse. Another young girl talked about how she had wanted to phone a helpline but the fear of the man seeing the number on an itemised phone bill prevented her phoning. Children need to be aware that helpline numbers will not show on phone bills.

In one family the woman had managed to find counsellors from a voluntary agency for three of the children, while the youngest went to child guidance. All the children were very positive about receiving counselling, as one of the children said:

It's that she [the counsellor] understands me and Tracy, 'cause she's been trained to ... to listen like as if she's been through it before and she's been told what it's about. (Aaron, aged 13)

Now Aaron feels that he understands things more thanks to counselling.

Two children interviewed, both boys, had attended groups run by two national children's charities for children who had experienced domestic violence. Both mothers and the two boys were very positive about these groups, as one woman said:

I think it does [help]: it's stirred things up inside him that I think he may be struggling to deal with. But then I am a firm believer that things like that can't be ... you shouldn't bury them. If they are there and you have a chance to deal with them at an early stage, then they are dealt with and you can put them behind you and move on away from them. (Lucy)

One of the boys stressed how, although he did not talk much in the group about his own experience, it was good to hear other children talk about similar things.

In relation to their experiences of counselling, children stressed the importance of trust, being believed and being given practical advice.

But with the NSPCC worker, she didn't focus on Dad that much at first, like she focused on that I couldn't sleep and things, and then, like, she'd like do me a tape with a relaxation, meditation thing on. And then, like, she'd like she'd go through the oils and found out which oils I liked to put on the fragrance burner when we had a session or whatever. So that she would put herself out for me kind of thing, which was like encouraging to know that she wanted to help. She wasn't just doing it because it was her job. (Fiona, aged 15)

One young boy said regarding his counsellor:

He's the only man I trust. (Terry, aged 8)

A girl who went to counselling for panic attacks and nightmares said:

That was good because she was like, she was really nice, sort of gave me advice really, I suppose. (Zara, aged 12)

Thus, children clearly appreciated having their experiences taken seriously and being able to define their needs and work through the issues from their perspective and at their own pace. If these conditions are not established then children are unlikely to engage in the process. This was clearly illustrated by one group of siblings who were attending family therapy with their mother. They described the process as boring and clearly felt that it was not something that was at all useful. From their individual interviews, it was apparent that the children felt that the therapist focused on their mother and her perspective and that their views were not sought or acknowledged.

Another young person said that he had been offered counselling before but at the time he was too much in crisis to be able to use it effectively. In fact because his mother insisted that he go initially, going to see the counsellor was experienced by him as added pressure when he was struggling to cope with his traumatic experiences. He had not been consulted about going to see a counsellor and acknowledged that he would have liked counselling a little later when he was not so much in crisis.

Not only is the timing of the counselling important but also how the service is perceived by children is crucial; that is, is the service seen as child-friendly and welcoming? Two of the mothers said that their children had been offered counselling but as it was housed within the psychiatric service the children would not go. They did not want to be labelled and were frightened of the stigma attached to psychiatric services.

Summary

Twenty-three families had stayed in a refuge at some point. Women said that they got more support from refuges than from anywhere else, including family and friends. The emotional support of refuge workers and other survivors of domestic violence was crucial, but equally valued was the help that women received in sorting out benefits, schooling, housing and legal matters. The main problem with refuge life was the difficulties associated with communal living.

Children were very positive about their experiences of refuges, especially in terms of having other children to talk to about domestic violence. As with their mothers they could find communal living difficult at times, and some children also felt that there should be more facilities for children living in refuges.

In terms of counselling women described a number of difficulties in accessing this kind of support while still in the relationship. Women did not find relationship counselling useful but were very enthusiastic about specialist domestic violence support projects. This was particularly so in relation to the groups for survivors of domestic violence run by these projects.

Children in twelve of the families had received some form of counselling. Children appreciated having their experiences taken seriously and being able to set the pace and content of the work. Building up trust in their counsellor was very important. Children emphasised the need to make services accessible, child centred and child friendly.

CHAPTER ELEVEN

Legal Remedies?

Currently, the legislation available to women and children to protect them from violence (in addition to that already referred to in the police response to domestic violence) is the Children Act 1989, the Housing Act 1996 and Part IV of the Family Law Act 1996. However, the interviews with women and children were carried out prior to the implementation of Part IV of the Family Law Act 1996 so their experiences refer to the previous rather than the current legislation.

Legal remedies were sought by forty-five of the mothers, making this the most commonly used method of seeking help.

Solicitors

Women consulted solicitors for a range of situations including divorce, contact arrangements, injunctions and in bringing criminal charges against their ex-partners. The major criticism of solicitors was that they did not appear to recognise domestic violence. Thus, for example, women were frequently told by their own solicitors that the man had a right to see the children so the woman should not oppose any application for contact.

> My solicitor, he, he nearly got me killed. I made an appointment. I said I want to divorce him. We filled out all the paperwork and this was before Christmas and he said, 'Right now, what do you want me to do?' And I said, 'Nothing until after Christmas. I will ring you and tell you when to send the papers.' And he said, 'Right, OK.' Three days later, because it was sheer fluke, I don't know, but [my partner] always picked up the post in the morning. And this particular morning he wasn't there. This big envelope came through addressed to him and I knew and I opened it and it was the divorce papers telling him that I was divorcing him for his behaviour and everything. So I hid those papers away. But had he have opened them; that particular week was a bad week, you know, and I was really cross about that. And the solicitor sort of going ahead anyway. But

he sort of said that, 'Women in your situation tend to put it off and put it off so I was giving you a helping hand'. (Margo)

My solicitor. Oh no. She said really ... Well, because basically he's seen him [son] every day of his life for nearly eight years, they're going to give him contact. And then they're going to give him staying contact. (Kim)

This solicitor also advised that Kim should give the man parental responsibility. In two cases women were referred to mediation by their solicitor. Mediation is generally strongly advised against in situations of domestic violence because of the obvious power imbalance between the violent man and the woman (Hester *et al.* 1999). There are clear safety concerns for the woman that are created by putting her in that position.

Marina described how she thought her solicitor was

very helpful, she was really good. (Marina)

But then she told the woman that her violent ex-partner had a right to see the children and to apply for parental responsibility. The woman said that her solicitor told her:

'At the end of the day they [the children] are going to want to know who their dad is, you know.' (Marina)

Women felt that their perception of the risk to their children from the violent man was completely overlooked by their solicitors and there was also no recognition of the danger to the woman in maintaining contact with the violent man. Instead, solicitors emphasised the man's rights, rather than the children's wishes, and voiced opinions regarding negative emotional outcomes for the children if contact with the violent man was not established and/or maintained.

One man told his ex-partner that if she agreed to him having contact with the children, he would not pursue residency. The woman was very scared of losing the children and agreed. She feels that her solicitor should have advised her against it and realised that she was not

in a fit state to make that decision. (Danielle)

Her solicitor told her that domestic violence would not be considered when making decisions about the children. Another woman said that when she described the violence she had experienced, her solicitor responded:

Well, that's not much is it? (Jacinta)

Thus, in disputes over the children, women were rightly critical of solicitors who advised the woman from the man's point of view, that is, advising that he has a right to see the children, rather than from the children's point of view, namely, what do the children want and how can that be facilitated?

On the other hand, women were very positive about solicitors who were clearly aware of the dynamics of the domestic violence and informed them of their options – including going to a refuge. Often the most supportive solicitors were those whom women were referred to by the police or other agencies who have experience of dealing with cases involving domestic violence. None of the solicitors appeared to consult the children involved, however.

Judges

None of the women interviewed discussed having contact with magistrates. However, it is likely that, in the examples given involving contact orders, women may in fact have been dealing with magistrates rather than judges.

Only three women were happy with the way judges had handled their cases. In one case the man had snatched the children and taken them to Spain. When the man returned to Britain, the judge said that he could not hand the children back to the woman until she had a permanent address (she was in a refuge). The judge had a letter written to the housing department on the woman's behalf. The woman felt that the case was not taken seriously until the judge got involved. In the other two cases, the women felt that in the dispute over contact and residency the judge considered the man's violence.

> He wanted custody of these and at this time the judge actually asked me, he said, if I've got Andy stood with me, he said, 'Which parent would he want to live with?', so I said, 'He'd want to live with his dad.' I answered everything as honestly as I could and he said, 'Well, all I can do is thank you for being candid, but I am giving you the children.' (Jacinta)

Women who criticised the judges did so because they felt that they had no awareness of domestic violence or how the woman was feeling.

One judge refused to grant the woman an ouster order against her violent partner because she would not show him her bruises in the courtroom. Another judge announced in court in front of the violent man that the woman was staying in the local refuge. Consequently the man was able to find her.

As the following quotes illustrate, women felt that they were seen as the guilty parties, not the violent men.

> I went to court in 1994, and what really got me is that this judge said to me, in court, he said to me, 'Why don't you just say no? No, you're not coming in, no. Why don't you just say that?' And he really gutted me. I was in pieces by the time he had finished with me. (June)

> He made this thing about if I had let him see his daughter he wouldn't have got so violent, but I stopped him. So the judge turned round and found him not guilty. Although there was a girl he had pushed out of the way to get at me, and she had gone to court as well. They found him not guilty and the judge said to me, 'I hope, Mrs [X], that you get things sorted out and you realise that he is the father at the end of the day.' I couldn't believe it. I came out of there and I broke my heart, and I thought that's it now, I've finished. I'd never go to the police again. (Marianne)

Clearly, some judges not only displayed a frightening ignorance of the dynamics of domestic violence but also treated the women as if they were to blame because of their irrational behaviour.

Injunctions

Consistent with the findings of Barron (1990) that injunctions did not effectively protect women, overall, women in this study did not have many positive things to say about injunctions. Specifically their criticism was of two types: the difficulties in actually getting an injunction and injunctions not working. Women were frustrated at how difficult it was to get an injunction. As one woman said:

> He [the solicitor] said I'm not to do anything, wait for him to do something; you know we were waiting for him to literally come here and attack me before we could take out an injunction or anything like that. (Bea)

Getting an injunction with power of arrest attached was described as being even harder.

> And the law seems to not understand, police don't seem to understand the difficulties the solicitors have, or the legal system has, in actually providing power of arrest, because they keep saying, 'Oh yes, you can get it with power of arrest, it shouldn't be that difficult'. And every time I tried to get it with power of arrest, I've been told by the judge, 'No,' and I said to him,

'So I have to be beaten up, do I? I have to be very physically harmed?'
(Larissa)

Over and over again women described injunctions as not working.

> I got an undersigning [undertaking] which is, he actually signed it to say
> he would keep away from me and he would be in contempt of court if he
> broke it. And he stepped outside of judge's chamber and broke it straight
> away but because I were too scared to go back, I could have gone straight
> back in and said, 'Look he's broke it, now I need something more than
> this'. When I got my second injunction, which lasted for six months, I had
> actually moved away by then. Because we had been apart for seven and a
> half months, so I couldn't get that power of arrest. They don't tell you
> what injunctions mean, which to me is wrong. You read it and you think
> OK, so if he breaks it he can get arrested and they don't tell you that it,
> you've got to take them back to court. If the police have actually seen it,
> then police can prosecute because they've actually witnessed it. We
> actually got him into court, he broke his injunction and so I took him to
> court. He attacked me outside the solicitor's office, dragged me off the
> street and round back of offices and attacked me there. Told me that I
> wouldn't walk out of court alive. I didn't manage to get into court; they set
> a date for hearing and between then and court date I actually left. I felt too
> threatened to go through with it. (Bernice)

> But he used to break the injunction, all they used to do was come and
> arrest him for breach of the peace. Apparently that's all they can arrest him
> for, breach of the peace. (Camilla)

> But it didn't stop him sitting outside, or following or phoning me. I had to
> get the phone changed. I couldn't do anything about him following us,
> because the injunction said it was to keep him out of our address, but he
> wasn't entering the house if he sat outside and watched the house.
> (Stephanie)

As one woman pointed out, violent men know how to 'work the system'.

> Because they are not stupid, they aren't going to do it while they've got a
> power of arrest on it. Most of these guys are clued up to the system and
> how it works. They can tell you about injunctions and everything about
> them. They can tell you that if they avoid being served it's no good. So
> they avoid being served because they know it's a well-known thing. It's
> not like they are stupid and they don't know what's going on. So if it's got
> a power of arrest they will wait till it hasn't. It only lasts for a certain

amount of time and when he hasn't done anything within that time of four weeks that they give the power of arrest they remove that. Then it starts again, because there's no power of arrest. All the police can say is, 'Go on your way and leave her alone.' Two seconds later he's back again – what good is that? That's not helping, no. (June)

Generally women felt that the odds were against them and their children when trying to seek legal redress against their violent ex-partners. Women spoke of being assaulted by their partners in court while waiting for their cases to be heard; of being threatened that he would harm the children unless she dropped the charges against him and of cases – their own and their children's – being thrown out by Crown Prosecution Service because of 'lack of evidence'. Women talked about how difficult it was for them not to see justice done but that it was even harder for their children.

If you do something bad and the police arrest you, then they can put you in prison. That's how a child sees it. But with him, he's done all these horrible things, he's not in prison, he's not locked away, he's [my son] still seeing him. To him [the perpetrator] is still free and he's his nightmare and nobody can do anything about him. (Stephanie)

Women referred to how much courage it took for them to press charges against their ex-partners. While waiting for a court date, they were left feeling vulnerable and unsupported, often while being threatened by their ex-partners.

Because he kept threatening me and because he held me hostage, for four days, and threatened to do various things to the children, I let the charges drop. Because I thought no, if he's going to do that to the kids I'll let the charges drop. It was the easiest way out. In a way I wish I had kept on going, but then if anything had happened to the children, I would have wished I hadn't, so I think that was when I had to leave [the area] indefinitely. (Camilla)

When they do drop charges because of the intimidation and their fear, women felt that they were then blamed.

One woman discussed how she thinks the court treats women and men differently. She and her children were witnesses to her friend being killed by her violent ex-partner who broke into the refuge where they were living. The man pleaded guilty due to diminished responsibility and the woman feels 'he got off lightly'.

He got off very lightly, you know; it's easy, let's plead insanity, you know. And it was obvious, I don't know how they did it, I don't honestly, it was obvious it was premeditated. He'd been sat outside of the house in a van for hours beforehand. He'd seen us go in and out but he waited 'til it were dark and he'd brought the knife with him. If it had been a woman that had done it to a man then you know, and then I look and I think of all the women on death row and all you know, and I think it's so, so unjust you know. But sadly that's the way. (Kathryn)

Court welfare officers

Of the fifteen families who had contact with court welfare officers (CWOs), eight of the mothers were unhappy that in writing their report they did not take the domestic violence into account. The view seemed to be that the domestic violence did not pose a risk to the children.

Because he wasn't at that point being violent to Ryan, that because he'd been violent to me, then that was not the issue. The point was that he wanted contact with Ryan and he was entitled to contact with Ryan. (Zoe)

Alternatively, some court welfare officers seemed to believe that the fathers' rights to see the children overrode the need to consider his violent behaviour.

But the welfare officer who was involved, she said that she'd say that regardless of what he's done, he would still have rights to see them, because at the end of the day he's their father. I'm thinking, how the hell can you say that after everything. (Marina)

In another case the court welfare officer expressed an opinion indicating that the mother's experience of violence could mean she could be viewed as a less capable parent.

This court welfare officer come to see if I could cope, mentally, because they said, 'Well you've been through so much, you could take it out on your children,' which really upset me more. (Denise)

This court welfare officer also told the violent man where his ex-partner was living.

Court welfare officers did not always talk to the children to ascertain their views, even where the children were of sufficient age and understanding to do this. Where they did speak to the children, children reported that they felt all right about that, although one girl said that she had been worried that the court welfare officer would directly ask her where she wanted to live and she did not want to be the one to make the decision.

Summary

Women more commonly sought legal remedies than any other form of help, but were often not pleased with either the process or the outcome. The major criticism of solicitors was that they did not recognise the domestic violence. With regard to settlements regarding the children it was often reported that they advised women from the viewpoint of the man's 'rights' rather than the children's wishes or best interests. Supportive solicitors advised women of all options available to them, including going to a refuge, and were usually those recommended by the police or other agencies experienced in dealing with domestic violence. None of the solicitors consulted with the children involved in this study.

Only three judges were viewed as helpful because they recognised the domestic violence and its impact. Unsupportive judges were perceived as demonstrating a complete lack of awareness of domestic violence as well as treating women insensitively, for example, asking to see a woman's bruising in court.

Overall, women were not positive about injunctions for two main reasons: the difficulties in getting an injunction, especially with powers of arrest attached and injunctions simply not working to protect them or their children.

Fifteen families had contact with court welfare officers and eight mothers were unhappy that they did not acknowledge the impact of the domestic violence on the children.

In general, legal remedies did not always offer the solutions women hoped for when they first set the process in motion. Women's experiences in this study lend credence to the statement by Hester et al. (1999):

> For abused women themselves, finding their way through the legal system is a complicated and difficult process, crucially dependent on their access to information, and to effective advocacy and representation. This is still too often simply a lottery, depending on where they live and their own financial and personal resources. (Hester et al. 1999, p.67)

PART FIVE

Overcoming
the Obstacles

CHAPTER TWELVE

Barriers to Seeking or Utilising Help

Barriers to women seeking help

Women described numerous things which had, over the years, inhibited them from seeking or being given help. Usually women encountered a number of obstacles rather than having to overcome a single difficulty. Help-seeking is clearly a process and the first step in this process is being able to name the violence and believe that the violent person is solely responsible. Women who have for years been told both by their violent partners and by societal messages that they are to blame for provoking the violence often struggle to overcome years of psychological and emotional abuse that has eroded their self-esteem. The effect of this is that women often come to believe that they deserve the violence.

Attitudinal barriers

Women may subscribe to widely held myths surrounding domestic violence, such as that only very poor women experience domestic violence or that it involves frequent and extreme levels of violence such as broken bones. They may not identify with the picture of the 'battered wife' and so feel that they are not deserving of help. For many, the characteristics of an abused woman are rigidly and stereotypically defined and if they do not meet those limited criteria they believe they will not be given help. For example, while Deirdre was living with Kevin she had considered approaching social services for help. In fact, she had gone so far as to go into their office. However, in the office she saw posters regarding domestic violence which she felt gave the impression that those who experience domestic violence

> live on council estates, all the pictures, as if you live on the fourteenth floor of a tower block. (Deirdre)

Deirdre decided not to say anything and walked out.

Two women referred to people's racism as individuals and in institutions and did not want to fulfil stereotypical expectations. In addition they were frightened about what would happen to their partners if they reported them:

> And because we know the history of the black men in prison. Some of us are wary of the system in that way and refuse to report our partners because we know they'll get sectioned or something. (Davina)

Another woman said:

> There are a lot of issues around black women and black men in these kind of relationships because of the racism that exists in society and how that's then used. And how situations can be manipulated, and sometimes as black women how we tolerate more and for longer, because of the racism out there and how it might be perceived. (Sheila)

Frequently women talked about not wanting to be stigmatised and how this stopped them looking for help:

> Anybody you come across and you say domestic violence, there is so much stigma to it. You are made to feel that you've done something wrong, it's like having a disease. So that alone, just sitting there, you feel empty in your stomach, you just feel gutted that you've got to sit there putting up with the questions and it's like [they're thinking] 'You're lying or trying to trap me'. 'Why didn't you do this then?' or 'Why didn't you do that then?' And you're like, 'But it's not like that.' It's really hard to explain why you didn't get out of it. (June)

In addition, women said they felt that people did not want to know, as the following quote illustrates:

> No one really takes any notice. I mean once he beat me up outside in the middle of the road. I mean I was on the floor and he was kicking me and people were stepping over me and walking past. No one stopped. I mean no one knew he was my husband. No one stopped and did anything. (Margo)

Such an experience can serve to reinforce the idea that domestic violence is tolerated and therefore there is no point in looking for outside intervention. Another woman described how her partner always hit her where the bruising would not show and she believed that if she wanted to seek help, she had no evidence to back up her claim. Women also said that they thought that no one would believe them, particularly in relation to psychological abuse. They described their isolation and their feeling that there was nobody they could turn to.

Only one woman said that she did not seek help because she hoped the man would change:

> We have a child and you think it's all gonna change, but you're caught in his web. It's easier to stay than sort of make a move somewhere else; it is hard. A lot of the time you stay in the situation thinking it will get better, because it's easier than making a fresh start somewhere else. (Vivien)

Other women said that they felt it was their responsibility to keep the family together and most importantly that they could not deprive the children of their father. There were a number of beliefs that women held which made it difficult for them to seek help regarding domestic violence. These beliefs encompassed not just attitudes about domestic violence but also views on children's needs as well as the nature of heterosexual relationships. In addition, some women feared that they or their children would suffer because of the stigma associated with domestic violence. Black and other ethnic minority women had to consider whether they would be exposing themselves, their children and their ex-partner to racism if they sought professional intervention. All of these factors were not merely idiosyncratic belief systems, but rather they reflected more widespread societal attitudes that affect not only when, where and how women do seek help but also the type of response they receive from others. For example, Imam (1994) pointed out that for many Asian women and children, 'the debilitating effects of racism may yet compel them to return to the abuse from which they had striven so hard to escape.' (p.189)

Practical obstacles

Many obstacles that women outlined were practical ones, which had to be overcome. As a first step, women and children need information on where to get help. Not knowing how to get help was a frequent barrier mentioned by women in the study. A number of women said that they did not know about the existence of refuges. For example, after years of Marguerite's approaching agencies for help, it was only when her social worker witnessed the domestic violence that she told her about refuges.

> She said, 'Right, for your own safety, I'll put you in a women's refuge,' and I thought, what's one of them? So she explained to me then, and I [said] straight away, 'Will I be safe?' and she said, 'Yeah, they will look after you,' and that's the first time I knew about anywhere that women could go. (Marguerite)

Once women know where to get help, they still physically have to make contact with that agency and for many women that was almost an impossible task. Women described two main types of constraints on their ability to seek help at this stage. First, they were unable to get away from their violent partners long enough to tell professionals what was happening. For example, Camilla did go to outside agencies for help once but when she did not get the support she needed, it meant that it was harder to be able to approach agencies the second time round, not least because of the difficulties in getting away from her partner to make the contact. Another woman wanted to tell the school what was happening but could not because her partner always went with her; she had to plan for an opportunity to see someone on her own.

> So it was something that I had to plan even when I knew that I needed to speak to him [headteacher]. It took a lot of planning to be able to speak to him, whereas otherwise I could have, you know, just had a quiet word. (Judith)

The second problem that women faced in contacting agencies was being physically able to get to the agencies they needed to go to, such as solicitors, the benefits agency or a support group, often without any money. This was particularly the case in rural areas, where women had to travel many miles to reach different offices. As well as being physically able to get help, women had to be emotionally strong enough, as one woman said, 'to convince' various professionals what was happening. Women spoke about not having the money to obtain an injunction that could cost several thousand pounds.

> I was convinced it was going to cost me a lot of money to do it, that I didn't have. All I could see was, I'll have nowhere to live, I'll have nowhere to go, I won't be able to keep my job. It's a vicious circle. I don't ... didn't as it's turned out, I haven't actually got legal aid for the injunction. I've got to pay that myself and it's about three grand. I've got to find that money. But I don't regret having taken that action. I wish, yes I wish it didn't cost me three grand but I don't regret having taken it because Francis is so much better off without [his father]. I'm so much better off without him, that I think that's money well spent. (Judith)

In addition mothers were scared that they would not be able to provide financially for their children on their own.

Having got to the point of feeling able to contact agencies for help, women at times found that it was not as straightforward as they had thought. Seven women said that they had asked for help and been rebuffed, as in Danielle's case:

> I remember calling the police once then and he was actually put in prison overnight because he'd threatened through someone else to shoot me. And I spoke to a policewoman then and she said, 'Well, you've got no marks on you.' That's after he'd kicked me and really there wasn't very much I could do about it. Just hope that he would leave me alone. (Danielle)

Women spoke about being turned away when they asked for help, being sent from agency to agency, being judged and feeling that professionals were not interested in helping. One woman described it as a constant battle to get help for her children:

> But it's like it's a constant struggle, it's an absolute battle all the way. It's like everybody you speak to and it's, 'Well, what do you want us to do?' 'Well, I don't know, you're supposed to be the professionals. I don't [know] ... I just know I need some help.' (Zoe)

Thus, women's fears about how agencies may react to their request for help may unfortunately be confirmed. Other difficulties that women described included not being able to get through to helplines and long waiting lists in order for their children to have counselling.

Fear of losing the children

Having children may effectively trap women in violent relationships, making it much harder emotionally and financially to leave their partners.

> Having the children probably made me stay longer, but it's like every time we split up I was pregnant, so I always went back. There was always a reason to stay and the kids were a reason to stay. I think having them made us stay together longer. (Jacinta)

Once they have children, one of the most important reasons, if not the most important reason, why women felt unable to seek help when they were experiencing domestic violence was the fear that professionals would remove their children:

> And I thought you don't go to social services and tell them your problems, not when they're the people who will take the children away and they're showing no sign of being supportive. (Marcia)

This fear of having the children removed meant that women felt that they could not be honest about the violence. They felt that they were the ones who would be blamed for the violence and would be punished by losing their children. For example, Marianne's first contact with social services came about when her neighbour contacted them. However, Marianne was so frightened of the children being removed that she felt she had to deny her partner's violence.

> Somebody reported Gerry [my partner] for hanging Sian [my daughter] out of the window, and the social services come and I was covered in bruises and I said, 'No, he hadn't done it'. I lied and that was it. (Marianne)

Jem said that if she had thought that there might be a chance that the children would be taken from her, she would never have approached social services and the consequences would have been disastrous:

> If I'd known that there was a risk of my children going on the child protection register, I mean it hasn't happened, but if there was that risk I don't think I would have gone. That would have been something that was just too negative for me at the time when I wouldn't have even gone to social services. I would have just carried on or just flipped in the end and killed him or whatever. (Jem)

It is vitally important that this fear is not underestimated if women and children are to be provided with help.

Fear of the violent man

Fear of their violent partner and what he might do to themselves or the children if he found out that the woman had looked for help also inhibited women telling anyone about the domestic violence. Women were very aware of what their partners were capable of doing and needed to be sure that seeking help would vastly improve the situation, not make it worse. One woman explained why she could not have taken an injunction against her ex-partner:

> Couldn't do that with John, you wouldn't be able to do that. He would just come in the night and slit my throat. He's too violent. (Jasmine)

Women often felt that they had to protect family and friends from the man's violence. For example, one woman told her neighbour not to call the police in case the man was then violent to him. Women tried to deal with it by themselves in case they exposed their family to risk:

To get away from him, I used to go to my mum's, but it's taking trouble to my mum's house then because he'd come there and start, want to fight my brothers you know. Always going to kill my mum and my family. That used to make me stay with him a lot because I was scared that maybe he would you know [harm others], so I used to try and stay, even when I knew I couldn't take it any more. (June)

Women talking to family about the domestic violence

Only seven women reported that their family had been aware of the domestic violence at the time because they had noticed what was happening. One man phoned his partner's mother and told her that he had just assaulted her daughter. However, it was still some time before this woman was able to talk to her mother about the violence. In the other cases, families had noticed the atmosphere or had witnessed the abuse or its outcomes.

Women who told their families about the domestic violence usually did so only after they had separated from the violent man. They often said that it came as a shock to their family to learn what had been happening.

> But up until after we split up, they hadn't got a clue. They knew he had an attitude problem and they didn't really like him, but they never thought that he were hitting me at all. Shocks me mum sometimes when I happen to let things slip. (Bernice)

> I didn't really talk to anybody until the day I got him arrested. That is the first I'd spoken to anybody. (Kim)

As we have seen earlier, many women did not tell their family about the violence because they tried to protect them both physically and emotionally.

Unsupportive response

The largest single group were those women who said that they did not receive a supportive response from their families when they told them about the violence (23 women).

One group of women reported that their parents reacted in some way as if they were let down by learning about the woman's experience of violence. In these cases women said that their families made them feel that they were disappointed in them. Other families reacted angrily; for example one woman said that her parents were very angry with her for having married and having children with her ex-partner when he had been violent before they married. Her getting a divorce also embarrassed them. Two women said that they knew that their fathers would not have wanted them to be hurt, but it was clear that their fathers would have preferred if they had stayed in the relationship.

> He wouldn't have wanted me to be hurt but he probably doesn't understand emotional abuse. And I think he thinks that it would look better if I would stay with him [my ex-partner]. Like I have a child from him and a family and all that and she's broke up from him and now and oh the shame, you know, that kind of thing. I think he still thinks that, which I find very kind of hurtful you know, that he would want me to go back to that. (Maisie)

Bernice also described how hurt she was by the fact that her father had not initially believed her.

> It wasn't until me dad saw him drag me out of car when I were going into hospital that he said, he snapped me dad, he said, 'Everything you told me is true, I just didn't want to believe it'. And it were a big jolt for me dad. So that were really hard for him to accept. (Bernice)

Four women discussed how hurt they were when their mothers did not support them.

> But all she would say was that kids need their father, and she didn't really listen. Which I was surprised, angry and shocked at. I thought she would understand. But as the years have gone by, she sort of seems to be a bit more understanding, she'll listen a bit more now. (Rita)

> I even asked her [my mother] for help. She wouldn't give me it, she didn't want to know. She used to say to me, 'You've made your bed, you lie in it.' (Marguerite)

Family was often the first place women turned to for help. When they were rebuffed, they felt that they had to deal with it alone, that they could not ask anyone else for help.

At times families could not understand why the woman would leave but keep going back to her violent partner. One woman could not cope with her family's frustration at her going back, so she cut off communication with them. Another woman found that her mother stopped speaking to her because she always went back to the violent man.

> My mum said, 'That's it, Deirdre, I wash my hands of you now. I've tried to convince you that he's no good, you keep running back. If it's going to take me to stop talking to you, then that's what I'll do.' And she hasn't spoken to me for two years now. (Deirdre)

Some women said that both their own and their partner's family knew about the violence, but they did not want to accept that it was happening or talk about it.

> Everybody knew what was going on but nobody wanted to accept it, nobody wanted to talk about it. My mother least of all wanted to discuss it. She knew what he was doing, but she never actually said, 'Oh no,' or 'Is it true?' or anything. His mother knew what was going on, but I don't think she wanted to accept it. I mean, she lived right at the back of us. She once said to me, 'Hit him over the head with a big pan. If you kill him, I'll stand up for you in court.' And that was as far as it got really. (Jacinta)

More than one woman reported that their families were actually supporting their violent partners rather than them. As Camilla describes:

> I went into the refuge and my parents had put my husband up. So no, they weren't very supportive. I think that happened several times. Every time I left my husband, I had to go and stay with friends because they would put him up, and they actually came to the refuge and begged me to go back with him. They saw the bruises. They actually told him the address of the refuge so that he could come and see me. And so no, my parents were never very supportive at all! (Camilla)

Supportive response

Ten women said that they had received a supportive response from their families.

> I mean they've been brilliant, all my family, they have been really supportive with whatever I'm going to do. And they said that I've really made the right decision now, and they will help me and they're always round to help me sort of thing, so I know I've done the right thing. (Vivien)

Families offered both emotional and practical support. One woman had not had much contact with her family, but got in touch with them after a particular violent assault and they were supportive. Another woman had been disowned by her family when she got married, but once they learned of the violence they were supportive. However, women did find that although their families may have been supportive, they often did not acknowledge the emotional abuse suffered by the women.

> But I think a lot of people don't see anything other than physical abuse as a reason for leaving home, so they assume that he used to beat me up. But he didn't. Never. (Carla)

June had experienced domestic violence in a previous relationship and at the time was unable to tell her family. When it happened in a later relationship, however, she told them everything.

> I think they more understood why my hands were tied and why I couldn't get out. And I had a lot of support from my family, just trying to get away from him, but even though everyone was scared as well, it wasn't just me that was scared, they all were scared too. (June)

Families offered practical support by giving the woman and children a place to stay when they left, or when they needed a break. One woman's sister would look after her children when she was hospitalised for extended periods. In other cases, family (usually fathers and mothers) would intervene to try to stop the violence. This usually meant that they would talk to (or threaten) the violent man in an attempt to make him stop. Finally, families offered support by physically helping women and children escape from the violent man.

Women talking to neighbours about the domestic violence

Neighbours were often the first to know about the domestic violence, either because they heard or saw what was happening or because women or children went to them for help. Women described a range of responses from neighbours, from not wanting to know to intervening physically to try to stop the violence.

> Most of me neighbours knew what were happening but didn't want to know. It weren't their problem. They didn't want to get involved, which I can understand. If I was getting threats to having me windows put in just for noticing things, I think I would have turned a blind eye as well. (Bernice)

Some neighbours would call to check on the woman after an assault or call the police. They also offered a place of safety for the woman and children to run to. One woman's neighbour gave her the phone number of the local Domestic Violence Unit and actually phoned them and told them to expect the woman.

At times women believed that without their neighbours' intervention, they would not be alive.

There was this woman, Susan, who lived next door. If it wasn't for her actually hearing me crying, calling out murder at the door, when he was getting ready to bash my head in, I could have been dead, you know. (Davina)

Overall, women frequently felt that neighbours should be more involved, particularly by calling the police. Women said that neighbours should not try to ignore it and pretend that it had nothing to do with them.

Women talking to friends about the domestic violence

As with family, frequently women are able to tell their friends about the violence only when they are ready to leave the violent man.

I started to tell personal friends and work colleagues, but only when I decided that I was going to get out. While I was in, it was still something I didn't want to talk about. So only recently. (Leah)

Most of the women who told their friends about the violence found that they were very supportive.

She's there to listen to me and whatever my decision is, she's supported me all the way through. But when I went ... when I told her and said to her that I was taking him to court, she was ready to come with me and hold my hand in court and make sure I did it, if I wanted her to. (Judith)

One woman found that her friend was the only person who believed her, that everybody else was 'fooled' by her partner's social charm. Others reported that their friends were aware of the violence and rather than wait for the woman herself to broach the subject, raised the issue of the domestic violence. In this way they were responsible for encouraging the woman to leave.

But my friend said, 'Well, you gave it a go but you can't stay in that relationship because he's gonna kill you. It won't get any better; you know it's getting worse. And he'll either injure you seriously or injure one of the children.' (Stephanie)

In a similar situation, another woman denied the violence when her friend asked her. She had been refused help from her mother and consequently felt that she could not admit it to her friend.

Some women found that their friends were also experiencing domestic violence and they would emotionally support each other. One woman said that she eventually left her violent partner after her friend went to stay in a refuge. Her friend persuaded her to come to the refuge to think about what she wanted to do and once there, the woman decided not to go back.

In addition to offering emotional support, friends provided practical assistance such as letting the woman and children stay with them once they had left the violent man and helping with childcare. In several instances, the women's friends also became targets of the man's violence. It was not uncommon for violent men to isolate the women from their friends. One woman described how her ex-partner tried to rape her best friend and tried to have her other friend's partner beaten up. Thus, the woman lost the support of her friends. Some men resented their partner's friends and would use the women's visits to friends as an excuse to trigger a row.

> I had a good friend and she was quite helpful in that she was there for me, but at the end of the day he resented her. He resented the relationship I had with her. So that caused a problem in itself. So even though she was there for me, it caused problems in that sense. (Maisie)

At times women's friends physically intervened to stop the violence.

> And she were actually physically helping me by fending him off. She did actually hit him one day when he stormed into her house, and she stood and took some blows for me as well. She's got in between us. (Bernice)

A small number of women found that their friends would not help them. These women talked at length about how hurt they were to discover that the people they considered friends did not understand and in fact blamed them for the men's violence.

> But where I could never talk to them because they've got no understanding whatsoever. It's like, 'All your fault, you should move out.' But if you move out you've got nothing, no money, you lose your home, everything. Other people say to uproot but it's not as easy as that. So really I had no one to talk to. (Vivien)

Lucy had been physically attacked in front of some male friends and was very angry that they had not done anything to help.

> On one occasion there was three blokes in there, all of whom I knew and I considered friends, and none of them interfered or intervened. They said, you know, it's difficult to know what to do between man and wife. I was so angry with them. (Lucy)

Barriers to women talking to family and friends about the domestic violence

The most common reason that women gave for not seeking informal help, particularly talking to family and friends about the violence, was that they were embarrassed or ashamed.

> I never used to tell anybody. You're ashamed of it. I do now. Given up lying for him, I'm not doing that any more. (Kim)

> It's also that you're so ashamed of it and it's also drummed into you that somehow it's your fault and you're a failure. I didn't tell anybody except my best friend. (Alma)

Women were afraid that they would be judged or seen to be bad mothers or that it would affect their job if people knew. Some women were clear that they had coped by denying the extent and meaning of the violence, which meant that they could not say anything about it. This was particularly true in relation to talking to their children.

> Ralph never really saw anything at that point and Shirley was still very young and I suppose by not talking to her about it, I could pretend it never happened. Obviously she did know. (Cheryl)

> For me I justified it by saying it was a new relationship, that it was because he wasn't used to kids and under pressure from work. You can justify it in all different ways so you can say it's not a problem, it's just a minor hiccup; even though you're sat there with your face busted to hell, it's still a minor hiccup. (Bernice)

Some women who had left their violent ex-partners said that they could still not really talk to their children about what had happened because they did not want the children to have to relive it.

> I think it's reliving it, because you've all gone through it together before. I think it's actually reliving it all with them. I can talk to them to an extent but I sort of clam up. I still find it quite difficult to talk about a lot of things with them. (Jacinta)

Other women said that they felt their children were trying to protect them by not talking about it, and when the violence was happening the women were too focused on day-to-day survival to discuss it.

> I think, because they couldn't really come to me and tell me what was ... how they were feeling and what was going on for them, because I was too

busy surviving and trying to keep them going. So ... and it was as though, the impression I got from Sabrina is, 'Mum's got enough to worry about, without this.' (Margo)

As well as fearing the consequences for others if they told them about the violence, women were also very afraid for themselves if they spoke out. Particularly in the early days of the relationship women emphasised that they had been in love with their partners and felt loyal to them. One woman said that she had been brought up with very strong religious beliefs, which dictated that marriage was for life. These beliefs were shared by her family and her close friends, which meant that she could not say anything to any of them. Finally, some women were so isolated by their ex-partners that there simply was not anyone to tell other than seeking formal intervention.

Children talking to mothers about the domestic violence

Only three children said that they did not want to talk about the domestic violence. All of these children were obviously very loyal to their fathers and found it very hard to accept that their father was violent to their mother. By far the majority of children were very clear that they did want to talk about the domestic violence.

Overall, twenty-one children had spoken to their mother about the domestic violence while it was happening. In sixteen cases it was the children themselves who had initiated the conversation. One teenage boy described how he had started to talk to his mother about what was happening and they then had family counselling.

However, the communication between the children and their mothers was not always straightforward. A teenage girl had told her mother that her father was sexually abusing her, but she felt that her mother had minimised what she had told her. Her mother realised afterwards that she had not understood the implications of what her daughter had told her. Another young person described how her mother had initially denied the violence, but Marilyn could see the evidence:

I hadn't heard anything, but I started seeing bruises when she was wearing her short sleeve tops and there was loads and loads of bruises and she'd get black eyes. (Marilyn, aged 15)

Tracy said that she had talked to her mother sometimes about the domestic violence but she was very aware of her mother's distress.

> Yeah, sometimes we'd sit down and talk, but most of the time she was crying like. But she wouldn't, like, sit down and cry, she'd be like tidying the house and you'd just see tears coming down her eyes, like, not making no noise or anything. (Tracy, aged 15)

A number of children referred to the fact that their mothers had, in fact, been the only source of support they had at the time. Children talked to their mothers about how they were feeling about the violence in an effort to understand what was happening. However, they also took an active role in trying to persuade their mother to leave. Children and young people would directly ask their mother to leave, or question her as to why she would not leave the violent man. Naomi talked at length about how frustrated she felt with her mother staying and that when they tried to talk about the domestic violence, they would only end up arguing.

> We'd just get angry about it though. It always ended up in an argument, because, like, I'd say, 'Why are you letting him do this. He's smashed up all the crockery again, he's broken anything valuable we've ever owned, he's ripped all your clothes up so you can't go anywhere.' (Naomi, aged 24)

A further five children had talked to their mothers while the violence was happening, but it was their mothers who had raised the issue. One mother described how she felt that it was very important to talk to the children and point out that the man's violent behaviour was not acceptable. A young boy had been able to talk to his mother about the domestic violence at the time, but later felt that he could not talk to her about his concerns regarding contact with his father. He asked his mother to arrange for him to see a social worker, which she did.

Six children said that there had been no discussion of the violence at the time, but the children had really wanted to talk about it. At times children said that their mothers had talked to them briefly about what was happening, but that they needed a more in-depth discussion.

> She didn't really have a big chat. I really wanted to know what was going on. Because some things I didn't understand and what's gonna happen next, and I really wanted to know, but she wouldn't tell me. She told me some things. (Rosita, aged 8)

Another child described how she had desperately wanted to say something or ask questions, but just was unable to. Instead the questions would run round and round in her mind.

Fear of getting into trouble for raising the issue could also prevent children from asking their mothers:

> I never really spoke to Mum about it, because I didn't know how she would accept it. I didn't speak to my father about it either because I thought he would go and do something [violent]. (Hannah, aged 15)

Darren described how he had asked his mother about the bruising she had. She told him that she had fallen. When it happened in the woman's next relationship, he said he knew immediately what was happening.

> I said, 'Why is that bruise there?' and she said, 'I fell over,' and then I remembered about what had happened with my dad, and I instantly knew. (Darren, aged 11)

Commonly, although children and mothers had not discussed the violence at the time, once they had left the violent perpetrator, they talked about it freely. Sixteen children said that since they were no longer living with the violent man, they could talk to their mothers about what happened and the children themselves initiated these discussions.

> Not until he [my father] were gone and out of way. (Kara, aged 10)

Children were also aware that their mothers were not talking about the violence in an effort to protect the child.

> I think she, she, I think she kind of thought that she was upsetting me. (Mona, aged 17)

A number of mothers explained how they had made a conscious decision not to initiate discussions about the domestic violence with their children. They wanted them to ask about it when they were ready.

> I just wanted him to naturally come out of himself and ask about it and then I'd answer him, which he did. But we really didn't elaborate on too many things. (Davina)

It is very important to children that any discussion of the violence is at the child's pace. For example, one young boy explained how he talks to his mother about the domestic violence but that sometimes he feels that he is not up to talking about it.

Children mostly felt that having left the violent man, they could now talk very openly with their mothers about the violence. This usually reflected a concerted effort on the part of the woman and her children in building their new life free from violence. Open communication within the family, about domestic violence and other issues, was clearly seen to be crucial. One young boy said:

> I let out all my feelings [to my mother]. (Damian, aged 9)

Another young girl described how talking to her mother about the violence resolved the issues for her.

> It just makes me feel like I'm getting things through to my mum and I can now forget about something now. (Shauna, aged 7)

Children and young people stressed how important it was for their mothers to explain about the violence once they had left.

> Question: What's it like now being able to talk to your mum about it?
>
> Answer: It makes me feel happy.
>
> Question: Why is that?
>
> Answer: Because I know what's happening, what happened there.
> (Seamus, aged 10)

Frequently children were able to tell their mothers about abuse that they had suffered themselves only after they were no longer living with the perpetrator. For example, one violent man had made his stepdaughter eat raw liver. Her mother described how she eventually began to talk.

> We'd gone in the butcher's and Sabrina said, 'What are we getting, Mum?' and I said, 'Liver,' and she just freaked out and she was on her knees begging me, 'Please don't buy it.' So I just brought her straight back here and when she told me, I phoned my mum. And my mum said, 'I know, she told me a couple of weeks ago.' And I was, oh I was hitting my head against the wall; I mean that is so sick and disgusting and she didn't tell me, because he used to say stuff to her like, 'It'll only cause an argument between me and your mum'. (Margo)

Another young girl had been sexually abused and because the perpetrator threatened to harm her mother if she told, she was silenced. However, when the young girl saw her mother assaulted by a group of men acting on behalf of the perpetrator, she was frightened into telling:

> And it was like he was playing a mental game with her, 'I'll beat her mother up and then she won't tell'. But it [witnessing the assault] done the reverse, she did tell. It frightened her that much she told. (Leila)

Once children and their mothers had left the violent man, children were not always able to talk to their mothers because they felt that they must protect them. The examples that children gave of this scenario fell into one of two types. Children felt that their mothers were making a new life and that it would be too painful for her if they started opening up old wounds, or they were experiencing problems to do with contact with their fathers but felt that telling their mothers would create additional pressures for the mother.

> Sometimes it brings memories back and I don't like to upset my mum bringing memories back. (George, aged 13)

> It's just that sometimes when I go there [for contact] and he [my father] does things, I need to tell someone about it and I can't just go and tell my mum because it puts more pressure on her and makes her feel upset. (Regina, aged 9)

Children talking to extended family about the domestic violence

Extended family can have an important role in supporting children experiencing domestic violence. Grandparents in particular were viewed by children as an important source of support. Children frequently told grandparents about the domestic violence in the hope that they would be able to stop it or help the woman and children escape.

> But they could like, help you get away and talk to you like, say how you can get away from it without being scared. (Sabrina, aged 10)

In some cases children made a point of telling grandparents about the violence when their mother was trying to cover it up.

> She said [to her grandmother], 'Because Daddy put Mummy's head in the sink, all her nose was bleeding. We went up the hospital, the police have been round, I'm frightened of my dad because he shouts at Mum all the time, banging doors, my mum's always crying' ... And I was gonna cover up for him, again. (Vivien)

The experience of a number of children was that grandparents did intervene, especially by talking to their parents to try to 'sort it out'. One teenage girl said that she felt phoning the police was not an option but she would call her grandparents to come and mediate.

> I used to go and phone my nan or his mum ... I never used to phone the police. I used to phone some member of the family that would, I thought would come and mediate. (Mona, aged 17)

Mona was one of the young people who used grandparents and other relatives as a place to escape to away from the violence, sometimes even going to live with them:

> My nan's house was my safe house. That was the one place that I could go and I knew, 'cause I was with my uncles and aunties, I knew that I was safe there. He couldn't trouble me there ... I don't know why, I just classed that as my safe house. (Mona, aged 17)

Although grandparents were generally viewed as being very capable and able to take action to protect children, at times they were also seen as vulnerable.

> I never told my nan, because I didn't really want her to know. I don't know why. Just in case it would hurt my nan to know that my dad was hurting my mum. (Darren, aged 11)

Where there were already tensions between the violent man and other family members, children said that they did not tell extended family in case it made the situation worse. After grandparents, children said that they were able to talk to their aunts and uncles.

Talking to siblings about the domestic violence

Siblings were an important source of support for children experiencing domestic violence.

> Yeah, me and my sister, we used to lay awake at night talking about it all the time. (Marilyn, aged 15)

Children emphasised that siblings understood how they were feeling because they shared the same experience of domestic violence. In addition, siblings, being close in age, shared a similar worldview.

> I think because adults think differently to children so it's easier for children to talk to people like friends or maybe cousins or brothers and sisters, but hard to talk to adults because their minds are different in a way. (Sheena, aged 12)

Older children clearly felt responsible for physically and emotionally protecting young brothers or sisters from the violence.

> Because I didn't want to tell him [my younger brother] the truth, because it will like get him all upset and that. (Rosita, aged 8)

During the assaults on their mother, younger children would go to older brothers or sisters for comfort.

> He'd just cry and I'd have to sit and cuddle him and sometimes he'd start coughing and being sick and stuff. (Regina, aged 9)

Sometimes, older children felt the pressure of trying to support younger siblings in addition to dealing with their own emotions concerning the violence.

> I went to talk to her [my older sister] about it. She said no. And I said why and she said because it's too sad. (Paul, aged 6)

In a minority of families, the children and the adults seemed locked into silence around the domestic violence so that although it went on for years and all the children were aware of it and distressed by it, nobody within the family discussed it. However, the more common trend was for children to discuss it among themselves.

Children talking to friends about the domestic violence

> I had my friends to talk to and that's all I needed to talk to. (Sheena, aged 12)

From children's interviews it was clear that, with the possible exception of their mothers, friends were their main source of emotional support. Over and over again children referred to talking to their friends about the violence and feeling better.

> I feel more happier when I talk about it, than keeping it inside. It helps because they know a bit what I've been through and they know what me mum's been through and it helps me a lot. (Kara, aged 10)

> Yeah, because I had like one friend that I would do everything with, told her a bit about it and she listened but then that was it, and I had another one that would sort of listen to it all and help me through it and stuff. (Laura, aged 14)

The most important thing children referred to in deciding to discuss the domestic violence with their friends was whether or not they felt they could trust them. Specifically, children needed to be sure that their friends would respect their confidentiality and not tell others.

> I've talked to my friends, but I told them to keep their mouths shut, like, I didn't exactly say it like that! I said, 'Oh please don't tell anyone,' and they said, 'Fair enough, I won't tell anyone,' because they are my best mates and they won't tell anyone. (Rosita, aged 8)

Children had two main concerns with regard to confidentiality. First, they did not want everybody knowing what they considered to be their private business and making them feel ashamed or humiliated. Children were clearly very aware of the stigma concerning domestic violence and did not want to be judged or stereotyped.

> Because they'll tell all other people and I don't want my business to go around to everyone. (Glenda, aged 9)

Second, children were frightened that if they told others what was happening, the violent man would get to know they had been talking about it and it would cause even further trouble.

> So we'd talk occasionally but I was too scared of what to say because if it ever got back I knew that I'd be the one that got in trouble. (Mona, aged 17)

Domestic violence is still very much a taboo subject and it was difficult for children to initiate discussions about it, particularly as they could feel disloyal to the family by talking about it outside:

> We were brought up to think that nobody was to know about this. This was within our family unit. Anyone who says anything outside the family unit is a traitor or whatever. (Naomi, aged 24)

Because of the difficulty in talking about domestic violence, but spurred on by their need for emotional support, children did talk to their friends. It was clear from the children's interviews, though, that they were able to talk about the domestic violence only on a very superficial level. In these situations children would tell their friends that they were upset because their parents 'had a row' but would not discuss the violence. Others would be very matter-of-fact about the violence, refer to the fact that it was happening but be unable to discuss how they felt about it.

Another way children coped with this dilemma was to confide only in friends who were going through similar experiences.

> There is one or two of my friends at school have had the same thing happen as well, so now I have got them to talk to as well. (Mona, aged 17)

Hannah described how she had only recently been able to tell her friend about the violence. Her friend was now also experiencing problems and this was why she had decided to tell her. Beforehand she had felt that her friend would not have been able to understand.

> I only felt comfortable telling her because she was actually getting problems of her own. And I didn't want to add to them or anything but, we've always been there for each other since … because, like, she could help me through anything and she knew that the feeling was mutual and I could help, so … (Hannah, aged 15)

On the other hand, a young boy said that he was unable to tell his friends about the domestic violence. He suspected that they were having a similar experience and did not want to upset them by talking about what was happening to him.

On the whole, children will often approach friends first for support. One young person said that he did not see the point of talking to adults about it when he can talk to his friends. Another young boy explained that if friends were too young to understand, it is important that children talk to adults. The implications were clear that talking to peers is very often the first choice for children. Children were also very clear that friends could meet their emotional needs but that they needed adults to provide practical help, to 'sort it out'.

Barriers for children talking about the domestic violence

Children gave a number of reasons why they were unable to tell anyone about the domestic violence. The most common reason given was fear. Children were generally frightened that they would get into trouble if their parents, particularly fathers, found out they were telling people about the domestic violence. Children were sometimes afraid that their mother would be cross if she knew they were talking about it. However, the most common fear reported was that the violent man would hear that the child had been telling people about his violence. Children were afraid of being beaten if this happened.

> And I was always scared, like I would say to [my teacher], 'Don't tell my dad because if he finds out I don't know what will happen then.' (Hannah, aged 15)

Sabrina explained that she could talk only to her mother and grandmother because she did not trust anyone else not to tell her father.

They would start telling [the violent man] that I had told how I feel and then maybe [he] might start hitting me too and I was scared. (Sabrina, aged 10)

Again, in terms of seeking formal help, the main barrier that children identified was the fear of making it worse:

But I was always really scared of telling anyone of that authority where I knew they could do something, and in a way I really wanted to tell people like that, but in another way I was scared of, like, would they get the backlash of his temper if he found out. That's the main reason why I didn't tell anyone. (Hannah, aged 15)

The usual situation envisaged by children was that they would tell someone in authority, such as a teacher, who would then either confront the violent man or pass on the information to someone else such as the police; the man when confronted would deny the allegations; the person would leave the home, the man would be furious that anybody had said anything and would be violent to the mother, children or both. Even if a more sensitive approach was taken by the person whom the child told, children still feared that the violent man would find out they had told somebody. One young girl who had been sexually abused by her stepfather was terrified that he would kill her if she told anybody anything of what was happening at home.

I did think about running away sometimes and ringing ChildLine or whatever. But I knew that if he ever caught me, I hate to think what he would do. Which is why I was scared to do it. I was scared to tell my mum. I told her not to tell anyone because I knew what would happen. Well, he told me that if I ever told anybody he would kill me. And he probably would have. (Shirley, aged 16)

Children also referred to the fact that even after they were no longer living with the abuser, they were still scared to talk about it in case it somehow got back to him and they would have to move again in order to escape.

Related to the fear of making it worse is children's fear of not being believed or of what they said being dismissed.

So sometimes I'd maybe think it wasn't worth talking to anybody 'cause they might not believe me. (Fiona, aged 15)

Children appeared to feel that if it came to a situation of their word against the violent man's, he would be believed, not them. Young people were often aware of how 'normal' the family as a whole and the violent man in particular appeared. Children feared that they would then be perceived as being naughty or causing trouble.

Children were very much aware of the stigma surrounding domestic violence and this clearly inhibited them from talking about what was happening. Children talked about being embarrassed by the violence.

> That's not an everyday thing. And therefore you know that makes you different, so that everyone else is going to see you as different. It's embarrassing; it's just really embarrassing because I know they're sitting there thinking 'Oh'. Do you know what I mean? It makes me feel below people, because, I don't know, it just makes me feel below people. (Mona, aged 17)

> It was just my dad beating my mum up that was different, and I just knew that it was different really, because people didn't go round beating people up, especially mums and dads. But I just felt a bit embarrassed really because, like, not many people get their mums beaten up by their dads. (Zara, aged 12)

Even quite young children were aware of the stigma surrounding domestic violence and were anxious that they should not be made to feel different. A young boy explained how he could not tell his best friend about the violence in case he told his mother, who would then no longer be friends with the boy's own mother. It suggests that even young children are aware of society's need to blame the victim. Children did not want people talking about the family and they did not want to be stereotyped. Children often talked about how difficult it was to explain and they were afraid that their friends would not understand. This was particularly so if they viewed their friends as having a 'perfect' life.

> Yeah, it did upset me, but I thought it was nothing to do with anyone else. Like, most of my friends at school, their lives are like perfect. They're, like, only childs [children] and everything so they don't really bother about anything like that. (Tracy, aged 15)

Related to the notion of stigma, children at times felt that it was a family secret and that it should not be discussed outside the family. In some cases, children were specifically told by the perpetrator not to say anything to anyone outside the family. In only one family had the mother specifically told her child not to discuss the domestic violence. This woman explained how this was an attempt on her part to prevent both herself and her child being stigmatised. More often, children had sensed a prohibition against telling people about the domestic violence, as illustrated by Shauna:

> I sort of wanted to [talk about it], but I didn't because my mummy didn't want me to tell anybody.
>
> Question: Is that what she said to you?
>
> Answer: No.
>
> (Shauna, aged 7)

Leah talked about how her daughter clearly felt guilty when her friend told Leah that she knew about the domestic violence.

> She [my daughter's friend] said, 'I knew this happened anyway, because Jane had told me before, haven't you, Jane?' And Jane looked at me very apologetic and said, 'I'm sorry,' and I told her it didn't matter. I was glad she was talking to somebody. (Leah)

Talking about the domestic violence could be emotionally distressing for children. However, only three children said that they had not been able to talk about it because it was too distressing.

> Upset, it just reminds me of the horrible things what he does to her. (Glenda, aged 9)

In the interviews children raised two salient points in relation to communicating about domestic violence, particularly in terms of discussing their experiences with adults. First, children referred to not having the necessary language skills to discuss the domestic violence.

> Because sometimes they ask you words that you didn't know, like really long words. (Theo, aged 9)

> It's the words that children use...it makes it hard for the mothers to understand. Yeah, and all the time when my mum is speaking to me, I have to say what does that mean, what does that mean and all that. (Don, aged 8)

This was true not only for young children but also for teenagers, who referred to the difficulty in finding words to express what was happening and how they felt about it. For example, teenagers said that they would say that their parents had been 'rowing' but did not feel able to detail the reality of their home life any more than this. Second, children felt that adults have a different worldview from children's and it could be difficult to bridge the gap. Children referred to adults having a different understanding of events, seeing things differently, and that this could hinder rather than facilitate communication between children and adults.

> In the way they see things, I think. Like my mum and me don't exactly see eye to eye sometimes. So I'll say something in the child's point of view. She'd tell me off, well not tell me off, but she'll say have a ... we'll have a sort of rivalry of her taking the adult's point of view. (Sheena, aged 12)

In order for children to talk to others about the domestic violence, they first of all have to define it as a problem or unacceptable. While children may feel distressed by the violence, having limited contact with other families might mean that they are not aware that violence does not frame every child's experience of home life. In addition, children have to have access to people they can tell. One teenage girl pointed out that she did not have anyone to talk to about it outside the family, because the abuser isolated them from everybody. This was not an unusual situation.

Services not being accessible to children was also a major barrier to help-seeking. Children, quite simply, just did not know where they could go to get help. Others talked about how their movements were so restricted, they could not seek support without the abuser finding out. For example, one young person said he did not have a phone at the time so was unable to call either the police or ChildLine. Another young person talked about how the violent man tape-recorded all the family's phone calls to ensure that nobody said anything about him. Others talked about not being able to seek support because where would they tell the abuser they had been? How would they get an excuse to leave the house other than going to school?

Summary

Help-seeking is clearly a process and women face numerous obstacles rather than a single one. Women described both psychological and practical hurdles that had to be overcome. The psychological obstacles they faced included recognising their experience as being domestic violence, overcoming their belief in the myths about domestic violence, accepting that they are not to blame, defeating their feelings of shame and stigma and refusing to believe that there is no point in seeking outside help. The practical barriers comprised not knowing where to get help, difficulties in being able to get to support agencies, a lack of money and being rebuffed by agencies. Fear of losing their children was perhaps the main reason why women did not contact outside agencies for help. Women believed that they would be blamed for the man's violence and viewed as an unfit mother.

Fear of the violent man was another very powerful reason stopping women seeking help. Women tried to protect not only themselves and their children but also extended family and friends. Leaving the violent man did at times place extended family and friends at risk, as the man harassed others to find the woman and children.

Most women told their families about the domestic violence only once they had left the abuser. Their main reason for this was that they were attempting to protect their family from the man's violence. The majority of women did not receive a supportive response from their families and even those families who were seen to be supportive, at times had difficulties recognising the emotional abuse that the woman had experienced.

As with family, many women told their friends about the violence only once they had left. Most said that their friends were supportive, although a small number of women reported that their friends actually blamed them for the violence.

As well as protecting family and friends, women found it difficult to talk to them because they felt embarrassed or ashamed by the violence. Mothers felt that by not talking to the children about the violence they were protecting them.

Only three children said that they had not wanted to talk about the domestic violence and it was obvious that loyalty to their father was the reason. Twenty-one children had discussed the violence with their mothers at the time of the violence. While mothers were often the only support that children had during the domestic violence, communication between child and mother could be somewhat difficult at times, with each trying to protect the other. Some children had wanted more in-depth discussions of the violence or said that their mothers had not talked about it at all.

Fear of the violent man frequently stopped children discussing the violence with anyone. Once they had left the abuser, children and mothers often spoke freely about the violence and it was not unusual for children to be able to tell their mothers about their own experiences of abuse only once they had left. Children were silenced by the threat that if they said anything, the perpetrator would hurt their mothers.

Grandparents were seen as an important source of support, particularly in terms of being able to 'sort it out'. Talking to siblings was clearly very important as they shared the same experiences of violence and, being close in age, had a similar worldview. Older siblings played an active role in protecting young children both physically and emotionally.

Apart from mothers, friends were the main source of emotional support for children. Even small children were aware of the stigma surrounding domestic violence and children were very careful to tell only those friends whom they knew they could trust to respect their confidentiality. An important point arising from the children's interviews is that children do not have the vocabulary to discuss domestic violence properly and how it makes them feel. It is the responsibility of adults to enable children to name the violence and provide them with the language skills needed to discuss their experiences.

The main barriers for children talking about domestic violence were

- fear of the violent man finding out (this was the most common)
- fear of not being believed
- fear of being stigmatised
- difficulty in talking to adults
- not having anyone to tell
- services not being accessible.

CHAPTER THIRTEEN

Conclusion

Thresholds of intervention

There are no circumstances under which domestic violence is justified and yet while we continue to ignore the consequences for women and children, we are conveying the message that it is acceptable. Women's and children's experiences of domestic violence portray a complex process of intimidation, control and brutality, whether physical or psychological. Their attempts to find help show that they cope with the violence in a context of isolation, desperation and frustration and this is a crucial factor often overlooked: women and children do find ways to cope with their experiences.

Ironically, having the resources to develop strategies for coping with or surviving the domestic violence may mean that women and children then find that sources of support are denied to them. Women who cope may be perceived as strong and capable and children who do not display overt behavioural problems may not be identified as being in need of support or even attention. This may particularly be the case for children who learn to cope with the violence by very controlled or conforming behaviour. It may also be true for those who, instead of failing in particular areas as is expected of children experiencing difficulties, actually learn to survive by excelling in some way, for example, by escaping into academic or sporting achievements which leave emotional and relationship stresses unresolved.

This point raises issues not only about thresholds of intervention but also about how we identify children in need. If services, including advice and support, are targeted solely at those displaying clearly visible signs of distress (externalising symptoms) then those who are equally distressed but not displaying that distress behaviourally (internalising symptoms) may not be helped. On the other hand, if all children are included in education campaigns on domestic violence and if information about sources of support is freely available, children could seek out assistance themselves instead of being totally dependent on adults identifying them as being in need of support.

Non-physical forms of abuse

As the women and children in the study have demonstrated, to experience domestic violence means many different things. However, central to all the forms of abuse that women and children are subjected to by known men is the total control of all aspects of their lives. Physical violence is an easily identifiable form of domestic violence. It is, for all that, just one form that the violence may take and its purpose is usually to reinforce the man's control of the woman and children. Both in terms of having their experiences named as domestic violence and in coping with the impact of the abuse, women and children referred to the difficulty that people have in recognising the non-physical forms of abuse. Yet, it was usually the psychological and emotional abuse that women and children said was the 'worst' and which had the most lasting impacts. Mothers and children described how living with a violent man meant that they had to be constantly alert, always waiting for the next abusive outburst. This constant anticipation is clearly an ongoing source of stress for both the women and children, never knowing what each day may bring. Attempting to quantify violence as episodic ignores the cumulative build-up of stress and anxiety which women and children experience as they try to cope with the unpredictability of the man's behaviour.

Children described witnessing all forms of violence to their mothers, including sexual violence. They also witness the non-physical forms of abuse; this is an aspect of their experience that is often minimised. Children need opportunities to describe the entirety of their experiences and it should not be assumed that it is witnessing only physical abuse that may traumatise them. For example, threats to kill the mother may be experienced as being equally as or more traumatic than seeing their mother being hit. It is the context of the abuse that is important and children need to be able to define that for themselves.

Domestic violence and child abuse

Although the numbers in this study are small, the findings confirm those of earlier studies which indicate that men who are violent to their partners may also abuse children living in the household. This may be particularly the case in terms of emotional abuse of the children (quite apart from any adverse emotional effects of seeing their mother abused). Domestic violence must be seen as a possible indicator of risk to children. It is vitally important that the source of that risk is clearly identified and that any intervention does not further threaten and therefore alienate the non-abusing parent.

Children who have been forced to become involved in the abuse of their mother carry the burden of guilt about their involvement. They may not be able to see clearly how they were coerced to behave as they did, or be able to attribute responsibility to the violent man. It is not unusual for children to blame themselves for the violence to their mother, especially if they have witnessed assaults apparently triggered by disagreements over childcare. When they feel themselves to have actually been involved in the abuse of their mother, how much more responsible do they feel? It is very important that children are given the opportunity to express their feelings of guilt and responsibility without these feelings simply being dismissed or ignored.

Thus, the available evidence indicates that the abuse of children and the abuse of their mothers frequently coexist. Where one form of abuse is perceived to exist, the presence of the other needs to be sensitively established or ruled out, as appropriate. In any case it must be recognised that children living with domestic violence are clearly children in need and they and their mothers merit support.

In responding to the needs of children experiencing domestic violence we must not rigidly apply set formulae, for example, placing children on the child protection register for emotional abuse, without ascertaining if there are other ways of offering support. It is also crucial that a comprehensive approach is taken which works with children and their mothers together while recognising that they also have separate and individual needs.

Barriers to help-seeking

In order to start seeking help, women have to recognise that what they are experiencing is domestic violence and that it is not acceptable. Many women themselves believe common myths about male violence and the first step in seeking help is to be able to let go of these beliefs. Women frequently referred to not wanting to be stigmatised by telling others about the domestic violence. They also referred to their belief that nobody would be interested and those who had been assaulted by their partners in public without anyone intervening certainly had very concrete reasons for this belief. Allied to this is the fact that women frequently said that they actually did not know where to go for help, they did not know which agencies to contact or how to go about getting information or advice. There is an obvious and immediate need for better advertising of services for women escaping domestic violence. The revised *Working Together* recognises that:

many families fear that revealing their problems will lead to punitive reactions by service providers. Promote a positive but realistic image of services to encourage and enable people to gain access to the help and advice they need. Families need information on how to gain access to services and what to expect if and when they approach services for help. (DoH, Home Office and Department for Education and Employment 1999, p.11)

Apart from not knowing where to get help, the main reason inhibiting mothers seeking formal help for the domestic violence was the overwhelming fear that their children would be removed and, as we have seen, this fear was then manipulated by the abuser. If professionals are to work productively with women and children experiencing domestic violence, it is imperative that the first step in this approach is to recognise women's abiding fear that telling a professional about the domestic violence will result in the removal of her children. Over and over again women said that this fear had stopped them contacting agencies for help, or, if they were involved with an agency, they tried to hide the domestic violence.

This fear appeared to be felt most acutely with regard to contact with social services but also extended to other professionals seen to be in authority such as doctors, health visitors, police or teachers. In effect, this meant that women felt unable to approach anyone for help and tried to cope with the violence by themselves. The most important thing for all women was keeping their children and they were prepared to cope with the man's abuse for years in order to ensure that happened. As we have seen, women commonly believe that the children are unaware of or unaffected by the violence, so mothers perceive that the only ones suffering are themselves. In fact, realising that the children are at risk, physically, psychologically or emotionally, is one of the commonest reasons for women leaving violent partners.

The main reason that children gave for not talking about the violence was fear of the violent man. They were afraid that telling someone could make the situation worse and put them and their mothers at greater risk. There was also a fear that they would not be believed and an awareness that their voices carry little weight. Children were acutely aware how easily they could be dismissed and even blamed for trying to cause trouble.

After mothers, friends were the main source of support for children experiencing domestic violence. Children were very careful with regard to which of their friends they talked to about the domestic violence.

Specifically, they chose friends they could trust to respect their confidentiality. Children are very aware of domestic violence being the 'family secret' and a number of children talked about how they felt that they would be betraying their family to tell others what was happening. For this reason they did not tell anyone.

In terms of seeking formal intervention, children did not know whom they could go to for help. In those instances where they did know of an agency that might help, children did not know how they could make contact. Services are simply not accessible to children. Adults who need help are often baffled over where to go; for children it is much more difficult. Even the most accessible services such as helplines are not very easy for children to contact. They often do not have the privacy at home to make a phone call without being overheard by the violent man. They also spoke of not being able to get through to helplines and also their fear that the number would show up on a phone bill. Advertising of free phone helpline numbers needs to make it clear to children that the number will not be itemised.

Why is help not forthcoming?

Earlier research has highlighted how women have to seek help on numerous occasions before that support is forthcoming; this study also found that both women and children did not always initially receive the assistance they needed. The type of response that women and children receive appears to reflect a complex interplay between the following factors:

- individual attitudes about domestic violence
- agency commitment to domestic violence training
- existence of policies and procedures on domestic violence
- agency willingness to accept 'ownership' of the area.

In society at large, many myths still abound about domestic violence, particularly as to the 'type' of family within which violence can be found. Women frequently are blamed for 'choosing' a violent partner or for 'provoking' physical violence by their 'nagging' and for 'failing to protect' their children. They are also blamed for not leaving as if, first, leaving is the only option available, and second, as if this can be achieved in one trouble-free move without need for external assistance. Domestic violence is commonly perceived as a woman's problem exemplified by the 'battered wife' rather than the battering man.

It is then expected that individuals can eschew these popular beliefs when operating in a professional capacity and provide appropriate assistance to women and children experiencing domestic violence. Why do we assume that professionals should be able to do this without any domestic violence training; a work environment which facilitates discussion and exploration of the intricacies of this area; a supportive management which enables the man's violence to be confronted or clear procedures to guide the structure of the work?

To respond to domestic violence in both proactive and reactive ways requires close cooperation between all local agencies that have contact with women and children. In order to achieve that close cooperation, joint initial and ongoing training is crucial not only to raise awareness of the issues but also to clarify areas of individual and shared agency responsibilities so that best practice can be achieved. This does not just apply to crisis intervention but to the whole area of prevention, which has, to date, largely been neglected.

What kind of support is needed?

Attention must be focused not just on what help is given but also on how that help is provided. This is particularly relevant in terms of the pace of the work or the intervention and applies equally to supporting women and children. Women and children who are experiencing domestic violence know the risks they face in seeking help better than anyone else. It is crucial that women feel that they are in control of decision-making about what to do to ensure their own and their children's safety. Having sought help, women may need a period of reflection to decide the best action to take once they are aware of the options available to them.

Children also need to progress at their own pace. Although children clearly want action taken to end the violence, they need to know what steps will be taken and what the implications of each step will be. It is vitally important that children are not made false promises of confidentiality and also that any intervention deemed necessary from what the child has said is planned in consultation with the child and the mother (where appropriate). If decisions are imposed on women and children by service providers, the outcomes might not necessarily be safe or positive. MacLeod (1999), examining calls to ChildLine regarding sexual abuse, also cautions professionals, 'Don't just do it,' and argues for a more flexible response that incorporates discussion with the child in question.

Not all children who experience domestic violence want or need formal intervention. What they do want, however, is for the violence to stop and the opportunity to talk about their experiences, whether that is with a trusted adult, a professional or other children. Peer counselling is an approach that has been used with children in relation to bullying (Sellors and Brown 1996) and bereavement (Quarmby 1993) and could be an approach that might benefit many children experiencing domestic violence. Schools-based peer counselling on domestic violence would be accessible to children, as would a telephone peer counselling service.

In terms of more traditional counselling methods, children need to be able to choose when they can avail themselves of counselling to their best advantage. Children who are not ready for any form of counselling may regard the obligation to attend a weekly counselling session as an added burden at a time when they are already struggling to cope, whereas they may feel more able to participate in the service some time later. Only two of the children interviewed had been offered group work for children who have experienced domestic violence and this was in fact the type of support most wanted by children. In Canada and the USA more attention has been paid to the development of group work programmes than in the UK. Mullender (1994a, 1994b) and Hester et al. (1999) have outlined such programmes. In addition, Peled and Davis (1995) have written a detailed manual for practitioners on setting up and running groups for children who have experienced domestic violence. It is hoped that more attention will be directed towards the setting up of such groups in the UK.

Over and over, children in this study spoke of their need for practical information about where to get help. Children also emphasised that schools are a place where such information could be available.

Perpetrators and parenting

And what of the perpetrators? Is it good enough that the yardstick of their ability to parent is the presence or absence of direct physical violence to their children? The answer can only be no, it is not good enough: children deserve more. While a mother's role encompasses all aspects of the care and protection of her children, the father's role is often perceived to be fulfilled simply by his mere presence in the family or in the child's life. It is interesting that these men appear confident that their own parenting skills are above reproach and have no fear of the consequences of others learning about their violence.

The quality of the parenting ability of violent men should be scrutinised more closely. When considering the perpetrator of domestic violence in his capacity as parent, the guiding consideration should be how the child is benefiting from the present or proposed arrangement. This is particularly so in relation to decisions about contact.

Where it was possible and safe for the children, women went out of their way to facilitate contact between the children and their father. Women were very conscious of not turning the children against their father and felt that the children were entitled to make their own minds up about seeing him. It is crucial, however, that the dangers to women at times of contact are not overlooked. As this work and a number of research studies have highlighted, women continue to be abused in the context of contact visits (Abrahams 1994; Hester and Pearson 1998; Hester and Radford 1996).

Communication

This study raised important issues about how we communicate with children about domestic violence. From children's perspectives it is apparent that we are not giving them opportunities to communicate about their experiences of domestic violence. There are a number of strands to this theme. First, children want domestic violence to be raised as a topic located within general discussions, for example, in schools within the context of bullying or relationships. Second, children want to talk about their own experiences of domestic violence; they want to talk to their family, their friends, concerned adults as well as professionals whom they have contact with, such as teachers or those working within the area of health. Third, children want access to counselling, particularly group counselling. They want to be able to access this counselling themselves and they want to have choices about where and when to avail of the service. Fourth, we need to furnish children with the concepts and language to discuss domestic violence. There are a number of resource packs available for communicating with children, such as *Turning Points* (NSPCC, Chailey Heritage and DoH 1997), and some which specifically address domestic violence, for example, STOP (London Borough of Islington 1995), *The Respect Pack* (Morley 1999), *I Wish the Hitting Would Stop* (Patterson 1990) and *Home Truths* (Leeds Animation Workshop 1999). In addition, there is a training pack available for professionals working with those experiencing domestic violence, *Making an Impact* (Barnardo's, NSPCC and University of Bristol 1998).

A salient finding to emerge from the children's interviews is that children simply do not have the vocabulary to talk to their friends and others about domestic violence. They might be able to tell their friends that their parents had a 'row' last night, but clearly do not have the words to describe what really happened or how it made them feel. Children referred to wanting to discuss the violence more, but just not knowing how to. Domestic violence is still very much a taboo topic and this is particularly so for children. Without adults having the courage to talk openly about domestic violence, it is unrealistic to expect children to break the taboo, especially when we do not furnish them with the concepts or language to do so. When adults cannot talk openly and honestly about children's experiences of violence, it reinforces both the stigma surrounding domestic violence and the notion that it is a shameful secret that must remain within the family.

In order to communicate we, as adults, have to face our own fears about talking with children about emotive topics such as domestic violence. If we refuse to accept that it is a problem which affects us all and do not seek to increase our understanding of just what domestic violence is, then we cannot hope to help those children who are already experiencing domestic violence or prevent it happening in the future. Not discussing domestic violence with children does not protect them from trauma; instead it prevents them from finding support to deal with the pain of domestic violence, either currently or prospectively.

Most mothers involved in the research said that, at the time, they believed, first, that they were successfully protecting the children from knowledge of the violence, and second, that where children were aware of the violence they were too young to be affected by it. Once they had left the relationship, mothers could see that the children had been aware of the violence and were affected by it. Mothers frequently expressed their surprise that children had remembered violent incidents from when they were very young. As part of their attempts to protect the children, women generally said that they had not talked to the children about the violence at the time, but once they had left they were more willing to talk about it. The majority of mothers felt that it was very important to talk to children about their experiences of domestic violence, both to communicate the message that domestic violence is wrong and to provide children with an opportunity to express their feelings. Mothers expressed their confusion over how best to talk to their children about their individual and shared experiences of violence. Women were very clear that they wanted information about the effects of domestic violence on children and that they needed guidelines on how best to communicate with children about it.

It was very clear from both children's and mothers' interviews that it can be very difficult for them to start talking to each other about the domestic violence. Apart from each wanting to protect the other, it can be difficult to be honest about how they feel. Mothers may feel ashamed that their children have witnessed them being hurt and degraded and children too may feel embarrassed at having seen their mother in this position.

Despite the difficulties, it is extremely important to children that at some point they are given the opportunity to talk to their mothers about the domestic violence. There are issues of their shared history of violence and of making a future together as a family that can be dealt with only as a family unit. There is a real and urgent need for mothers and children who have experienced domestic violence to be offered a service that would facilitate their talking to each other.

Communication was the key factor differentiating those mother–child relationships that became closer from those which became strained. Mothers and children who were able to talk about the violence (not necessarily at the time) judged their relationship as closer than those who were unable to talk about their experiences. Mothers and children did point out that it could be very difficult for them to talk to each other about the domestic violence, usually because they are trying to protect or avoid upsetting each other. Mothers and children both felt that it would be very useful to have counselling support as a family unit which would facilitate them talking to each other about their experiences and their feelings.

It is also important that siblings are able to talk to each other about their shared experiences of violence and most children did talk to brothers and sisters. Older children are frequently very protective of their younger siblings and younger children clearly did rely on older brothers and sisters for comfort. Sometimes older children did feel somewhat pressurised by the responsibility of protecting and comforting their younger siblings. However, most older children seemed to appreciate having something tangible to focus on while their mother was being assaulted. Taking care of younger children made them feel less powerless.

The strongest message that children gave throughout the research is that they want to talk about domestic violence.

Education

How can we work to ensure that future generations will not tolerate the use of violence in intimate relationships or against children? A study carried out in 1992 by Edinburgh District Council found that 71 per cent of adolescent boys surveyed said that there was some likelihood of their using violence in future relationships and over 50 per cent of girls said that they expected to experience violence from future partners (Edinburgh District Council 1992). Clearly there is much work to be done.

It is noteworthy that numerous children, including quite young children, were aware of the stigma associated with domestic violence and felt degraded and humiliated by it. There is a clear need for awareness raising and educational work with children and young people to correct the myths about domestic violence. Children who cope with the fear and restrictions of living with a violent man should not have to cope with the added pressure of social stigma, which serves to reinforce the impact of the domestic violence.

Children who live with domestic violence need to be told that their first priority during an assault on their mother is to protect themselves. It is unrealistic not to expect children to want to protect their mother and ignoring these intense feelings is not helping children cope with their experiences. Children are saying very clearly that they want to know of practical ways they can help their mother. Providing children with the skills and perhaps, more importantly, the permission to call the police or seek help in some other way enables them to protect not only their mothers but also themselves. Their overwhelming desire to stop the violence often means that children physically try to intervene thereby placing themselves in immediate physical danger.

Even if they do not physically intervene, children are evidently traumatised by being forced to listen to the sounds of the violence and their mother's terror and distress. They believe that their mothers may be killed and feel extremely guilty that they do not know how or if they should call for help. Just as children are taught skills to protect themselves from sexual abuse, they need to be taught how to protect themselves both physically and psychologically from domestic violence. It is clear that children feel degraded because of their experiences of domestic violence and this feeling is compounded by popular belief systems which view those who experience domestic violence, but not those who perpetrate it, as tainted by their experiences. It is particularly disheartening to learn that such beliefs are held by children as well as adults and internalised by those who experience domestic violence, both young and old.

Friends appear to be very often the first people whom children who are experiencing domestic violence will turn to for help. Programmes with children raising awareness of domestic violence would no doubt have huge impacts on the quality of support that children could expect from friends.

We need to communicate with children about where they can get help if they are experiencing domestic violence. This should include practical advice which children can follow in order to activate support for themselves or their mothers. Much greater use should be made of the media, particularly radio, television, billboards and the Internet, to deliver the message that domestic violence is unacceptable, as well as indicating where children and young people can get help.

Domestic violence can affect all areas of children's lives and some of these affects may be persistent. It must be acknowledged that leaving the violent relationship commonly does not mean an end to the violence. Women and children may have to keep moving in order to escape the violence and harassment. Outreach support for both women and children who have moved to a new area to escape domestic violence would have enormous benefits. Refuges, women's support, outreach and advocacy services are best placed to provide this help. However, resources are needed to ensure that all local refuges can offer this service and that it is extended to children, not just their mothers.

In recent years there has been a much greater interest in domestic violence with both legislative change (Part IV of the Family Law Act 1996, Protection from Harassment Act 1997 and the Crime and Disorder Act 1998 under which local crime audits are expected to identify the prevalence of domestic violence in the area) and policy initiatives (e.g. Cabinet Office, Women's Unit and Home Office 1999). The revised *Working Together* (DoH, Home Office and DfEE 1999) for the first time specifically addresses issues of best practice when children are experiencing domestic violence. It encourages links between area child protection committees (ACPCs) and domestic violence forums with the suggestion that ACPC membership should include representation from the local domestic violence forum. It also emphasises the importance of agencies working in partnership to protect and support children. In addition, at the time of writing, the Lord Chancellor's Department is considering the report of the Children Act Sub-committee of the Advisory Board on Family Law regarding domestic violence and contact.

However, much thinking in this area remains polarised: we focus on (and then allocate sparse resources to) either women or children; perpetrators or victims; prevention or therapy; child abuse investigations or family support. We have come a long way in recognising the problem and we have identified how it should be addressed. The next challenge is to adopt a more encompassing view of domestic violence instead of parcelling off particular areas to work on as if they have a truly meaningful existence in this independent fashion.

It would be naïve to expect that this work could be achieved without additional resources. This is an area that crucially needs a committed source of funding. However, there are also resources that could be capitalised on, particularly in the area of skills and expertise that already exist. In addition, children are a resource that could be used to support others. What should our starting point be?

Just to talk to us, get people to go out and talk to children in their houses, schools and community halls, places like that. (Seamus, aged 10)

CHAPTER FOURTEEN

Recommendations

In their interviews, women and children made a number of recommendations as to how those experiencing domestic violence could best be protected and supported.

Information

- There is a need for greater information for women experiencing domestic violence, both in terms of posters advertising services and information packs about where to get practical and emotional support both for themselves and their children. They also need guidance on legal remedies. This information needs to be available in places that are frequented by women as part of their daily routine such as post offices, doctors' surgeries, housing services and shopping centres.

- Posters advertising domestic violence services should not rely on depictions of worst case scenarios, that is, extreme physical violence, as this may alienate large numbers of women who do not identify with such images.

- Children and young people also need information about domestic violence, including practical advice. Leaflets aimed at young people should be available through schools and community centres.

Awareness raising and education

- There needs to be a nation-wide, long-term, adequately resourced public education campaign aimed at both adults and children which addresses domestic violence and other forms of violence against women and children. Running the zero tolerance campaign nationally would be the first step in this education process.

- Children and young people's media programmes need to raise the issue of domestic violence, directing young people to where they can get information and support.

- Schools need to address domestic violence both as a general issue for discussion and awareness raising as well as offering on-site specific support for children who are experiencing domestic violence or its aftermath.

Legal protection

- Women and children need to be protected from domestic violence. To do this, every police officer who attends a 'domestic' needs to treat it as a crime. When called out because of domestic violence, police officers need to check the physical safety and emotional welfare of all children in the home.

- The application of the law was perceived by women to be biased against them and their children. There is an urgent need for ongoing training for the judiciary on domestic violence, particularly in terms of the impact of non-physical forms of abuse and the effect of domestic violence on children.

- Children's cases within the criminal justice system need to be dealt with more quickly so those children can receive therapeutic support.

- Children need ongoing information about what is happening to their case and what they can expect from being involved in the criminal justice system.

- Mothers and children both need support when children are involved in the criminal justice system.

Professionals' knowledge

- Professionals from all of the agencies likely to be in contact with women and children experiencing domestic violence need mandatory initial and ongoing training on domestic violence. This is particularly crucial for housing officers, education staff (not just teachers), health professionals (including those working in the field of mental health), police, probation and social workers.

- All of these agencies need to have established policies and procedures on domestic violence. These policies and procedures should be subjected to regular review to assess their effectiveness in protecting and supporting women and children.

- Professionals need training on how to communicate with children who have experienced domestic violence. There needs to be a recognition that skills professionals already have are transferable to this area but attention needs to be focused on addressing the specific difficulties which may arise in working with children with experience of domestic violence. The first step in this process is to be confident in addressing children's experience of violence directly without using language which minimises or obscures what that experience has been.

Support services

- Domestic violence comprises more than physical assaults and the existence and impact of psychological and emotional abuse need greater recognition.

- Intervention thresholds for children should not be dependent on physical signs of abuse or distress. Children experiencing domestic violence are often very resilient; however, most children will benefit from some form of support in dealing with their experiences. Children who have experienced domestic violence should be considered children in need. This is particularly true for children living in refuges or other temporary accommodation.

- As the sole agencies dedicated to helping women and children who have experienced domestic violence, there needs to be committed government funding for refuges. This is particularly urgent in relation to provision for children in refuges.

- Outreach support should be available for women and children who have escaped domestic violence to enable them to work through the issues facing them as a reformed family unit coming to terms with their individual and shared experiences. Refuges are the best places to provide this outreach support not just to women and children who have left the refuge but to those living in the community also, including in temporary accommodation. Again funding is the key issue.

- Age and culturally appropriate counselling should be available to every child who has experienced domestic violence. Furthermore this counselling should be made available as and when the child most needs it. Some children will need extensive counselling support whereas others would benefit from a one-off session that enables them to express their feelings about their experiences.

- Children who have experienced domestic violence will often benefit most from group work. There are a number of locations where such group work could easily be offered to children without them feeling stigmatised. Youth centres and schools are places which are familiar to children and where children could easily access such support.

- Counselling should be available for women who have experienced domestic violence.

- Mothers need advice about how to help their children come to terms with their experiences of domestic violence and also information about possible impacts of domestic violence on children. Leaflets addressing children's experiences of domestic violence and suggestions on how to talk to children about it should be available for mothers.

- In setting up counselling services for children who have experienced domestic violence, agencies should consult with and involve young people in the planning of such services to ensure that the service will be accessible to children and young people and will retain a true child-centred focus.

- Young people were particularly keen to see the establishment of a dedicated twenty-four hour helpline for children experiencing domestic violence which would operate not just as a counselling service but also as a source of information.

Contact

- Children's contact with violent fathers should be decided on the basis of considerations of the child's safety (including the potential psychological harm to the child of witnessing his or her mother being further abused in the context of contact arrangements) and the wishes of the child not on an assumption of the father's rights.

- A national network of contact centres offering assessments and supervised contact needs to be established.

- Children's wishes regarding contact change over time; children need ongoing opportunities to express their feelings and possibly revise, instigate or end contact arrangements.

- Accordingly, children need clear information about their rights in relation to contact with their fathers and details of the different types of contact so they can make informed decisions.

Appendix

The interview procedure

Once a woman and/or child had received information about the research and they were interested in taking part, they contacted the researchers either by telephone or in writing. A suitable time was arranged for the interview to take place in their home or where they were living at the time. All those taking part were offered the option of doing the interview somewhere other than their home, particularly if there were safety concerns about going to the home. In the majority of cases the interviews were held in the woman and children's home.

Once contacted by someone interested in taking part, the researcher sent an information pack which included further details of the research and a copy of the ground-rules for interviews, including the name and address of who to contact if the person had any complaints about the interview. This ensured that if there were any concerns about the interviewer or the research generally, women and children were able to voice those concerns without having to do so through the interviewer. No complaints were ever made.

With reference to the available literature and practice knowledge in this area, semi-structured interview schedules were designed for mothers and children or young people, broken down into three age groups of children. Two forms were also designed to be completed by the interviewer, one collecting demographic information and the other detailing allegations of child abuse or neglect. At the start of each interview, all participants completed a consent form.

Interview schedules for 5–8-year-olds

It was initially expected that non-verbal means of communication would be used with this age group during interviews, for example a 'story path' adapted from commonly used life-story techniques was formulated. In practice, however, it soon became obvious that children wanted to verbalise their experiences in a question and answer or storytelling format.

The interview questions for this group of children concentrated on whom children talked to about the domestic violence and how support could be improved for children with these experiences. It was decided not to ask children about specific incidents of abuse they had witnessed or experienced as, first, the focus of the study was on support services for children, and second, in a one-off interview it could be distressing for the child to concentrate on recalling numerous incidents of violence, particularly if support services were not in place to support that child. In total the interview schedule consisted of five questions. When asking the first question, the interviewer clearly stated that she had been talking to the child's mother about when Daddy (or perpetrator's name) was hurting Mummy. This served three purposes:

1. It made it clear to the child exactly why the interviewer was talking to her/him.

2. It openly acknowledged the domestic violence. Adults generally shy away from talking about domestic violence with children and when they do they use vague or woolly terms rather than name the violence directly. Children need a direct approach in order to discuss their experiences.

3. It gave the child 'permission' to break the secret of the violence by being clear that the mother (and possibly siblings) had already spoken about it.

Before the interview proceeded, the interviewer explained that she wanted the child to practise refusing to answer questions so that if a question came up in the interview which the child was unhappy with, the child would feel able to refuse to answer that question. Children were told that the interviewer would first of all ask them some questions that had nothing to do with the 'project' and that she wanted the child to respond, 'No, I don't want to answer that.' Until the child was clearly able to refuse to answer the researcher's questions, the interview did not proceed. All children were able to do this.

Children were then asked

- what they knew about the violence
- who they could talk to about it
- what makes it easy or hard to talk to adults
- how things could have been improved for the child.

Finally, the children were asked if there was anything they wanted to add. This was important in that the interview did not completely follow the researcher's agenda but allowed the children more control over the kinds of things they wanted to tell the interviewer. It also meant that the children were not left with unmet expectations about being able to express their view of their experiences. It was not unusual for a child to have very little to say in response to the first four questions but to talk at some length in response to the final one. At times it was also evident that when the child's mother had discussed the possibility of taking part in the research, the child had decided prior to the interview which aspects of their experience they wanted to tell the interviewer. Without the last question children would often have been disappointed. Children frequently chose to describe particular incidents of violence in response to the last question and for these children it was important that they could take the opportunity to do that without a request or pressure from the interviewer to do so.

Interview schedules for 8–11 year olds

With this age group of children the questions more directly addressed the children's experience of witnessing or overhearing the violence to their mother as well as times they were hurt or frightened. The same first and last questions were used as for the younger children.

Interview schedules for teenagers

Interviews with teenagers included questions not only on their awareness of the violence and their relationship with the perpetrator but also on their views of the impact of the violence on themselves and their relationship with their mother.

Interview schedules for mothers

Interviews with the mothers covered areas such as the nature of the violence suffered and its course over time, relationships between members of the family, and her perception of the children's awareness of the domestic violence. Questions also elicited information about the help-seeking process and the support received for the children.

Useful Contacts

Careline
020 8514 1177
Confidential counselling line for children, young people and adults

ChildLine
Freepost 1111
London N1 0BR
www.childline.org.uk
0800 1111
24-hour helpline for children

Domestic Violence Intervention Project
PO Box 2838
London W6 9ZE
Women's support service
020 8463 7983

Freecall Message home
0500 700740
Confidential, non-traceable message service for those who have left home.

London Rape Crisis Centre
020 7837 1600
24-hour helpline

National Children's Bureau
8 Wakely Street
London EC1V 7QE
www.ncb.org.uk
email@ncb.org.uk
020 7278 9441

NSPCC Child Protection Helpline
www.nspcc.org.uk
0808 800500
24-hour helpline
Textphone 0800 056 0566

Samaritans
0345 909090
24-hour confidential counselling

Shelterline
0808 800 4444
Emergency access to refuge services

Southall Black Sisters
52 Norwood Road
Middlesex UB2 4DW
email: sbs@leonet.co.uk
020 8571 9595

Women's Aid Federation in Britain and Northern Ireland
National helplines

Women's Aid in England
PO Box 391
Bristol BS99 7WS
www.womensaid.org.uk
email: info@wafe.co.uk
0345 023 468

Women's Aid Federations:
Women's Aid in Ireland
1800 341900

Women's Aid in Scotland
0131 475 2372

Women's Aid in Wales
01222 390874

REFUGE
0870 599 5443
24-hour national domestic violence hotline

References

Abrahams, C. (1994) *The Hidden Victims: Children and Domestic Violence.* London: NCH Action for Children.

Andrews, B. and Brown, G.W. (1988) 'Marital violence in the community: A biographical approach.' *British Journal of Psychiatry 153*, 305–312.

Barnardo's, NSPCC and University of Bristol (1998) *Making an Impact: Children and Domestic Violence. A Training Pack.* Leicester: NSPCC Training Centre.

Barron, J. (1990) *Not Worth the Paper ...? The Effectiveness of Legal Protection for Women and Children Experiencing Domestic Violence.* Bristol: Women's Aid Federation of England.

Bernard, C. (1997) 'Black mothers' emotional and behavioural responses to the sexual abuse of their children.' In G. Kaufman-Kantor and J.L. Jasinski (eds) *Out of the Darkness: Contemporary Perspectives on Family Violence.* London: Sage.

Bowker, L.H., Arbitell, M. and McFerron, J.R. (1988) 'On the relationship between wife beating and child abuse.' In K. Yllö and M. Bograd (eds) *Feminist Perspectives on Wife Abuse.* Newbury Park, CA: Sage.

Bowstead, J., Lall, D. and Rashid, S. (1995) *Asian Women and Domestic Violence: Information for Advisers.* London: University of Greenwich Women's Equality Unit.

Brandon, M. and Lewis, A. (1996) 'Significant harm and children's experiences of domestic violence.' *Child and Family Social Work 1*, 33–42.

Cabinet Office, Women's Unit and Home Office (1999) *Living Without Fear: An Integrated Approach to Tackling Violence Against Women.* London: Cabinet Office.

Casey, M. (1987) 'Domestic violence against women: The women's perspective.' Social and Organisational Psychology Research Unit. Dublin: University College Dublin.

Clark, A. (1994) 'A needle in a haystack: Finding support as a survivor of domestic violence.' In M. Wilson (ed) *Healthy and Wise: The Essential Health Handbook for Black Women.* London: Rage.

Cleaver, H. and Freeman, P. (1995) *Parental Perspectives in Cases of Suspected Child Abuse.* London: HMSO.

Clifton, J., Jacobs, J. and Tulloch, J. (1996) *Helping Women Survive Domestic Violence: A Report to the Sussex Domestic Violence Multi-Agency Consultative Group.* Falmer, Sussex: University of Sussex Centre for Social Policy and Social Work.

Davis, L. and Carlson, B.E. (1987) 'Observations of spouse abuse: What happens to the children?' *Journal of Interpersonal Violence 2*, 3, 278–291.

Department of Health and Dartington Social Research Unit (1995) *Child Protection: Messages from Research.* London: HMSO.

Department of Health, Home Office and Department for Education and Employment (1999) *Working Together to Safeguard Children: A Guide to Interagency Working to Safeguard and Promote the Welfare of Children.* London: Stationery Office.

Dobash, R.E. and Dobash, R.P. (1980) *Violence against Wives: A Case Against the Patriarchy.* London: Open Books.

Dobash, R.E. and Dobash, R.P. (1992) *Women, Violence and Social Change.* London: Routledge.

Dominy, N. and Radford, L. (1996) *Domestic Violence in Surrey: Developing an Effective Inter-Agency Response.* London: Surrey County Council and Roehampton Institute.

Edleson, J.L. (1995) 'Mothers and Children: Understanding the Links between Woman Battering and Child Abuse.' Paper presented at the Strategic Planning Workshop on Violence Against Women. Washington, DC, National Institute of Justice. Quoted in M. Hester, C. Pearson and N. Harwin (1999) *Making an Impact: Children and Domestic Violence. A Reader.* London: Jessica Kingsley.

Edinburgh District Council (1992) *Adolescents' Knowledge about and Attitudes to Domestic Violence.* Edinburgh: Women's Equality Unit.

Epstein, C. and Keep, G. (1995) 'What children tell ChildLine about domestic violence.' In A. Saunders, C. Epstein, G. Keep and T. Debbonaire, *It Hurts Me Too: Children's Experiences of Domestic Violence and Refuge Life.* Bristol: WAFE/ChildLine/NISW.

Evason, E. (1982) *Hidden Violence: Battered Women in Northern Ireland.* Belfast: Farset Co-operative Press.

Fantuzzo, J.W., DePaola, L.M., Lamber, L., Mariono, T., Anderson, G. and Sutton, S. (1991) 'Effects of interpersonal violence on the psychological adjustment and competencies of young children.' *Journal of Consulting and Clinical Psychology 59,* 258–265.

Farmer, E. and Owen, M. (1995) *Child Protection Practice: Private Risks and Public Remedies.* London: HMSO.

Frost, M. (1997) 'Health visitors' perceptions of domestic violence.' *Health Visitor 70,* 7, 258–259.

Gibbons, J., Conroy, S. and Bell, C. (1995) *Operating the Child Protection System: A Study of Child Protection Practices in English Local Authorities.* London: HMSO.

Goddard, C. and Hiller, P. (1993) 'Child sexual abuse: Assault in a violence context.' *Australian Journal of Social Issues 28,* 1, 20–33.

Hague, G., Kelly, L., Malos, E., Mullender, A. with Debbonaire, T. (1996a) *Children, Domestic Violence and Refuges: A Study of Needs and Responses.* Bristol: Women's Aid Federation of England.

Hague, G. and Malos, E. (1994) 'Domestic violence, social policy and housing.' *Critical Social Policy 14,* 3, Issue 42. 112–125.

Hague, G. and Malos, E. (1998) *Domestic Violence: Action for Change,* 2nd edn. Cheltenham: New Clarion Press.

Hague, G., Malos, E. and Dear, W. (1996) *Multi-Agency Work and Domestic Violence.* Bristol: Policy Press.

Hanmer, J. and Saunders, S. (1993) *Women, Violence and Crime Prevention.* Aldershot: Avebury.

Hester, M., Humphries, J., Pearson, C., Qaiser, K., Radford, L. and Woodfield, K. (1994) 'Domestic violence and child contact.' In A. Mullender and R. Morley (eds) *Children Living with Domestic Violence: Putting Men's Abuse of Women on the Child Care Agenda.* London: Whiting and Birch.

Hester, M. and Pearson, C. (1998) *From Periphery to Centre: Domestic Violence in Work with Abused Children.* Bristol: Policy Press.

Hester, M., Pearson, C. and Harwin, N. (1999) *Making an Impact: Children and Domestic Violence. A Reader.* London: Jessica Kingsley.

Hester, M. and Radford, L. (1992) 'Domestic violence and access arrangements for children in Denmark and Britain.' *Journal of Social Welfare and Family Law 1,* 57–70.

Hester, M. and Radford, L. (1996) *Domestic Violence and Child Contact Arrangements in England and Denmark.* Bristol: Policy Press.

Hiller, P.C. and Goddard, C.R. (1990) 'Family violence and the sexual and physical abuse of children: Some empirical light on theoretical darkness.' In M. Slattery (ed) *VICSPAN Third Annual Conference: Proceedings.* Port Melbourne, Vic.: Victorian Society for the Prevention of Child Abuse and Neglect.

Hilton, N.Z. (1992) 'Battered women's concerns about their children witnessing wife assault.' *Journal of Interpersonal Violence 7,* 1, 77–86.

Hoff, L. (1990) *Battered Women as Survivors.* London: Routledge.

Homer, M., Leonard, A. and Taylor, P. (1984) *Private Violence: Public Shame. A Report on the Circumstances of Women Leaving Domestic Violence in Cleveland.* Cleveland: Cleveland Refuge and Aid for Women and Children.

Hughes, H. (1988) 'Psychological and behavioural correlates of family violence in child witnesses and victims.' *American Journal of Orthopsychiatry 58,* 1, 77–90.

Hughes, H. (1992) 'Impact of spouse abuse on children of battered women.' *Violence Update 1,* 9–11.

Humphreys, C. (2000) *Social Work, Domestic Violence and Child Protection: Challenging Practice.* Bristol: Policy Press.

Imam, U.F. (1994) 'Asian children and domestic violence.' In A. Mullender and R. Morley (eds) *Children Living with Domestic Violence.* London: Whiting and Birch.

Jaffe, P., Wolfe, D.A. and Wilson, S.K. (1990) *Children of Battered Women.* Newbury Park, CA: Sage.

Jones, A. (1989) 'Domestic violence.' *Home Office Research Study 107.* London: HMSO.

Kelly, L. (1988) *Surviving Sexual Violence.* Cambridge: Polity Press.

Kelly, L. (1994) 'The interconnectedness of domestic violence and child abuse: Challenges for research, policy and practice.' In A. Mullender and R. Morley (eds)

Children Living with Domestic Violence: Putting Men's Abuse of Women on the Child Care Agenda. London: Whiting and Birch.

Kelly, L. (1999) *Domestic Violence Matters: An Evaluation of a Development Project.* London: Home Office.

Kelly, L. and Radford, J. (1991) 'Nothing really happened.' *Critical Social Policy 30,* 39–53.

Leeds Animation Workshop (1999) *Home Truths.* Leeds: Leeds Animation Workshop.

Lloyd, S. (1995) 'Social work and domestic violence.' In P. Kingston and B. Penhale (eds) *Family Violence and the Caring Professions.* London: Macmillan.

London Borough of Hackney (1993) *The Links between Domestic Violence and Child Abuse: Developing Services.* London: Hackney Council Press and Publicity Team.

London Borough of Islington (1995) *STOP: Schools Take on Preventing Domestic Violence.* London: Women's Equality Unit, London Borough of Islington.

McGee, C. (1997) 'Children's experiences of domestic violence.' *Child and Family Social Work 2,* 1, 13–23.

McGee, C. (2000) 'Children's and mothers' experiences of support and protection following domestic violence.' In J. Hanmer and C. Itzen (eds) *Home Truths about Domestic Violence: Feminist Influences on Policy and Practice.* London: Routledge.

McGee, C. and Westcott, H. L. (1996) 'System abuse: Towards a greater understanding from the perspectives of children and parents.' *Child and Family Social Work 1,* 3, 169–180.

MacLeod, M. (1999) 'Don't just do it: Children's access to help and protection.' In N. Parton and C. Wattam (eds) *Child Sexual Abuse: Responding to the Experiences of Children.* Chichester: NSPCC/Wiley.

McWilliams, M. and McKiernan, J. (1993) *Bringing it Out in the Open: Domestic Violence in Northern Ireland.* Belfast: HMSO.

Malos, E. and Hague, G. (1993) *Domestic Violence and Housing: Local Authority Responses to Women and Children Escaping from Domestic Violence.* Bristol: Women's Aid Federation of England and University of Bristol.

Mama, A. (1996) *The Hidden Struggle: Statutory and Voluntary Sector Responses to Violence against Black Women in the Home.* London: Whiting and Birch.

Mezey, G.C. and Bewley, S. (1997) 'Domestic violence and pregnancy.' *British Medical Journal 314,* 1295.

Mooney, J. (1994) *The Hidden Figure: Domestic Violence in North London.* London: Islington Police and Crime Prevention Unit.

Morley, R. (1999) *The Respect Pack.* London: City and Hackney Community Services, N.H.S. Trust.

Morley, R. and Mullender, A. (1994) 'Domestic violence and children: What do we know from research?' In A. Mullender and R. Morley (eds) *Children Living with Domestic Violence: Putting Men's Abuse of Women on the Child Care Agenda.* London: Whiting and Birch.

Mullender, A. (1994a) 'Groups for child witnesses of woman abuse: Learning from North America'. In A. Mullender and R. Morley (eds) *Children Living with Domestic Violence: Putting Men's Abuse of Women on the Child Care Agenda*. London: Whiting and Birch.

Mullender, A. (1994b) 'School-based work: Education for prevention.' In A. Mullender and R. Morley (eds) *Children Living with Domestic Violence: Putting Men's Abuse of Women on the Child Care Agenda*. London: Whiting and Birch.

Mullender, A. (1996) *Rethinking Domestic Violence: The Social Work and Probation Response*. London: Routledge.

Mullender, A. and Morley, R. (eds) (1994) *Children Living with Domestic Violence: Putting Men's Abuse of Women on the Child Care Agenda*. London: Whiting and Birch.

Nazroo, J. (1995) 'Uncovering gender differences in the use of marital violence: The effect of methodology.' *Sociology 29*, 3, 475 494.

NSPCC, Chailey Heritage and Department of Health (1997) *Turning Points: A Resource Pack for Communicating with Children*. London: NSPCC.

O'Hara, M. (1994) 'Child deaths in contexts of domestic violence: Implications for professional practice.' In A. Mullender and R. Morley (eds) *Children Living with Domestic Violence: Putting Men's Abuse of Women on the Child Care Agenda*. London: Whiting and Birch.

Pahl, J. (1985) *Private Violence and Public Policy*. London: Routledge.

Pahl, J. (1995) 'Health professionals and violence against women.' In P. Kingston and B. Penhale (eds) *Family Violence and the Caring Professions*. London: Macmillan.

Patterson, S. (1990) *I Wish the Hitting Would Stop: A Workbook for Children Living in Violent Homes*. Fargo, ND: Rape and Abuse Crisis Centre.

Peled, E. and Davis, D. (1995) *Groupwork with Children of Battered Women: A Practitioner's Manual*. Thousand Oaks, CA: Sage.

Quarmby, D. (1993) 'Peer group counselling with bereaved adolescents.' *British Journal of Guidance and Counselling 21*, 2, 196–211.

Reder, P., Duncan, S. and Gray, M. (1993) *Beyond Blame: Child Abuse Tragedies Revisited*. London: Routledge.

Ross, S.M. (1996) 'Risk of physical abuse to children of spouse abusing parents.' *Child Abuse and Neglect 20*, 7, 589–598.

Sellors, A. and Brown, R. (1996) 'School-age counsellors.' *Young Minds 24*, 7–8.

Silvern, L. and Kaersvang, L. (1989) 'The traumatised children of violent marriages.' *Child Welfare 68*, 4, 421–436.

Stanko, E.A., Crisp, D., Hale, C. and Lucraft, H. (1998) *Counting the Costs: Estimating the Impact of Domestic Violence in the London Borough of Hackney*. London: Crime Concern.

Stark, E. and Flitcraft, A. (1988) 'Women and children at risk: A feminist perspective on child abuse.' *International Journal of Health Services 18*, 1, 97–118.

Women's Aid Federation of England (WAFE) (1997) *Annual Report*. Bristol: WAFE.

Legislation

Children Act 1989. Chapter 41. London: HMSO.

Crime and Disorder Act 1998. Chapter 37. London: Stationery Office.

Family Law Act 1996. Chapter 27. London: HMSO.

Housing Act 1996. Chapter 52. London: HMSO.

Offences Against the Person Act 1861. Chapter 100. London: HMSO.

Police and Criminal Evidence Act 1984. Chapter 60. London: HMSO.

Protection from Harassment Act 1997. Chapter 40. London: HMSO.

Subject Index

abortions, forced 36, 43, 169
Accident and Emergency (A&E) departments 155–8
  supportive response 155–6
  unsupportive response 156–8, 161
adoption 47, 118
African-Caribbean children, over-representation in care system 20
agencies
  failures to help 217–18
  overview of research 20–3, 112
  professionals' knowledge recommendations 228–9
  support services recommendations 229–30
  type of support needed 218–19
  see also individual agencies
agency records, confidentiality 15
aggressive behaviour, children's 71, 74–5, 92, 93
  boys, against mothers 74, 82
  gender differences 74
  in school 74, 79, 93
  teenage girls 74–5, 92
aims of research 14
alcohol abuse
  accusations against women 36
  teenage girls 92

as trigger 27, 29, 52
alcoholism 29
anger
  as effect of domestic violence 74–5, 93
  towards fathers 85–6
antidepressants 152–3, 160
area child protection committees (ACPCs) 224
Asian women and children 15
  difficulties accessing help 112
  effects of racism 187
  housing needs 21
associated persons concept 21–2
awareness of violence, children's 95–6, 109
awareness raising 222–3, 227–8

bedwetting 65, 71, 84, 100
behavioural problems 71
  cessation on leaving violent relationship 100
  as coping strategies 106, 110
  effect on mother-child relationships 48
  health professionals' responses 151, 152, 153
  improved in refuge 74, 167
  and levels of exposure to violence 69
  in school 144, 146, 147
  see also aggressive behaviour
birth of children, and onset of violence 30
black women and children
  barriers to help-seeking 112, 185–6, 187
  children's identity 78

distrust of police 23
effects of violence on children 69
fear of removal of children 20
housing needs 21
research sample 15
terminology 16
blame
  children blaming mothers 83, 87
  see also self-blame
boys
  aggressive behaviour 74, 82
  favourable treatment 86
  likelihood of violence in future relationships 222

child abuse
  links with domestic violence 18–20, 45–6, 214–15
  types of violence experienced 48–57, 58–9
  see also child sexual abuse
child deaths 44
child guidance 159, 171
Child Protection: Messages from Research (1995) 113
child protection register 135, 190, 215
  and social work support 120–1, 124, 126
child protection work
  domestic violence a factor 113
  key areas of development 20–1
  prosecution 56
child sexual abuse 56–7, 59
  disclosure to mothers 198, 201
  disclosure prevented by fear 56, 207

245

Author Index

Abrahams, C. 20, 48, 51, 61, 63, 69, 220
Andrews, B. and Brown, G. W. 42

Barnado's, NSPCC and University of Bristol 220
Barron, J. 178
Bernard, C. 20
Bowker, L. H., Arbitell, M. and McFerron, J. R. 19
Bowstead, J., Lall, D. and Rashid, S. 112
Brandon, M. and Lewis, A. 19, 113

Cabinet Office, Women's Unit and Home Office 224
Casey, M. 22
Clark, A. 20
Cleaver, H. and Freeman, P. 19
Clifton, J., Jacobs, J. and Tulloch, J. 20, 21, 22, 69

Davis, L. and Carlson, B. E. 69
Department of Health and Dartington Social Research Unit 113
Deparment of Health, Home Office and Department for Education and Employment 216, 224
Dobash, R. E. and Dobash, R. P. 16, 17

Dominy, N. and Radford, L. 20, 21, 22, 23

Edinburgh District Council 222
Edleson, J. L. 20
Epstein, C. and Keep, G. 51
Evason, E. 69

Fantuzzo, J. W., DePaola, L. M., Lamber, L., Mariono, T., Anderson, G. and Sutton, S. 69
Farmer, E. and Owen, M. 19, 113
Frost, M. 22

Gibbons, J., Conroy, S. and Bell, C. 19, 113
Goddard, C. and Hiller, P. 56

Hague, G., Kelly, L., Malos, E., Mullender, A. with Debbonaire, T. 78
Hague, G. and Malos, E. 16, 17, 21
Hague, G., Malos, E. and Dear, W. 22
Hanmer, J. and Saunders, S. 112
Hester, M., Humphries, J., Pearson, C., Qaiser, K., Radford, L. and Woodfield, K. 18, 32, 78, 92, 113, 129, 142, 176, 182, 219
Hester, M. and Pearson, C. 45–6, 96, 220
Hester, M., Pearson, C. and Harwin, N. 17
Hester, M. and Radford, L. 16, 18, 32, 46, 57, 82, 101, 220
Hiller, P. C. and Goddard, C. R. 19
Hilton, N. Z. 83
Hoff, L. 58

Homer, M., Leonard, A. and Taylor, P. 112
Hughes, H. 20, 69
Humphreys, C. 20, 120

Imam, U. F. 18, 21, 112, 187

Jaffe, P., Wolfe, D. A and Wilson, S. K. 13, 65, 80
Jones, A. 20

Kelly, L. 18, 23, 32, 45, 57, 70, 92, 113
Kelly, L. and Radford, J. 18

Leeds Animation Workshop 220
Lloyd, S. 21
London Borough of Hackney 19
London Borough of Islington 220

McGee, C. 16, 18, 20
McGee, C. and Westcott, H. L. 14
MacLeod, M. 218
McWilliams, M. and McKiernan, J. 18, 20, 22, 23, 65
Malos, E. and Hague, G. 46
Mama, A. 18, 23, 69, 112
Mezey, G. C. and Bewley, S. 42, 58
Mooney, J. 17, 20
Morley, R. 220
Morley, R. and Mullender, A. 20, 47
Mullender, A. 20, 113, 219

Nazroo, J. 17
NSPCC, Chailey Heritage and Department of Health 220

O'Hara, M. 20–1, 45

253

Printed in the United Kingdom
by Lightning Source UK Ltd.
105412UKS00001B/220-237